Heraldic Illustrations,

COMPRISING THE ARMORIAL BEARINGS

OF THE PRINCIPAL

FAMILIES OF THE EMPIRE; WITH PEDIGREES

AND ANNOTATIONS,

BY JOHN BURKE, ESQ.

AUTHOR OF THE PEERAGE AND BARONETAGE, DICTIONARY OF THE LANDED GENTRY, ETC.

AND

JOHN BERNARD BURKE, ESQ.

OF THE MIDDLE TEMPLE, BARRISTER-AT-LAW.

LONDON:

E. CHURTON, 26, HOLLES STREET.

1844.

TREU · UND · FEST

WORKS devoted altogether to the display of Armorial Bearings are met with frequently on the Continent. In Germany more especially, where the inheritance of a Shield of manifold Quarterings has ever been essential in the formation of Alliances, and indispensable in the attainment of Honours, the collections are voluminous and authoritative, while in England, although the pride and pomp of Heraldry are hardly less regarded, there has hitherto been no attempt whatsoever to produce a Uniform Collection of Heraldic Engravings, if we except the slight and ill executed etchings that ever and anon disfigure our antiquarian and genealogical literature; why or wherefore, it is now unnecessary to enquire,—sufficient to refer to the existence of such a desideratum, and to state that the " Heraldic Illustrations " have been undertaken to supply it.

CONTENTS.

HERALDIC ILLUSTRATIONS.

———∞✢∞———

His Royal Highness

Prince Albert, of Saxe Coburg Gotha, K. G.

THE Family of Saxe-Coburg is one of the most ancient and illustrious of the Sovereign Houses of Europe. Its Princes, who frequently commanded armies and acquired great military renown, were as eminent in peace as the munificent Patrons of Art, Science, and Literature. Originally Counts of Wettin, they became, by inheritance, Margraves of Meissen and Landgraves of Thuringia: and of the latter potent Race sole Representatives at the decease of HERMANN, Landgrave of Thuringia and EMPEROR OF GERMANY.

The Reigning Duke of Saxe Coburg Gotha is Chief of the Saalfeld Branch of the ERNESTINE Line of the House of Saxony. In that Line the Electorate vested at the decease of Albert III. in 1422, and remained until JOHN FREDERICK, the *Magnanimous*, was deprived of his dominions by the Emperor CHARLES V. who conferred them, with the dignity of Elector of Saxony, on Duke Maurice of Meissen, Representative of the Albertine branch, and direct Ancestor of the present KING OF SAXONY. Thus, but for the misfortunes of the Elector John Frederick, (Prince Albert's immediate Progenitor) the Chief of his House—the Grand Duke of Saxe Weimar—would now be invested with the Sovereignty of Saxony. His Royal Highness PRINCE ALBERT bears for

Arms.—Quarterly, first and fourth, the Royal Arms of the British Empire, differenced by a label of three points, on the centre point a cross gu. Second and third, barry of ten, or and sa. a bend treflé vert, for SAXONY. The QUARTERINGS are very numerous and splendid, including THURINGIA, MEISSEN, CLEVE, BERG, ANHALT, HENNEBERG, &c.

Crests.—The various Cognizances of the House of Saxony.

Supporters.—Two lions ramp. or, crowned ppr. each charged on the shoulder with a label, as in the Arms.

Motto.—Treu und Fest.

Conrad the Great, Count de Wettin,[1] Margrave of Meissen and Margrave of Lower Lusatia, son of Thimo, Margrave of Meissen, and grandson of Theodric II. Count de Wetten, Representative of that distinguished Line, (by Matilda, his wife, dau. and heir of Eckard, Margrave of Meissen,) d. in 1156. This Prince joined the Crusade, and on his return assumed the religious habit: he first granted to the city of Leipsic the privilege of holding two annual fairs.

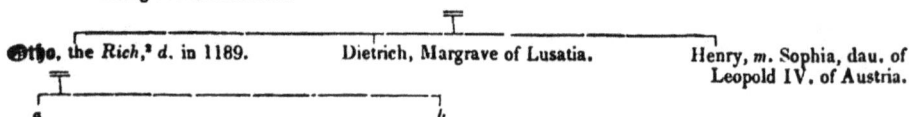

Otho, the *Rich*,[2] d. in 1189.   Dietrich, Margrave of Lusatia.   Henry, m. Sophia, dau. of Leopold IV. of Austria.

H. R. H. PRINCE ALBERT.

a

Albert the *Proud*, poisoned in 1195.

b

Theodric, Margrave of Meissen, m. Jutta, dau. of Herman, Landgrave of Thuringia,[3] and was poisoned in 1222.

Henry the *Illustrious*,[4] Margrave of Meissen and Thuringia, d. in 1288.

Albert the *Degenerate*,=Margaret, dau. of the Landgrave of Thuringia, d. in 1314. | Emperor Frederick II. 1st wife.

Theodric, Margrave of Meissen, d. in 1283.

Frederick, d. in 1316.

Frederick *with the Bitten Cheek*, Margrave of=Elizabeth, dau. of Otho Meissen and Thuringia, d. in 1324, leaving the | Von Arnshaug. reputation of a great and excellent Prince.

Diezman, a distinguished soldier, killed in 1307 by an assassin.

Frederick the *Serious*, aided John, King of=Mechtild, dau. of the Emperor Lewis VI. m. in France, in his war with Edward III. of Eng- | 1329. land, d. in 1349.

Frederick the *Severe*, acquired Coburg by his=Catherine, dau. of Count Henry de Henneberg. marriage in 1347, d. in 1380.

Frederick I. the *Warlike*, purchased the town and castle of Saalfeld, and became possessed, by gift of the Emperor Sigismund, in 1422 (the Ascanian line of the Electors of Saxony becoming extinct with Albert III.) of the Duchy of Upper Saxony and the dignity of Elector and Arch Marshal of the Roman Empire. He d. in 1428.

Frederick II. the *Good*, Elector of Saxony, d. in 1464.

William, Duke of Thuringia, d. without male issue in 1483. This Prince refused the Crown of Bohemia.

Ernest,[5] **Elector of Saxony**, d. in 1486.

Albert[5] the *Courageous*, one of the most celebrated warriors of his time, d. in 1500.

Frederick the *Wise*,[6] the patron of Luther, d. unm. in 1525.

John the *Constant*, Elector of Saxony, d. in 1532.

George the *Rich*, d. in 1539.

Henry the *Pious*, d. in 1541.

John Frederick the *Magnanimous*,[7] Elector of Saxony, distinguished for his unbending integrity and many sufferings, dispossessed by the Emperor of his dignities and dominions, which were conferred on Maurice his cousin. He formed the plan of the celebrated seminary at Jena, which was afterwards completed by his son: m. in 1597, Sibylla, dau. of John, Duke of Cleve, and sister of Anne of Cleve, Queen of HENRY VIII. King of England, d. in 1554.

Maurice, Elector of Saxony, d. in 1553.

Augustus, Elector of Saxony, d. in 1586.

John Frederick II. Founder of the House of Saxe Gotha, b. in 1567, d. in 1595.

John William, Founder of the House of Saxe Weimar, one of the suitors of Queen Elizabeth. He m. Dorothy-Susanna, dau. of Frederick III. Elector Palatine, and d. in 1573.

Christian I. Elector of Saxony, d. in 1591.

John Casimir,=Arma, dau. of the Elec- d. in 1633, | tor Augustus of Sax- s. p. | ony, 1st wife. Mar- garet, Princess of Brunswick, 2nd wife.

John Ernest, d. in 1638 s. p.

Frederick William, of Altenburg, whose line became extinct in 1672.

John, Duke of Wei-=Dorothea Maria, dau. mar, d. in 1605, in | of Prince Joachim his 36th year. | Ernest of Anhalt.

Christian II. Elector of Saxony, d. in 1611.

John George, Elector of Saxony, d. in 1656.

William, Duke of Saxe Wei- mar, *died* in 1662.

Other issue.

Albert of Eisenach, d. s. p. in 1644.

Ernest the *Pious*,=Elizabeth Sophia, Duke of Saxe | only dau. of Gotha, d. in | John Philip, 1675. | Duke of Alten- burg.

Bernard, the celebrated military com- mander, so distinguished at Lützen, d. in 1639.

John George, Elector of Saxony, d. in 1680.

a   *b*   *c*   *d*   *e*   *f*   *g*   *h*   *i*

H. R. H PRINCE ALBERT.

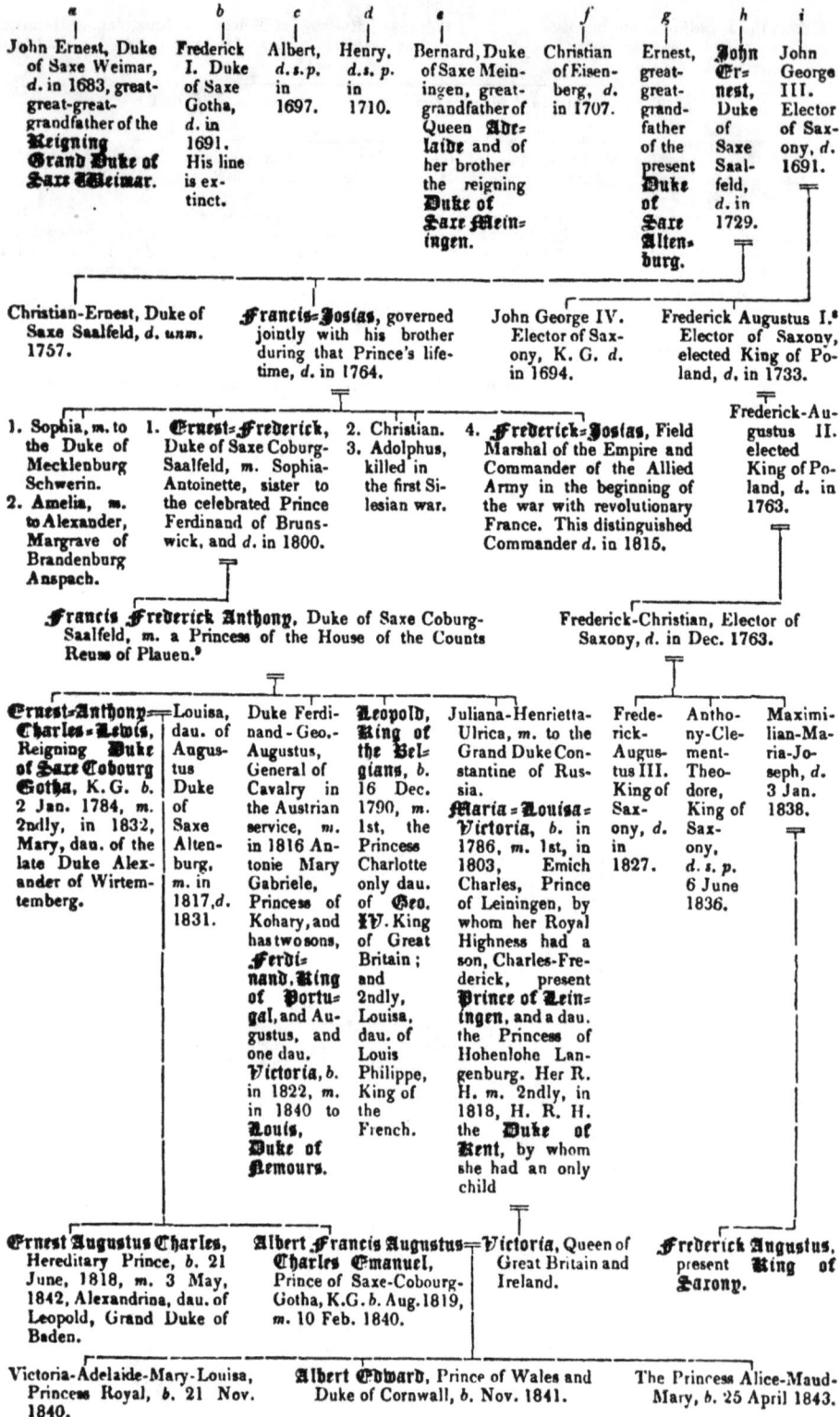

a	b	c	d	e	f	g	h	i

a John Ernest, Duke of Saxe Weimar, d. in 1683, great-great-great-grandfather of the **Reigning Grand Duke of Saxe Weimar**.

b Frederick I. Duke of Saxe Gotha, d. in 1691. His line is extinct.

c Albert, d. s. p. in 1697.

d Henry, d. s. p. in 1710.

e Bernard, Duke of Saxe Meiningen, great-grandfather of Queen **Adelaide** and of her brother the reigning **Duke of Saxe Meiningen**.

f Christian of Eisenberg, d. in 1707.

g Ernest, great-great-grandfather of the present **Duke of Saxe Altenburg**.

h **John Ernest**, Duke of Saxe Saalfeld, d. in 1729.

i John George III. Elector of Saxony, d. 1691.

Christian-Ernest, Duke of Saxe Saalfeld, d. unm. 1757.

Francis-Josias, governed jointly with his brother during that Prince's lifetime, d. in 1764.

John George IV. Elector of Saxony, K. G. d. in 1694.

Frederick Augustus I. Elector of Saxony, elected King of Poland, d. in 1733.

---

1. Sophia, m. to the Duke of Mecklenburg Schwerin.
2. Amelia, m. to Alexander, Margrave of Brandenburg Anspach.

1. **Ernest-Frederick**, Duke of Saxe Coburg-Saalfeld, m. Sophia-Antoinette, sister to the celebrated Prince Ferdinand of Brunswick, and d. in 1800.

2. Christian.
3. Adolphus, killed in the first Silesian war.

4. **Frederick-Josias**, Field Marshal of the Empire and Commander of the Allied Army in the beginning of the war with revolutionary France. This distinguished Commander d. in 1815.

Frederick-Augustus II. elected King of Poland, d. in 1763.

Francis Frederick Anthony, Duke of Saxe Coburg-Saalfeld, m. a Princess of the House of the Counts Reuss of Plauen.[9]

Frederick-Christian, Elector of Saxony, d. in Dec. 1763.

Ernest-Anthony-Charles-Lewis, Reigning **Duke of Saxe Cobourg Gotha**, K. G. b. 2 Jan. 1784, m. 2ndly, in 1832, Mary, dau. of the late Duke Alexander of Wirtemberg.

Louisa, dau. of Augustus Duke of Saxe Altenburg, m. in 1817, d. 1831.

Duke Ferdinand-Geo.-Augustus, General of Cavalry in the Austrian service, m. in 1816 Antonie Mary Gabriele, Princess of Kohary, and has two sons, **Ferdinand, King of Portugal**, and Augustus, and one dau. **Victoria**, b. in 1822, m. in 1840 to **Louis, Duke of Remours**.

Leopold, King of the Belgians, b. 16 Dec. 1790, m. 1st, the Princess Charlotte only dau. of **Geo. IV.** King of Great Britain; and 2ndly, Louisa, dau. of Louis Philippe, King of the French.

Juliana-Henrietta-Ulrica, m. to the Grand Duke Constantine of Russia. **Maria-Louisa-Victoria**, b. in 1786, m. 1st, in 1803, Emich Charles, Prince of Leiningen, by whom her Royal Highness had a son, Charles-Frederick, present **Prince of Leiningen**, and a dau. the Princess of Hohenlohe Langenburg. Her R. H. m. 2ndly, in 1818, H. R. H. the **Duke of Kent**, by whom she had an only child

Frederick-Augustus III. King of Saxony, d. in 1827.

Anthony-Clement-Theodore, King of Saxony, d. s. p. 6 June 1836.

Maximilian-Maria-Joseph, d. 3 Jan. 1838.

Ernest Augustus Charles, Hereditary Prince, b. 21 June, 1818, m. 3 May, 1842, Alexandrina, dau. of Leopold, Grand Duke of Baden.

Albert Francis Augustus Charles Emanuel, Prince of Saxe-Cobourg-Gotha, K. G. b. Aug. 1819, m. 10 Feb. 1840.

Victoria, Queen of Great Britain and Ireland.

Frederick Augustus, present **King of Saxony**.

Victoria-Adelaide-Mary-Louisa, Princess Royal, b. 21 Nov. 1840.

Albert Edward, Prince of Wales and Duke of Cornwall, b. Nov. 1841.

The Princess Alice-Maud-Mary, b. 25 April 1843.

NOTES.

[1] Some writers deduce the House of Saxony from WITTEKIND, the celebrated Saxon opponent of CHARLEMAGNE, and, though the proof they adduce is not absolutely conclusive, yet as Dietrich, or Theodoric, Count of Wetten, was the undoubted progenitor of the Electors of Saxony, and as Wittekind's descendants did certainly possess the Castles of Zörbeg and Wettin, this presumed descent is most probable. Meissen, the Margravate acquired by THEODRIC II. COUNT OF WETTIN, in right of his wife, Mathildis, sister and heir of Herman, Margrave of Meissen, was anciently inhabited by the Hermanduri and Suardones, and subsequently by the Sorabi or Winithi, a great Sclavonian Tribe, whom the Emperor Henry I. subdued. He annexed the territory to the empire, and its governors were appointed by his successors until OTHO III. made ECKHARD, son of Gunther, first Proprietary Margrave of Meissen. This Eckhard was father of Mathildis, wife of Theodric II. Count of Wettin, ancestor of Prince Albert.

[2] Surnamed the *Rich* from the silver mine discovered at Freyberg in 1170.

[3] In 1039, the Emperor Conrad II. conferred various Lordships in Thuringia on his kinsman, LEWIS, the *Bearded*, son of Charles, Duke of Lorraine, and grandson of Lewis IV. of France. Lewis was father of LEWIS II. surnamed the *Leaper*, whose son Lewis III. Landgrave of Thuringia and Hessen, *d.* in 1149, leaving a son and successor, LEWIS IV. surnamed *Ironside*, Landgrave of Thuringia, who *m.* Judith, dau. of the Emperor Conrad III. and dying in 1172, was *s.* by his son LEWIS V. surnamed the *Pious*, Landgrave of Thuringia, who *d. s. p.* in 1192, and was *s.* by his brother HERMANN I. Landgrave of Thuringia, who was involved in war with Albert the *Proud*, Margrave of Meissen. He *m.* 1st, Sophia, dau. and heiress of FREDERICK V. Palatine of Saxony, and 2ndly, Sophia, dau. of Otto, Duke of Bavaria, and *d.* in 1215, leaving issue, I. LEWIS VI. the *Saint*, Landgrave of Thuringia, who *m.* Elizabeth (canonized in 1235), dau. of Andrew II. King of Hungary, and dying in 1227, on his way to Palestine, left a son, HERMANN II. who *d. s. p.* II. HENRY Raspe, Landgrave of Thuringia, elected EMPEROR in 1246, *d. s. p.* in 1248. III. JUTTA, *m.* 1st to THEODRIC, MARGRAVE OF MEISSEN, and 2ndly, to Poppo XIII. Count of Henneberg.

[4] HENRY the *Illustrious*, one of the most powerful Princes of his time, inherited the Landgravate of Thuringen, in right of his mother, Jutte, daughter of Hermann, Landgrave thereof, descended from Lewis the *Bearded*, son of Charles, Duke of Lorraine, and grandson of Lewis IV. of France.

[5] These Princes, after governing their country conjointly, according to their father's will, for more than twenty years, finally determined on a partition of their dominions, by which ERNEST obtained the greater part of Thuringen, with the Electoral dignity, and ALBERT, who was one of the most distinguished warriors of his time, acquired Meissin. In this partition originated the distinctions of the ERNESTINE and ALBERTINE line, which still subsist in the House of Saxony.

[6] At the decease of the Emperor Maximilian, in 1519, CHARLES, King of Spain, and Francis I. of France offered themselves as candidates for the imperial diadem. The Electors, however, objecting to both as foreigners, wished to place the crown on the head of FREDERICK the *Wise*, but that Prince—then far advanced in years—declined the dignity, and gave his support to the King of Spain.

[7] This Elector, a zealous supporter of the Reformation, suffered much from the consequent hostility of the Emperor Charles, who, at length, deprived him of the Electoral dignity, and all his dominions, and conferred them on his cousin, Duke Maurice of Meissen, who agreed to give up Weimar, with some other towns and districts, to the children of the deposed Prince.

[8] Frederick Augustus I. (the opponent of CHARLES XII. of Sweden) had, by the Countess of Konigsmark, an illegitimate son, MAURICE, Count de Saxe, the celebrated Marshal of France, Commander-in-chief at Fontenoy.

[9] The two eldest daughters of Duke Francis of Saxe Coburg Saalfeld are both dead—one was married to Count Mensdorf, an Austrian nobleman, and the other to Duke Charles Alexander Frederick of Wurtemberg.

PLATE I.

Hopper, of the county of Durham.

This quartered Coat is borne by Augustus M. Hopper, Esq. son of Walter C. Hopper, of Belmont, Esq. by Margaret, his wife, daughter of the late Ralph Shipperdson, of Piddinghall Garth, Esq. The family of Hopper is of ancient standing in the County of Durham. (See Burke's *Landed Gentry*.) The Arms of Carlos, which are quartered with the paternal bearing, were granted in 1658 by Charles II. to Colonel William Carlos, his preserver in the Royal Oak, and in his escape subsequent to the battle of Worcester, " in perpetuam rei memoriam," as it is expressed in the Patent, the record of which is still preserved in the College of Arms.

Arms.—Quarterly, first and fourth, gyronny of eight sa. and erm. a tower or, for Hopper. Second and third, or, on a mount in base, an oak tree vert, over all, on a fesse gu. three regal crowns of the first, for Carlos.

Crests.—First, a tower ppr. for Hopper. Second, a sword ar. hilt and pomel or, and a sceptre of the second, crossed in saltire, enfiled with an oaken civic crown vert, fructed of the second, for Carlos.

Motto.—Subditus fidelis Regis et salus regni.

Sykes, of London.

The family of Sykes of London, now represented by John Sykes, of London and Highbury, Esq. merchant, is a branch of the Sykes's of Drighlington, co. York, who derived their descent from George Sykes, of Vicar Lane, Leeds, fourth son of William Sykes, of Leeds, living *temp*. Henry VII. The Escutcheon of Pretence is borne by Mr. Sykes in right of his wife, Catherine, daughter and co-heir of John Jackson, of London, Esq.

Arms.—Ar. a chev. sa. betw. three heraldic fountains ppr. On an Escutcheon of Pretence, for Jackson, Ar. on a chev. sa. betw. three hawks' heads erased az. as many cinquefoils or.

Crest.—An ox pass. charged on the shoulder with a fountain ppr.

Motto.—Quod facio valde facio.

The Chisholm, Erchless Castle, co. Inverness.

This Clan was founded in the twelfth century by Harald, Thane or Earl of Caithness, Orkney, and Shetland, one of the most formidable Northern Chiefs of that period. In the risings of '15 and '45, the Chisholms adhered with devotion to the Royal House of Stewart, and suffered severely in consequence. (See Burke's *Landed Gentry*.) The Chief is always styled the " The Chisholm," and bears, as such, the Supporters depicted in the Engraving. The present Chieftain is Duncan Macdonell Chisholm, of Erchless Castle.

PLATE I.

MARY, wife of JAMES GOODEN, of London, Esq. merchant, is only child and heir of Alexander Chisholm, the Chisholm, who died in 1793.

Arms.—Gu. a boar's head erased ar.

Crest.—A dexter hand, holding a dagger erect ppr. on the point a boar's head couped gu.

Supporters.—Two naked men, wreathed about the loins, with clubs over their shoulders, ppr.

Mottoes.—Vi aut virtute. And, *above the Crest*, Feros ferio.

Armstrong, of Ballycumber, King's County.

THE Armstrongs of Ballycumber, now represented by JOHN WARNEFORD ARMSTRONG, of that place, Esq. descend from the family of Armstrong of Giltknock Hall, in Eskdale, of which was the renowned JOHN ARMSTRONG, so celebrated in the wars and minstrelsy of the Scottish border. The Arms are allusive to the name and martial prowess of the family.

Arms.—Gu. three dexter arms vambraced ar. hands ppr.

Crest.—A dexter arm, vambraced in armour, ar. the hand ppr.

Motto.—Vi et armis.

Standish, of Durbury Park, co. Lancaster.

UNDER the will of the late FRANK HALL-STANDISH, of Duxbury, Esq. WILLIAM STANDISH CARR, of Cocken Hall, co. Durham, Esq. as representative of the Standishes of Duxbury, succeeded to the estates, and assumed, by Sign Manual in 1841, the surname and Arms of STANDISH only. The Duxbury family is derived from Hugh Standish, second son of Ralph Standish, and grandson of Thurstan de Standish, of Standish, living *temp.* Henry III.

Arms.—Az. three standing dishes, two and one, ar.

Crest.—A cock ar. combed and wattled gu.

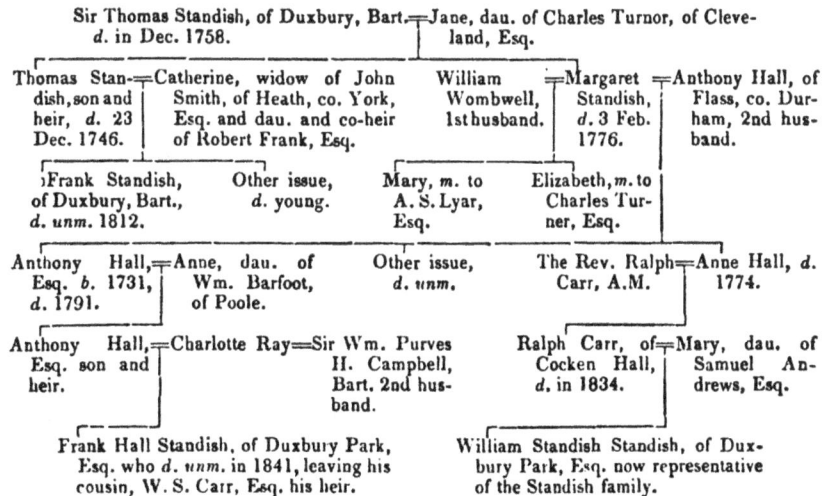

Sir Thomas Standish, of Duxbury, Bart.=Jane, dau. of Charles Turnor, of Cleveland, Esq. d. in Dec. 1758.

| Thomas Standish, son and heir, d. 23 Dec. 1746. | =Catherine, widow of John Smith, of Heath, co. York, Esq. and dau. and co-heir of Robert Frank, Esq. | William Wombwell, 1st husband. | =Margaret Standish, d. 3 Feb. 1776. | =Anthony Hall, of Flass, co. Durham, 2nd husband. |

| Frank Standish, of Duxbury, Bart., d. unm. 1812. | Other issue, d. young. | Mary, m. to A. S. Lyar, Esq. | Elizabeth, m. to Charles Turner, Esq. |

| Anthony Hall, Esq. b. 1731, d. 1791. | =Anne, dau. of Wm. Barfoot, of Poole. | Other issue, d. unm. | The Rev. Ralph Carr, A.M. | =Anne Hall, d. 1774. |

| Anthony Hall, Esq. son and heir. | =Charlotte Ray=Sir Wm. Purves H. Campbell, Bart. 2nd husband. | | Ralph Carr, of Cocken Hall, d. in 1834. | =Mary, dau. of Samuel Andrews, Esq. |

| Frank Hall Standish, of Duxbury Park, Esq. who d. unm. in 1841, leaving his cousin, W. S. Carr, Esq. his heir. | William Standish Standish, of Duxbury Park, Esq. now representative of the Standish family. |

PLATE I

AUGUSTUS M. HOPPER, ESQ.
CO. DURHAM.

JOHN SYKES, ESQ.
HIGHBURY, CO. MIDDLESEX.

THE CHISHOLM.
ERCHLESS CASTLE, INVERNESS.

JOHN WARNEFORD ARMSTRONG, ESQ.
BALLYCUMBER.

WILLIAM STANDISH STANDISH, ESQ.
DUXBURY PARK, CO. LANCASTER.

PLATE II.

Maze, of Bristol.

These Arms were granted in July, 1840, to Peter Maze the younger, of Berkeley Square, in the city and county of Bristol, Esq. sometime High Sheriff of the said county.

> *Arms.*—Erm. on a bend engr. az. betw. two eagles displ. another bend plain or, charged with three lions pass. ppr.
>
> *Crest.*—An eagle displ. erm. charged on the breast and on either wing with a cinquefoil gu.
>
> *Motto.*—Garde ta bien aimée.

Best, of Wierton, co. Kent.

These Arms were granted, a century since, 18 December, 1742, to Mawdistly Best, of Park House, Esq. High Sheriff of Kent in 1730. His son, James Best, of Park House, Esq. High Sheriff in 1751, had four sons : the eldest, Thomas, was father of the present James Best, of Park House, Esq. and the youngest, George, of Chelston Park, co. Kent, M.P. was father of the present Thomas Fairfax Best, of Wierton, Esq. who impales the coat of Brett in right of his wife, Margaret-Anna, daughter of J. George Brett, Esq.

> *Arms.*—Sa. a cinquefoil pierced, and in chief two cross-crosslets fitchée or ; impaling, for Brett, Or, a lion ramp. within an orle of cross-crosslets gu.
>
> *Crest.*—A demi ostrich ar. issuing out of a mural crown, and holding in the beak a cross-crosslet fitchée or.

Coulthart, of Collyn, co. Dumfries.

William Coulthart, of Collyn, Esq. is the representative of the ancient Scottish family of Coulthart, of Largmore, co. Kirkcudbright. (See Burke's *Landed Gentry*.)

> *Arms.*—Quarterly : first, ar. a fesse betw. two colts at full speed sa. Second, or, a chev. chequy sa. and ar. betw. three water bougets of the second. Third, sa. an inescutcheon chequy ar. and az. betw. three lions' heads erased ar. Fourth, quarterly ar. and sa. a cross per cross indented counterchanged.
>
> *Supporters.*—*Dexter*, A war horse, completely accoutred for the field, ar. *Sinister*, A hart of the last, attired and ducally gorged or.
>
> *Crest.*—A nag's head caparisoned ar.
>
> *Motto.*—Virtute non verbis.

Allan, of Blackwell Grange, and Blackwell, co. Durham.

The ancient family of Allan of Blackwell Grange, a scion, originally, of the Allans of Buckenhall and Brockhouse, co. Stafford, quarters the Arms of Pemberton, Hindmarsh, Killinghall, Herdewyk, Lambton, and Dodsworth.

PLATE II.

Arms.—Quarterly: first, sa. a cross potent, quarter pierced, or, charged with four guttes de sang, in chief two lions' heads erased of the second, all within a bordure engr. erminois, for ALLAN. Second, ar. a chev. erm. betw. three griffins' heads sa. for PEMBERTON. Third, gu. in a marsh a hind lodged ppr. for HINDMARSH. Fourth, gu. a bend raguly ar. betw. three garbs or, for KILLINGHALL. Fifth, or, a maunch sa. betw. three martlets gu. for HARDEWYK. Sixth, sa. a fesse betw. three lambs pass. ar. a trefoil gu. on the fesse for cadency, for LAMBTON. Seventh, ar. a chev. sa. charged with three bezants, betw. as many bugle horns, stringed, of the second. for DODSWORTH.

Crest.—A demi lion ramp ar. ducally crowned gu. holding in the dexter paw a cross potent or, and supporting with the sinister a rudder of the second.

Motto.—Fortiter gerit crucem.

The right to these quarterings is shown in the following pedigree:

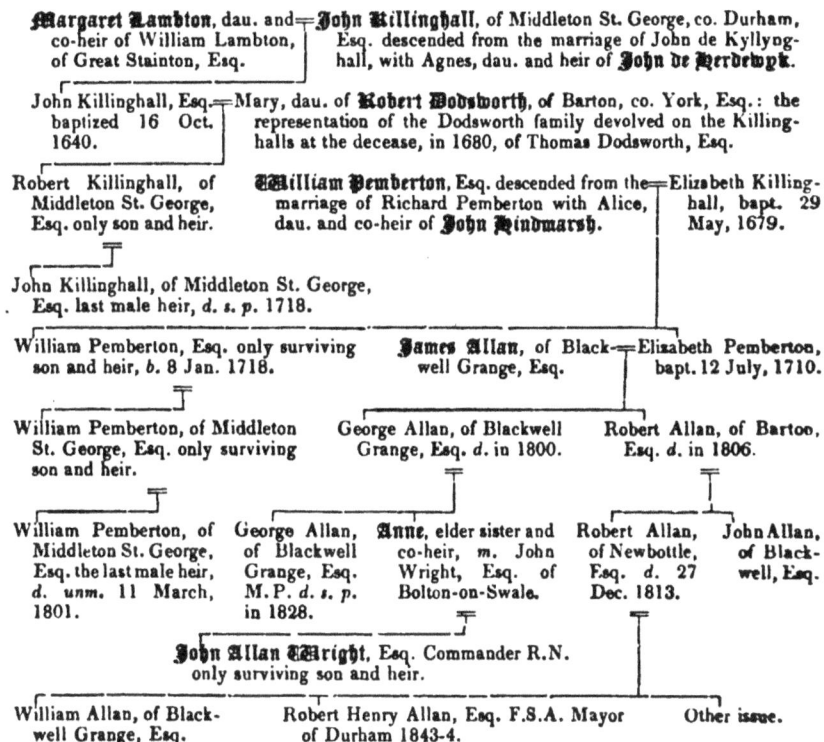

Margaret Lambton, dau. and co-heir of William Lambton, of Great Stainton, Esq. ═ John Killinghall, of Middleton St. George, co. Durham, Esq. descended from the marriage of John de Kyllynghall, with Agnes, dau. and heir of John de Herdewyk.

John Killinghall, Esq. baptized 16 Oct. 1640. ═ Mary, dau. of Robert Dodsworth, of Barton, co. York, Esq.: the representation of the Dodsworth family devolved on the Killinghalls at the decease, in 1680, of Thomas Dodsworth, Esq.

Robert Killinghall, of Middleton St. George, Esq. only son and heir.

William Pemberton, Esq. descended from the marriage of Richard Pemberton with Alice, dau. and co-heir of John Hindmarsh. ═ Elizabeth Killinghall, bapt. 29 May, 1679.

John Killinghall, of Middleton St. George, Esq. last male heir, d. s. p. 1718.

William Pemberton, Esq. only surviving son and heir, b. 8 Jan. 1718.

James Allan, of Blackwell Grange, Esq. ═ Elizabeth Pemberton, bapt. 12 July, 1710.

William Pemberton, of Middleton St. George, Esq. only surviving son and heir.

George Allan, of Blackwell Grange, Esq. d. in 1800.

Robert Allan, of Barton, Esq. d. in 1806.

William Pemberton, of Middleton St. George, Esq. the last male heir, d. unm. 11 March, 1801.

George Allan, of Blackwell Grange, Esq. M.P. d. s. p. in 1828.

Anne, elder sister and co-heir, m. John Wright, Esq. of Bolton-on-Swale.

Robert Allan, of Newbottle, Esq. d. 27 Dec. 1813.

John Allan, of Blackwell, Esq.

John Allan Wright, Esq. Commander R.N. only surviving son and heir.

William Allan, of Blackwell Grange, Esq.

Robert Henry Allan, Esq. F.S.A. Mayor of Durham 1843-4.

Other issue.

Walker, of Norton Villa, Kempsey. co. Worcester.

THESE Ensigns have been confirmed by the College of Arms to GEORGE JAMES ALEXANDER WALKER, of Norton Villa, Esq. and his cousin, the Rev. THOMAS WALKER, Prebendary of Wolverhampton, and Rector of Abbots Moreton, co. Worcester, descendants of an ancient Staffordshire family.

Arms.—Per pale az. and vert, on a fesse dancettée, betw. three mural crowns or, a crescent gu. betw. two torteaux.

Crest.—A lion's gamb erect and erased gu. charged with a mural crown or, betw. two plates in pale.

Motto.—In Domino confido.

PLATE II

PETER MAZE, ESQ. JUN.
BRISTOL.

THOMAS FAIRFAX BEST, ESQ.
WIERTON.

WILLIAM COULTHART, ESQ.
COLLYN, CO. DUMFRIES.

ALLAN OF BLACKWELL, GRANGE,
AND BLACKWELL.

GEORGE JAMES ALEX. WALKER, ESQ.
NORTON VILLA.

PLATE III.

Dunscombe, of Mount Desert, co. Cork.

THIS Family, of Saxon origin, was first settled in Devonshire, and subsequently in the city of London. Towards the close of Queen Elizabeth's reign (A. D. 1590), Edward Dunscombe, Esq. son of Captain Clement Dunscombe, and grandson of William Dunscombe, born in London in 1475, by Miss Clement, his wife, established himself in Cork, and founded the Mount Desert Family, now represented by NICHOLAS DUNSCOMBE, of Mount Desert, Esq. (*See* BURKE's *Landed Gentry*.)

    Arms.—Ar. a chev. betw. three talbots' heads erased.
    Crest.—Out of a ducal coronet or, a horse's hind leg sa. shoe ar.
    Motto.—Fidelitas vincit.

Temple, of Stowe, co. Buckingham.

THE Temples of Stowe, whose male Representative is Sir GRENVILLE TEMPLE TEMPLE, Bart., and from whom the Dukes of Buckingham maternally derive, deduce their descent from LEOFRIC, Earl of Chester, in the time of Edward the Confessor, and consequently bear the Black Eagle displayed on a field of gold—the Arms of the Heptarch kingdom of Mercia—in the first quarter of their shield of quarterings : the bars charged with martlets is the paternal Coat of Temple. The present Baronet, Sir GRENVILLE TEMPLE, is entitled to quarter, in addition, the Ensigns of Sheppy, Everton, Heritage, Spencer, Deverell, Lincoln, Warsted, Heritage, and Lee.

    Arms.—Quarterly, first and fourth, or, an eagle displ. sa. for LEOFRIC, Earl of Mercia ; second and third, ar. two bars sa. each charged with three martlets or, for TEMPLE.
    Crest.—On a ducal coronet or, a martlet gold.
    Motto.—Templa quam dilecta.

Cobbe, of Newbridge, co. Dublin.

ROBERT COOKE, Clarenceux King of Arms, certified these " to be the armes and creste of Thomas Cobbe, of Swarraton, in the countie of Southampton, gentleman, descended to him from his ancestors, and allowed, ratified, and confirmed to and for the said Thomas Cobbe and his posteritie in the tyme of the Visitation of Hampshire in 1575." A younger son of this ancient Hampshire family, CHARLES COBBE, D.D. an eminent divine, became Archbishop of Dublin, and founded the House of Cobbe, of Newbridge, now represented by CHARLES COBBE, of Newbridge, Esq. High Sheriff of the county of Dublin in 1821.

    Arms.—Gu. a fesse ar. in chief two swans ppr.
    Crest.—Out of a ducal coronet gu. a pelican vulning itself ppr.
    Motto.—Moriens cano. *Over the Crest*—In sanguine vita.

PLATE III.

Twemlow, of Cheshire.

THESE Ensigns are borne by JOHN TWEMLOW, of Hatherton, Esq. as a descendant of the Twemlows, of Arclyd. (See BURKE's *Landed Gentry*, Article TWEMLOW of PEATSWOOD.) The first quarter exhibits the ancient, the second, the modern Arms.

Arms.—Quarterly, first and fourth, ar. a chev. or betw. three squirrels sejant gu.; second and third, az. two bars engr. or, charged with three boars' heads, two and one, erect, couped, sa.

Crest.—On the stump of a tree erect a parrot ppr.

Motto.—Teneo tenuere majores.

Evans, of Ashhill, co. Limerick.

THE first and second quarters are for EVANS, the third for WILLIAMS, and the fourth for MORRICE. The present EYRE EVANS, of Ashhill Towers, and Miltown Castle, Esq. derives his right to the two latter quarterings from his mother.

Arms.—Quarterly, first, ar. three boars' heads couped sa. for EVANS. Second, gu. a lion ramp. reguard. or. Third, gu. a lion ramp. within a bordure or, for WILLIAMS. Fourth, or a lion ramp. reguard. sa. for MORRICE.

Crest.—A demi lion reguard. or, holding betw. his paws a boar's head couped sa.

Motto.—Libertas.

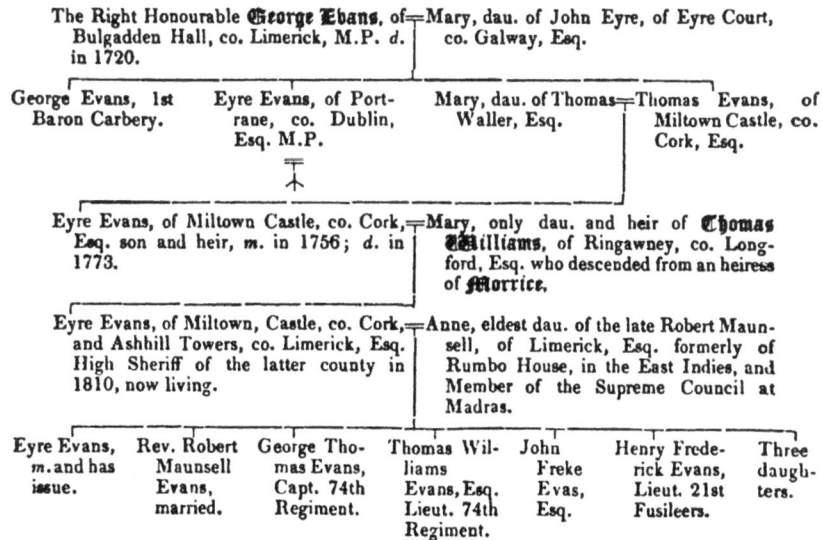

The Right Honourable **George Evans**, of Bulgadden Hall, co. Limerick, M.P. *d.* in 1720.=Mary, dau. of John Eyre, of Eyre Court, co. Galway, Esq.

George Evans, 1st Baron Carbery. — Eyre Evans, of Portrane, co. Dublin, Esq. M.P. — Mary, dau. of Thomas Waller, Esq.=Thomas Evans, of Miltown Castle, co. Cork, Esq.

Eyre Evans, of Miltown Castle, co. Cork, Esq. son and heir, m. in 1756; d. in 1773.=Mary, only dau. and heir of **Thomas Williams**, of Ringawney, co. Longford, Esq. who descended from an heiress of **Morrice**.

Eyre Evans, of Miltown, Castle, co. Cork, and Ashhill Towers, co. Limerick, Esq. High Sheriff of the latter county in 1810, now living.=Anne, eldest dau. of the late Robert Maunsell, of Limerick, Esq. formerly of Rumbo House, in the East Indies, and Member of the Supreme Council at Madras.

| Eyre Evans, m. and has issue. | Rev. Robert Maunsell Evans, married. | George Thomas Evans, Capt. 74th Regiment. | Thomas Williams Evans, Esq. Lieut. 74th Regiment. | John Freke Evans, Esq. | Henry Frederick Evans, Lieut. 21st Fusileers. | Three daughters. |

PLATE III

DUNSCOMBE OF MOUNT DESART.
CO. CORK.

SIR GRENVILLE TEMPLE TEMPLE, BART.

CHARLES COBBE, ESQ.
NEWBRIDGE, CO. DUBLIN.

JOHN TWEMLOW, ESQ.

EYRE EVANS, ESQ.
ASH HILL CO. LIMERICK.

PLATE IV.

King, of Loxwood House, co. Sussex.

THESE Arms were granted by Camden to the family of King, of London, and are now borne by JOHN KING, of Loxwood House, co. Sussex, Esq.

Arms.—Sa. on a chev. betw. three crosses crosslet or, as many escallops of the field.
Crest.—A dexter arm embowed in armour, holding a broken spear, all ppr.

Chadwick, of Swinton Hall, co. Lancaster.

THE Armorial Bearings of the old Lancashire family of Chadwyke, of Chadwyke, slightly differenced, were confirmed by the Herald's College to the present ELIAS CHADWICK, of Swinton Hall, Esq. and the other descendants of his father, the late ELIAS CHADWICK, of Swinton Hall, Esq. derived from a younger branch of Chadwick, of Chadwick.

Arms.—Gu. an inescutcheon or, within an orle of martlets ar. all within a bordure engr. of the second, charged with eight crosses crosslet sa.
Crest.—In front of two crosses crosslet fitchée in saltire, the flower and stem of a white lily, all ppr.
Motto.—In candore decus.

Moubray, of Cockairny House, Fifeshire.

COLONEL SIR ROBERT MOUBRAY, Knt. K.H. of Cockairny, represents the great House of Moubray, of Barnbougle, derived from the marriage of Philip de Moubray, younger brother of William de Mowbray, ancestor of the Dukes of Norfolk, with Galiena, daughter of Waldeve, Earl of Dunbar. Sir Robert is son of the late Robert Moubray, of Cockairny, Esq. by Arabella, his wife, daughter of Thomas Hussey, of Wrexham, Esq. and great-grandson of John Moubray, of Cockairny, Esq. who is described in Nisbet's Heraldry, as undoubted heir, in a direct and uninterrupted male line, of William Moubray, of Cockairny, who had a charter of those lands from his nephew, Sir John

PLATE IV.

Moubray, of Barnbougle, in 1511.   The Coat impaled by Sir Robert, is that of Hobson, in right of his wife, Laura, fourth daughter of William Hobson, of Markfield, co. Middlesex, Esq.

Arms.—Gu. a lion ramp. crowned ar. within a bordure engr. of the last, impaling for HOBSON, sa. a cinquefoil erm. a chief chequy or and az.

Crest.—A demi lion ramp. ar.

Supporters.—*Dexter*, a knight in court dress. *Sinister*, a woman habited ppr.

Mottoes.—*Over the Crest*, Fortitudine. *Under the Arms*, Let the deed shaw.

Beedham, Ashfield, Kimbolton, co. Huntingdon.

THESE Arms were confirmed to the present JOHN BEEDHAM, of Ashfield, Esq. who is married to Anne, daughter of Elizabeth, (wife of Josiah Claughton, of Hasland House, co. Derby, Esq.) one of the co-heirs of the last lineal descendant of a branch of the ancient family of Brailsford, co. Derby.

Arms.—Az. on a chev. engr. erm. betw. three birds ar. beaked and legged gu. as many human hearts of the last.

Crest.—On a mural crown ppr. a bird, wings expanded ar. beaked and legged gu. resting its claw on an escutcheon of the second, charged with a human heart of the third.

Motto.—God be in my bede.

Taylor, of Todmorden Hall, co. Lancaster.

THE present JAMES TAYLOR, of Todmorden Hall, Esq. as representative through his mother, of the senior branch of the ancient Lancashire family of CROSSLEY, of Scaitcliffe, quarters the Arms of CROSSLEY.

Arms.—Quarterly first and fourth, per pale ar. and or, an escarbuncle az. on a chief nebulée of the last, a ducal crown betw. two escallops of the second for TAYLOR ; second and third, per pale or and az. in chief a Tau gu. betw. two crosses potent fitchée of the second.

Crest.—A demi lion az. charged with a bezant, holding betw. his paws an escutcheon or, charged with a Tau gu.

Motto.—Natale solum dulce.

Anthony Crossley, of Scaitcliffe, Esq.═Betty, elder dau. of Abraham Gibson, of purchased in 1795, the estate of Tod-│ Briggroyd, co. York, Esq. morden Hall ; *d.* in 1810.

Anne Crossley, of Todmorden Hall, only═James Joseph Hague Taylor, Esq. *d.* 8 Jan. dau. and heir. │ 1810.

James Taylor, of Todmorden Hall, Esq.═Betty, second dau. of James Maden, of magistrate for Lancashire, and for the │ Greenshouse, in the Forest of Rossen-West Riding of Yorkshire ; living 1843. │ dale, co. Lancaster, Esq. *m.* 22 June, │ 1831 ; *d.* 19 Feb. 1838.

Issue.

PLATE. IV

JOHN KING, ESQ.
LOXWOOD HOUSE, SUSSEX.

ELIAS CHADWICK, ESQ.
SWINTON HALL, LANCASHIRE.

COLONEL SIR ROBERT MOUBRAY, Kt K.H.
COCKAIRNY HOUSE, FIFESHIRE.

JOHN BEEDHAM, ESQ
ASHFIELD KIMBOLTON HUNTS

JAMES TAYLOR, ESQ.
TODMORDEN HALL, LANCASHIRE

PLATE V.

Erle-Drax, of Charborough Park, co. Dorset.

JOHN SAMUEL WANLEY SAWBRIDGE-ERLE-DRAX, of Charborough Park, co. Dorset, and of Ellerton Abbey, co. York, Esq. son of Samuel Elias Sawbridge, of Olantigh, co. Kent, Esq. and grandson of John Sawbridge, Esq. Lord Mayor of London in 1775, and M. P. for the city, succeeded to the estates in right of his wife, JANE-FRANCES, only daughter of RICHARD-ERLE-DRAX-GROSVENOR, Esq. and assumed in consequence the name and arms of ERLE-DRAX. The marshalling of the Shield, which is quarterly, first and fourth, DRAX, second ERLE, and third SAWBRIDGE, with GROSVENOR, DRAX, and ERLE on the Escutcheon of Pretence, will be explained by the following Pedigree :

Arms.—Quarterly, first and fourth, chequy or and az. on a chief gu. three ostrich feathers in plume, issuant of the first, for DRAX ; second, gu. three escallops ar. a bordure engr. of the last, for ERLE ; third, or, two bars az. each charged with a barrulet dancettée ar. a chief indented of the second.

An Escutcheon of Pretence.—Quarterly, first and fourth, az. a garb or, for GROSVENOR ; second, DRAX ; third, ERLE.

Crests.—First, a demi wivern or, for DRAX. Second, a demi lion ramp. az. holding in his paw a handsaw erect or, for SAWBRIDGE.

Motto.—Mort en droit.

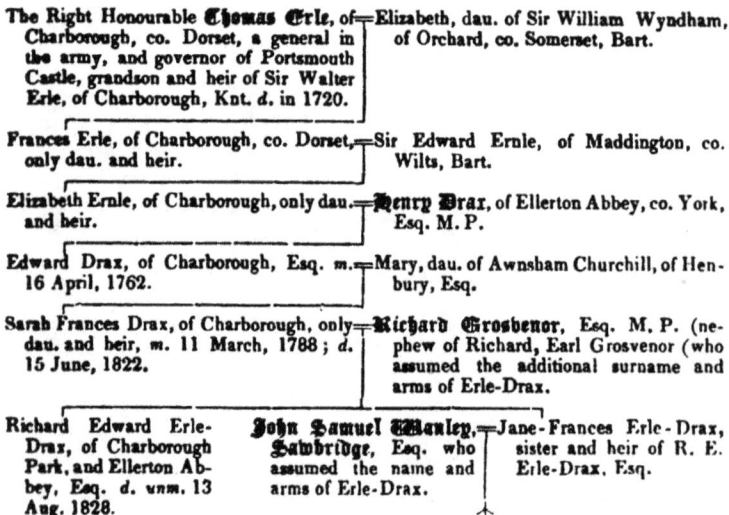

The Right Honourable **Thomas Erle**, of Charborough, co. Dorset, a general in the army, and governor of Portsmouth Castle, grandson and heir of Sir Walter Erle, of Charborough, Knt. *d.* in 1720.=Elizabeth, dau. of Sir William Wyndham, of Orchard, co. Somerset, Bart.

Frances Erle, of Charborough, co. Dorset, only dau. and heir.=Sir Edward Ernle, of Maddington, co. Wilts, Bart.

Elizabeth Ernle, of Charborough, only dau. and heir.=**Henry Drax**, of Ellerton Abbey, co. York, Esq. M. P.

Edward Drax, of Charborough, Esq. *m.* 16 April, 1762.=Mary, dau. of Awnsham Churchill, of Henbury, Esq.

Sarah Frances Drax, of Charborough, only dau. and heir, *m.* 11 March, 1788 ; *d.* 15 June, 1822.=**Richard Grosvenor**, Esq. M. P. (nephew of Richard, Earl Grosvenor (who assumed the additional surname and arms of Erle-Drax.

Richard Edward Erle-Drax, of Charborough Park, and Ellerton Abbey, Esq. *d. unm.* 13 Aug. 1828. | **John Samuel Wanley Sawbridge**, Esq. who assumed the name and arms of Erle-Drax.=Jane-Frances Erle-Drax, sister and heir of R. E. Erle-Drax, Esq.

PLATE V.

Fleeming Fryer, of the Wergs, co. Stafford.

WILLIAM ELEEMING FRYER, Esq. son and heir of Richard Fryer, of the Wergs, Esq. late M. P. for Wolverhampton, bears his paternal Arms quartered with the Coat of FLEMING, in right of his mother, the heiress of the ancient family of Fleming, of the Wergs.

Arms.—Quarterly, first and fourth, or, semée of oak leaves vert, betw. two flaunches az. each charged with a castle ar. for FRYER ; second and third, erm. on a chev. engr. gu. betw. three crosses patée fitchée sa. a Cornish chough betw. two crescents ar. for FLEEMING.

Crests.—First, a castle ar. entwined by a branch of oak fructed ppr. thereon a cock sa. combed and wattled gu. for FRYER.   Second, on a mount vert, a cross patée fitchée or, thereon perched a Cornish chough ppr. for FLEEMING.

Richard Fryer, Esq. late M. P. for Wolverhampton, son of the late Richard Fryer, of Wednesfield, Esq.	**Mary Fleming**, only child of William Fleming, Esq. and niece and sole heiress of John Fleming, Esq. of the Wergs, m. in 1794.

William Fleeming Fryer, Esq. son and heir.

Brisbane, of Brisbane, co. Ayr.

GENERAL SIR THOMAS MAKDOUGALL BRISBANE, of Brisbane, co. Ayr, Bart. G. C. B. G. C. H. LL.D. and F. R. S. is Representative of the Brisbanes of Brisbane, confessedly the chief of the name.   In 1826, Sir Thomas assumed, by Sign Manual, the surname of MAKDOUGALL before his patronymic, having married Anna Maria, daughter and heiress of Sir Henry Hay Makdougall, Bart., and Quarters, in consequence, the Arms of MAKDOUGALL, with his paternal Coat.

Arms.—Quarterly, first and fourth, a chev. chequy or and gu. betw. three cushions of the second, in the collar point a representation of one of the gold medals conferred on General Sir Thomas Brisbane by his late Majesty, for BRISBANE : second and third, az. a lion ramp. ar. crowned with an antique crown or, armed and langued gu. within a bordure of the second, charged with six fraisers of the first, for MAKDOUGALL.

Crests.—First, a stork's head erased, holding in its beak a serpent wavy ppr. for BRISBANE.   Second, a lion issuing guard. ppr. holding in his dexter paw a cross crosslet fitchée gu. for MAKDOUGALL.   Third, a goat's head erased ar. armed or, for HAY.

Supporters.—Two talbots ppr.

Mottoes.—*Over the Brisbane Crest*, Certamine summo.   *Over the Makdougall Crest*, Fear God.   *Over the Hay Crest*, Spare nought.

PLATE V.

Irbine, of Castle Irbine, co. Fermanagh.

THE Engraving represents the Arms of IRVINE, quartered with MERVYN; bearing on an Escutcheon of Pretence, D'ARCY, JUDGE, NUGENT, and CUMING. The descent of the Quarterings is as follows:

Arms.—Ar. a fesse gu. betw. three holly leaves ppr. quartering MERVYN.
An Escutcheon of Pretence.—Quarterly, I. D'ARCY; II. JUDGE; III. NUGENT; and IV. CUMING.

Crest.—A dexter arm in armour fesseways, issuant out of a cloud, hand ppr. holding a thistle, also ppr.

Motto.—Dum memor ipse mei.

Christopher Irbine, of Castle Irvine, son=Eleanor, dau. and co-heir of Audley Mer-
of Col. William Irvine, who was heir of | byn, of Trelick, co. Tyrone, Esq. m.
Sir Gerard Irvine, Bart. | Aug. 1718.

William Irvine, of Castle Irvine, b. 15 July,=Sophia, dau. of Gorges Lowther, of Kilrue,
1734, M.P. for co. Fermanagh. | co. Meath, Esq. M.P.

| | 1st wife. | 2nd wife. |
Sir Gorges Marcus D'Arcy=Elizabeth Judge D'Arcy,=Sarah-Catherine, dau. of
Irvine, of Castle Irvine, | only dau. and heir of | Thomas Napper, Esq. of
b. 26 Nov. 1760, assumed | Judge D'Arcy, of Dun- | Shropshire.
the additional surname of | mow, co. Meath, and
D'Arcy. | Grangebeg, co. West-
| meath, Esq. descended
| from heiresses of Judge,
| Nugent, and Cuming.

Morris, of York.

THE Rev. FRANCIS ORPEN MORRIS (eldest son of Captain Henry Gage Morris, R. N. by Rebecca Newenham-Millerd, his wife, daughter of the Rev. Francis Orpen, Vicar of Kilgarvon, grandson of the late Lieutenant-Colonel Roger Morris, of York, by Mary, his wife, daughter of Frederick Philipse, of New York, Esq. and great-grandson of Roger Morris, Esq. by Mary, his first wife, daughter of Sir Peter Jackson, Knt.) bears the quartered Coat as a descendant of an ancient Welsh Family which derived from CADWGAN, son of Elystan Glodrydd, Prince of Ferlys, Founder of the IV Royal Tribe of Wales.

Arms.—Quarterly, first and fourth, gu. a lion ramp. reguard. or; second and third, ar. three boars' heads couped sa.

Crest.—A lion ramp. reguard. or.

Motto.—Marte et Mari faventibus.

PLATE V

I.S.W. SAWBRIDGE ERLE DRAX, ESQ.
CHARBOROUGH PARK, CO. DORSET.

WILLIAM FLEEMING FRYER, ESQ.
THE WERGS, CO. STAFFORD.

GEN. SIR THOMAS MAKDOUGALL BRISBANE, BART. G.C.B.
BRISBANE.

IRVINE, BART.
CASTLE IRVINE, CO. FERMANAGH.

THE REV. FRANCIS ORPEN MORRIS.

PLATE VI.

———

The Duke of Sutherland, K. G.

His Grace George Granville, second and present Duke of Sutherland, K. G. bears a Coat of eight Grand Quarterings, marking the representation of the great houses from which he derives.

Arms.—Quarterly of eight.—

I. Quarterly, first and fourth, Barry of eight ar. and gu. over all a cross patonce, sa. for Gower ; second and third, Az. three laurel leaves or, for Leveson.

II. Barry of eight ar. and gu. over all a cross patonce sa. for Gower.

III. Gu. three organ rests or sufflues or, for Granville, Earl of Bath.

IV. Ar. a lion ramp. gu. betw. three pheons' heads sa. for Egerton, Duke of Bridgewater.

V. Ar. on a bend az. three bucks' heads cabossed or, for Stanley.

VI. Gu. two lions passant ar. for Strange, of Knockyn.

VII. Barry of ten ar. and gu. over all a lion ramp. or, crowned, per pale of the first and second, for Brandon, Duke of Suffolk. On a canton chequy or and az. a fesse gu. for Clifford, Earl of Cumberland.

VIII. Royal Arms ; quarterly, first and fourth, France ; second and third, England, to mark the Duke of Sutherland's descent from Henry VII.

Over all, on an escutcheon of pretence, surmounted by an earl's coronet, gu. three mullets within a bordure or, charged with a double treasure, flory and counter-flory of the field, being the arms of the ancient Earls of Sutherland, to mark their descent from King Robert Bruce.

Crests.—First, a wolf passant ar. collared and lined or. Second, a cat-a-mountain sejant guardant ppr.

Supporters.—Two wolves ar. each collared and lined or.

Motto.—Frangas non flectes.

The descent of the Quarterings is deduced in the annexed Pedigree :—

PLATE VI.

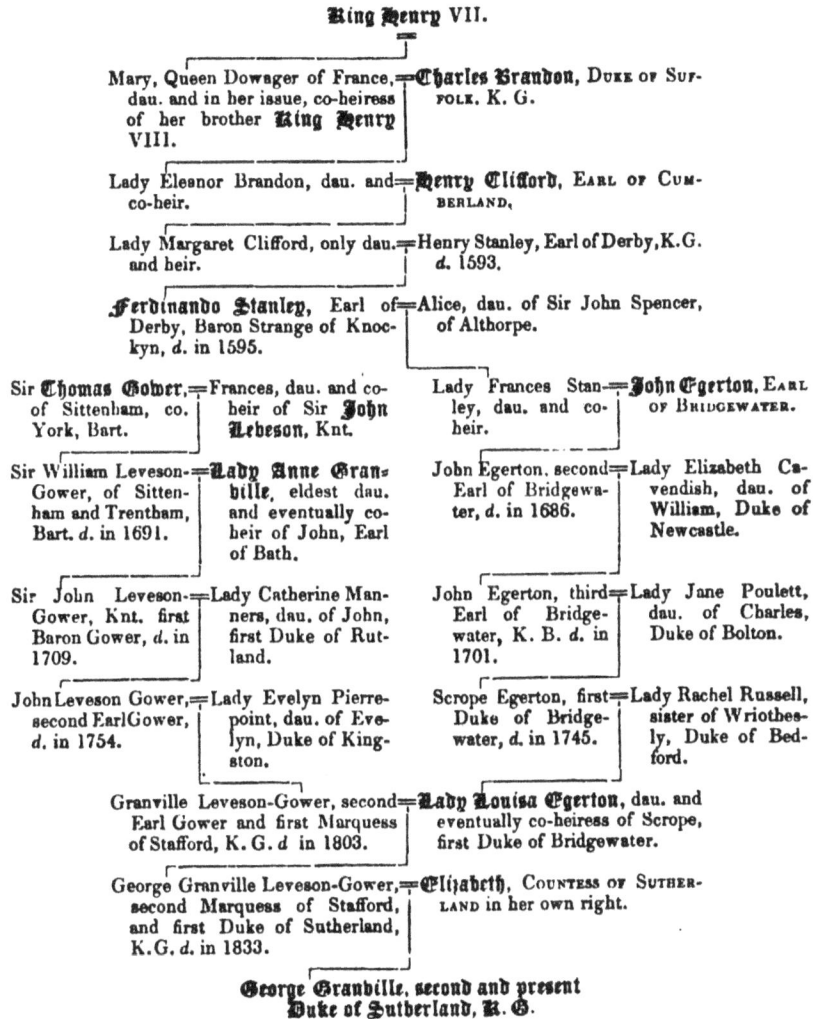

King Henry VII.

Mary, Queen Dowager of France,=Charles Brandon, Duke of Suf-
dau. and in her issue, co-heiress | folk. K. G.
of her brother King Henry
VIII.

Lady Eleanor Brandon, dau. and=Henry Clifford, Earl of Cum-
co-heir. | berland,

Lady Margaret Clifford, only dau.=Henry Stanley, Earl of Derby, K.G.
and heir. | d. 1593.

Ferdinando Stanley, Earl of=Alice, dau. of Sir John Spencer,
Derby, Baron Strange of Knoc- | of Althorpe.
kyn, d. in 1595.

Sir Thomas Gower,=Frances, dau. and co-   Lady Frances Stan-=John Egerton, Earl
of Sittenham, co. | heir of Sir John   ley, dau. and co- | of Bridgewater.
York, Bart. | Leveson, Knt.   heir.

Sir William Leveson-=Lady Anne Gran-   John Egerton, second=Lady Elizabeth Ca-
Gower, of Sitten- | ville, eldest dau.   Earl of Bridgewa- | vendish, dau. of
ham and Trentham, | and eventually co-   ter, d. in 1686. | William, Duke of
Bart. d. in 1691. | heir of John, Earl | Newcastle.
              | of Bath.

Sir John Leveson-=Lady Catherine Man-   John Egerton, third=Lady Jane Poulett,
Gower, Knt. first | ners, dau. of John,   Earl of Bridge- | dau. of Charles,
Baron Gower, d. in | first Duke of Rut-   water, K. B. d. in | Duke of Bolton.
1709. | land.   1701.

John Leveson Gower,=Lady Evelyn Pierre-   Scrope Egerton, first=Lady Rachel Russell,
second Earl Gower, | point, dau. of Eve-   Duke of Bridge- | sister of Wriothes-
d. in 1754. | lyn, Duke of King-   water, d. in 1745. | ly, Duke of Bed-
              | ston. | ford.

Granville Leveson-Gower, second=Lady Louisa Egerton, dau. and
Earl Gower and first Marquess | eventually co-heiress of Scrope,
of Stafford, K. G. d in 1803. | first Duke of Bridgewater.

George Granville Leveson-Gower,=Elizabeth, Countess of Suther-
second Marquess of Stafford, | land in her own right.
and first Duke of Sutherland,
K.G. d. in 1833.

George Granville, second and present
Duke of Sutherland, K. G.

The Most Noble George Granville Leveson-Gower,

Duke of Sutherland,

Knight of the Garter.

F. I. Becker, sc.

London, Edward Churton, [illegible]

PLATE VII.

———

Harris, of Cork, Ireland.

THE Family of Harris, of Cork, descends from William Harris, a Quaker, who died at Park's Grove, co. Kilkenny, in 1658, and is believed to have been son of Sir Thomas Harris, who, in 1654, made an unsuccessful attempt to surprise the Castle of the Foregate, Shrewsbury, in order to favour the restoration of Charles II.

> Arms.—Barry of ten az. and erm. three annulets or.
> Crest.—A hare, holding, in the forepaws, two ears of wheat ppr.
> Motto.—Sola virtus invicta.

Raffles, of Liverpool.

THE present Rev. THOMAS RAFFLES, LL.D. and D.D. of Liverpool, heir male and representative of the late distinguished Sir THOMAS STAMFORD RAFFLES, Lieut.-Governor of Java, bears on an escutcheon of pretence, the arms of HARGREAVES in right of his wife, an heiress of that family.

> Arms.—Erminois, an eagle with two heads displayed gu. charged on the breast with an eastern crown or, a chief vert, thereon a cross crosslet, fitchée of the third : an escutcheon of pretence, quarterly or and vert. on a fesse erm. betw. three stags courant counterchanged, a fret gu.
> Crest.—Out of an eastern crown or, a griffin's head purpure, beaked and gorged with a collar gemel, gold.
> Motto.—In Cruce triumphans.

Cleland, of Rath Gael House, co. Down.

JAMES-DOWSETT ROSE-CLELAND, of Rath Gael House, Esq. quarters the Arms of ROSE, BENNET, ALLEN, MURDOCH, and CLELAND.

> Arms.—Quarterly, first, Az. a hare saliant ar. with a hunting-horn vert, hanging about the neck, garnished gu. for CLELAND. Second, Sa. on a pale ar. three roses gu. seeded and slipped ppr. for ROSE. Third, Gu. a bezant betw. three demi-lions ramp. ar. for BENNET. Fourth, Ar. a chev. betw. three roses gu. stalked and leaved vert, for ALLEN. Fifth, Ar. two ravens hanging paleways sa. with an arrow through both their heads fesseways ppr. for MURDOCH. Sixth, Az. a hare saliant ar. betw. a hunting-horn and rose both of the second for CLELAND.
> Crests.—First, A falcon standing on a sinister hand glove ppr. for CLELAND. Second, A rose gu. seeded and slipped ppr. betw. two wings erm. for ROSE.
> Supporters.—Two greyhounds ppr. collared or.
> Mottoes.—Je pense a qui pense plus (under the Arms). Non sibi (over the Cleland Crest). Flourish (over the Rose Crest.)

Thomas Rose, of Charlestown, South Caro-=Elizabeth Bennet, an heiress, m. 1704.
lina, America, Esq., settled there about 1700.

Richard Rose, of Abingdon, co. Berks, Esq.=Elizabeth, only child and heir of William
died 14 Jan. 1784.　Allen, of Grove, Wantage, Berks, Esq.

Richard Rose, of Abingdon, Esq. died in 1768.=Agnes, dau. and eventual heir of John Cleland, of Whithorn, co. Wigton, Esq. (de-
scended from Cleland of that Ilk) by his
wife, Margaret Murdoch, an heiress.

James-Dowsett Rose-Cleland, of Rath Gael House, co. Down, Esq. High Sheriff in 1805.

PLATE VII.

Cole, of Brandrum, co. Monaghan.

OWEN BLAYNEY COLE, of Brandrum, co. Monaghan, Esq. (descended from Edward Cole, of Twickenham, Esq. born in 1579,) impales the arms of MONCK, having married Lady Frances Monck, daughter of the Earl of Rathdowne.

> **Arms.**—Ar. within a bordure sa. bezantée, a bull gu. and for augmentation (to mark the descent, through the Blayneys, of Mr. Cole, of Brandrum, from the noble house of Drogheda), on a canton erm. a nag's head ppr. over which on a chief or, three estoiles gu. Impaling gu. a chev. betw. three lions' heads erased ar. for MONCK.
>
> **Crest.**—A demi dragon vert, bearing in the dexter paw a javelin armed or, feathered ar.
>
> **Motto.**—Deum cole Regem serva.

Wilson, of Knowle Hall, co. Warwick.

WILLIAM HENRY BOWEN JORDAN WILSON, of Knowle Hall, Esq. bears a shield of six quarterings, and an escutcheon of pretence in right of his wife, the dau. and co-heir of Richard Le Hunte, of Artramont, co. Wexford, Esq.

> **Arms.**—Quarterly, First, Sa. a wolf saliant or, in chief a rose ppr. betw. two estoiles gold, for WILSON. Second, Gu. a lion ramp. regard. or, for FITZGERALD. Third, Ar. on a fesse sa. three cross-crosslets of the field, for NEWSHAM. Fourth, Az. on a chev. betw. three fleurs-de-lis ar. as many estoiles gu. for SHEPPERD. Five, Az. three mullets pierced or, for HARRIES. Sixth, quarterly first and fourth, Gu. a lion ramp. within an orle of cross-crosslets fitchée or; second and third, Az. three catherine wheels or, on a chief of the second, a greyhound courant, sa. for JORDAN. On an escutcheon of pretence for LE HUNTE, vert a saltire ar.
>
> **Crest.**—A wolf's head.
>
> **Motto.**—Fortiter et fideliter.

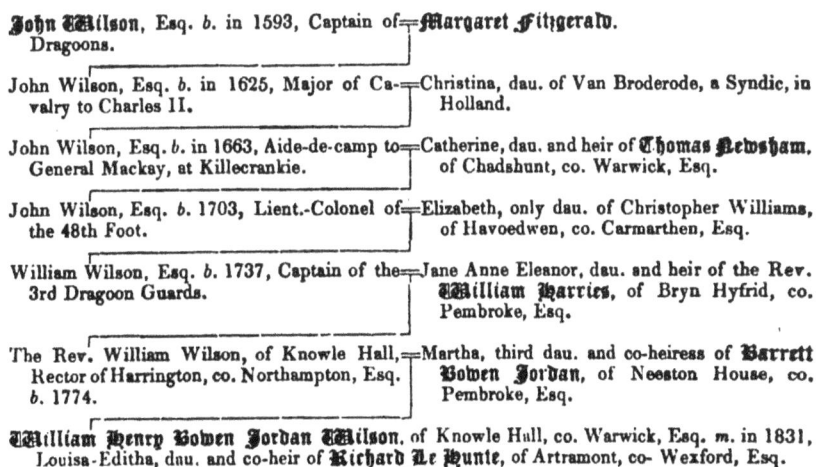

John Wilson, Esq. b. in 1593, Captain of Dragoons.=Margaret Fitzgerald.

John Wilson, Esq. b. in 1625, Major of Cavalry to Charles II.=Christina, dau. of Van Broderode, a Syndic, in Holland.

John Wilson, Esq. b. in 1663, Aide-de-camp to General Mackay, at Killecrankie.=Catherine, dau. and heir of Thomas Newsham, of Chadshunt, co. Warwick, Esq.

John Wilson, Esq. b. 1703, Lient.-Colonel of the 48th Foot.=Elizabeth, only dau. of Christopher Williams, of Havoedwen, co. Carmarthen, Esq.

William Wilson, Esq. b. 1737, Captain of the 3rd Dragoon Guards.=Jane Anne Eleanor, dau. and heir of the Rev. William Harries, of Bryn Hyfrid, co. Pembroke, Esq.

The Rev. William Wilson, of Knowle Hall, Rector of Harrington, co. Northampton, Esq. b. 1774.=Martha, third dau. and co-heiress of Barrett Bowen Jordan, of Neeston House, co. Pembroke, Esq.

William Henry Bowen Jordan Wilson, of Knowle Hall, co. Warwick, Esq. m. in 1831, Louisa-Editha, dau. and co-heir of Richard Le Hunte, of Artramont, co- Wexford, Esq.

PLATE VII

HARRIS OF CORK.

THE REV? THOMAS RAFFLES, LLD. DD.
LIVERPOOL.

NON SIBI   FLOURISH

JAMES DOWSETT ROSE CLELAND, ESQ.
RATH GAEL HOUSE, CO. DOWN.

OWEN BLANEY COLE, ESQ.
BRANDRUM CO. MONAGHAN.

W. H. B. J. WILSON, ESQ.
KNOWLE HALL. CO. WARWICK.

London, Edward Churton, 26 Holles Street, Cavendish Square, 1842.

PLATE VIII.

Warrington, of Lancashire.

THE Ensigns borne by Captain WILLIAM HENRY WARRINGTON, late of the 3rd Dragoon Guards, are those of the ancient family of Warrington of Aigberth, co. Lancaster, quartered with the Arms of STRUDWICK.

    Arms.—Quarterly, first and fourth, per chev. or and az. three lions ramp. counterchanged, for WARRINGTON. Second and third, per pale erm. and sa. a lion ramp. or, holding in the paws a cross pattée fitchée of the last, for STRUDWICK.

    Crest.—Out of a ducal coronet gu. a demi eagle displ. or.

The Rev. George Warrington, Rector of Pleasley, co. Derby, and Vicar of Hope, co. Flint, grandson of John Warrington, of Aigberth, Esq.	=	Mary, only dau. and heir of Henry Strudwick, Esq. descended from the Baronetical families of Hanmer and Broughton.		
George Henry Warrington, who m. the heiress of Carew, of Carew Castle and Crowcombe, and assumed, in 1811, the name and arms of Carew.	Hanmer Warrington, Esq. Major 4th Dragoon Gds. Consul-general at Tripoli. =	Jane Elizabeth, only dau. of Charles Price, Esq.	Thornhill Warrington, Esq. Capt. 8th Light Dragoons.	Other issue.

1. Hanmer George Warrington.	2. William Henry Warrington, Capt. 3rd Dragoon Gds.	3. Charles Thornhill, 11th Light Dragoons, d. in 1839.	4. Frederick. 5. Herbert, H.M. Vice-consul at Tripoli.	Osman, 77th Regt.	Henry.

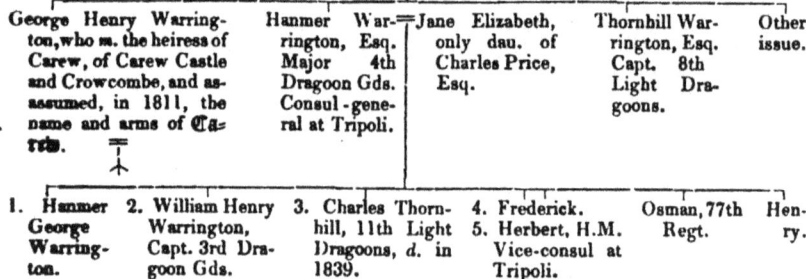

Bracebridge, of Morville House, co. Warwick.

WALTER HENRY BRACEBRIDGE, of Chetwode Priory, co. Bucks, Esq. now residing at Morville House, near Warwick, lineally descended from the marriage of Peter de Bracebrigg, of Bracebrigg, co. Lincoln, with Amicia, grand-daughter and ultimately heiress of TURCHILL DE ARDEN, EARL OF WARWICK, bears the ancient Coat of Bracebridge, differenced by a crescent of cadency, and quartered with that of Turchill de Arden; and impales (in right of his wife, Mary-Holte, only dau. of the late Abraham Bracebridge, of Atherstone, Esq. the head of the family) the Arms of Bracebridge, without the crescent, and with the quarterings of HOLTE and BRERETON.

    Arms.—Quarterly, first and fourth, vairé ar. and sa. a fesse gu. charged with a crescent for difference, for BRACEBRIDGE; second and third, chequy or and az. a chev. erm. for TURCHILL DE ARDEN; impaling, first and fourth, vairé ar. and sa. a fesse gu. for BRACEBRIDGE; second, az. two bars or, in chief a cross formée fitchée of the second, for HOLTE; third, ar. two bars sa. for BRERETON.

    Crest.—A staff ragulée ar.

    Motto.—Be as God will.

PLATE VIII.

Peter de Bracebrigg, of Bracebrigg : from which marriage derived ═ Amicia, grand dau. and heir of **Curchill de Arden**. Earl of Warwick.		**Sir Charles Holte**, of Aston, co. Warwick, Bart. great grandson of Sir Robert Holte, Bart. by Jane, his wife, dau. and eventual heiress of **Brereton of Brereton**, co. Chester.
Walter Bracebridge, Esq. 2nd son of Abraham Bracebridge, of Atherstone, Esq. ═ Harriet, dau. of H. Streatfield, Esq.	**Abraham Bracebridge**, of Atherstone, Esq. elder son of Abraham Bracebridge, of Atherstone, Esq. ═ Mary-Elizabeth, only dau. and heir of Sir Charles Holte, Bart.	

Harriet Anne, m. to Henry Ogle, Esq.	Elizabeth, d. unm.	**Walter Henry Bracebridge**, of Morville House, Esq. ═ Mary-Holte Bracebridge, only dau.		Charles Holte Bracebridge, Esq.

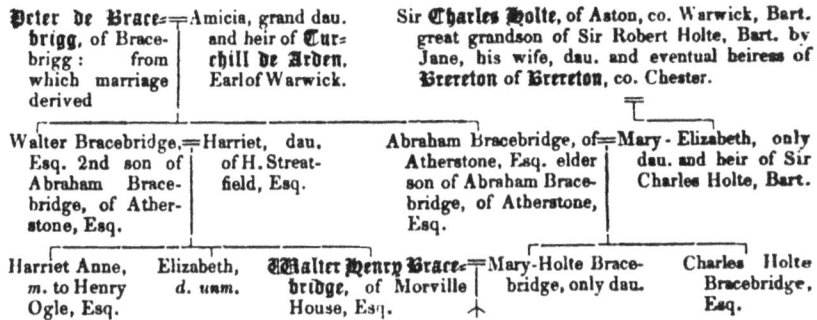

Forbes, of Culloden, co. Inverness.

THE Family of Forbes, of Culloden, derive, through the Tolquhon branch, from the noble House of Forbes, and bear its Arms, with the addition of three unicorns' heads. The present representative is ARTHUR FORBES, of Culloden House, Esq. great-great-grandson of the Right Hon. Duncan Forbes, fifth Laird of Culloden, the celebrated Lord President of the Court of Session.

> **Arms.**—Az. on a chev. betw. three bears' heads ar. muzzled gu. as many unicorns' heads erased sa.
> **Crest.**—An eagle displ. or.
> **Motto.**—Salus per Christum.

Cardale.

THESE Arms were borne by WILLIAM CARDALE, of Dudley, A. D. 1670, son of William Cardale, of Hagley, and grandson of William Cardale, living in 1590. The existing representatives are JOHN BATE CARDALE, and EDWARD THOMAS CARDALE, of Bedford Row, Esqrs. sons, by Mary Anne Bennett, his wife, grand-daughter and co-heir of Say, of the late William Cardale, Esq. who was son of William Cardale, of Bedford Row, Esq. who died in 1816, and grandson of Fernando Cardale, Alderman of Worcester, son of John Cardale, who was the eldest son of William Cardale, of Dudley. The Rev. Joseph Cardale, Vicar of Bulkington, co. Warwick, and of Hinckley, co. Leicester, fourth son of William Cardale, of Dudley, was father of the Rev. George Cardale, D. D. Vicar of Rothley, co. Leicester, whose only son was the Rev. GEORGE CARDALE, Rector of Millbrook, co. Bedford.

> **Arms.**—Az. a chev. ar. betw. three linnets ppr. [Carduelis, a linnet, dict. qd. Carduorum semine pascatur.]
> **Crest.**—A linnet ppr.
> **Motto.**—Studendo et contemplando indefessus.

The family of Cardonnay (varied from Chardonneret Carduelis) Seigneur de Courtieres, &c. Generalité de Rouen, maintained their right to the same charges on a field gu. in 1668. *Vide Nobiliare de Normandie, Cardonnay.*

Dyson, of Willow Hall.

THE Arms borne by THOMAS FOURNIS DYSON, of Willow Hall, co. York, and Everton, co. Lancaster, Esq. are DYSON and EDWARDS quarterly, the latter in right of his descent from the family of Edwards, of Northowran, co. York.

> **Arms.**—Quarterly, first and fourth, per pale or and ss. the sun, also per pale sa. and gold, for DYSON. Second and third, per bend sinister erm. and ermines, a lion ramp. or, for EDWARDS.
> **Crests.**—First, for DYSON, on a mount vert a paschal lamb ar. with a banner and flag. Second, for EDWARDS, a demi lion per bend sinister, erm. and ermines.
> **Motto.**—Cruci dum spiro fido.

WILLIAM, HENRY, WARRINGTON, ESQ.
LATE CAPT.^N 3RD DRAGOON GUARDS.

WALTER, HENRY, BRACEBRIDGE, ESQ.
MORVILLE HOUSE, CO. WARWICK.

ARTHUR FORBES, ESQ.
CULLODEN, CO. INVERNESS.

CARDALE.

T. F. DYSON, ESQ.
WILLOW HALL, HALIFAX.

London, Edward Churton,

PLATE IX.

Baker, of Bayfordbury, co. Herts.

WILLIAM ROBERT BAKER, of Bayfordbury, Esq. High Sheriff of the county in 1836, is son of the late William Baker, of Bayfordbury, Esq. grandson of William Baker, Esq. member for Hertfordshire in five successive parliaments, and great-grandson of Sir William Baker, Knt. who purchased the manor of Bayford.

Arms.—Per pale erm. and gu. a greyhound courant betw. two bars invected, in chief two quatrefoils, and another in base, all counterchanged.

Crest.—A cockatrice per fesse, indented erminois and pean, combed and wattled gu. gorged with a collar az. and in the beak a quatrefoil slipped vert.

Currie, of Bush Hill, Co. Middlesex.

THIS family, settled at Dunse, co. Berwick, in 1571, derived from CUTHBERT CURRIE, a Cadet of the family of that Ilk, in Annandale, and has always borne the same arms as the Chief of the house. The present ISAAC CURRIE, of Bush Hill, Esq. is son of the late WILLIAM CURRIE, Esq. banker of London, by Madeleine Lefevre, his wife, grand aunt of the Right Honourable C. Shaw Lefevre, Speaker of the House of Commons.

Arms.—Gu. a saltire ar. in chief a rose of the second, barbed and seeded ppr.

Crest.—A cock gu.

Crawfurd, of Newfield, co. Ayr.

REPRESENTATIVE OF CRAWFURD OF CRAWFURD, OF LOUDOUN AND OF CROSBY.

COLONEL CRAWFURD, of Newfield, as male representative of the great Scottish house of Crawfurd, bears the supporters and quartered coat—first and fourth, Crawfurd, of Crosby; second and third, Crawfurd, of Crawfurd.

REGINALD DE CRAWFURD, living in the beginning of the twelfth century, is supposed, from the strongest presumptive evidence, identity of Arms, &c. to have sprung from a younger son of the old Earls of Richmond.

Arms.—Quarterly, first and fourth, Erm. two tilting spears saltirewise, gu. for CRAWFURD of Crosby; second and third, gu. a fesse erm. for CRAWFURD of Crawfurd.

Crest.—A phœnix rising from flames, gu.

Supporters.—Two stags gu.

Mottoes.—God shaw the right. *Above the Crest*, I bide my time.

PLATE IX.

Tempest, of Tong, co. York.

JOHN PLUMBE-TEMPEST, of Tong Hall, co. York, Esq. and of Haughton, co. Lancaster, Colonel of the First Royal Lancashire Militia, bears the arms of Tempest and Plumbe quarterly, as depicted in the Engraving; quartering in addition, the ensigns of LEGGARD, HEBDEN, RYE, BOLLING, MIRFIELD, TONG, SAVILLE, CHOLMLEY, and FRANK, heiresses of which families his ancestors had married.

> **Arms.**—Quarterly, first and fourth, Ar. a bend betw. six martlets sa. for TEMPEST; second and third, Erm. a bend vaire betw. two cotises sa. for PLUMBE.

> **Crests.**—First, A griffin's head erased per pale, ar. and sa. beaked gu. for TEMPEST. Second, on a mount vert. a greyhound sejant ar. collared gu. spotted or, for PLUMBE.

> **Motto.**—Loywf as thow fynds.

Sir **John Tempest**, of Tong Hall, co. York, Bt. representative of the marriage of Henry Tempest, eighth son of Sir Richard Tempest, of Bracewell, Knt. with Ellenor, dau. and heir of **Christopher Mirfield**, of Tong Hall, Esq. = Henrietta Catharina, dau. and heir of Sir **Henry Cholmley**, of Newton Grange, co. York, Knt.

Sir George Tempest, of Tong Hall, Bart.: died in 1745. = Anne, dau. and heir of **Edward Frank**, of Campsal, Esq.

Sir Henry Tempest, Bart. — John Tempest, of Nottingham, Esq. Captain in Churchill's Dragoons. = Elizabeth, fourth dau. of William Seremshire, of Cotgrave, Notts. Esq.

Sir Henry Tempest, d. s. p. 1819. — **Elizabeth Tempest**, dau. and eventual heiress. = **Thomas Plumbe**, Esq. son and heir of William Plumbe, of Wavertree Hall and Aughton, Esq.

John Plumbe Tempest, of Tong Hall, Esq.

Guerin, of Norton Fitz Warren.

THE REV. J. GUERIN, of Norton Fitz Warren, co. Somerset, derives from a noble French family, established at Champaign, Isle of France and Auvergne.

> **Arms.**—Or, three lions ramp. sa. langued armed and crowned gu.

> **Crest.**—A demi lion, as in the Arms.

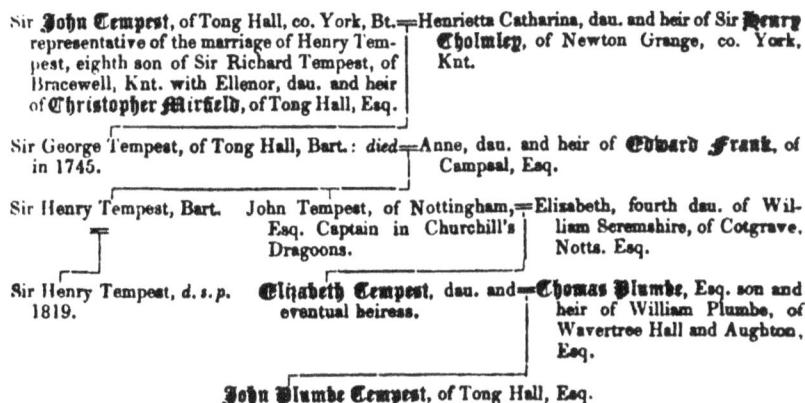

PLATE. IX

WILLIAM BAKER, ESQ.
BAYFORDBURY, HERTS.

I BIDE MY TIME

RAIKES CURRIE, ESQ.

COLONEL CRAWFURD, OF NEWFIELD, CO. AYR.
REPRESENTATIVE OF CRAWFURD, OF CRAWFURD, AND CROSBY.

JOHN PLUMBE TEMPEST, ESQ.
TONG HALL, CO. YORK

THE REV. J GUERIN
NORTON FITZWARREN, CO. SOMERSET

PLATE X.

Hibbert Ware, of Edinburgh.

Samuel Hibbert-Ware, M.D. of Edinburgh, whose patronymic is Hibbert, assumed, by sign manual, in 1837, the additional name and arms of Ware, as representative of the eldest branch of the family of Sir James Ware, the historian of Ireland, and now bears the ensigns of Ware and Hibbert quarterly.

    Arms.—First and fourth, Or, two lions passant az. within a bordure of the second, charged with escallops of the first, for Ware. Second and third, barry of eight or and vert, a pale counterchanged, for Hibbert.

    Crests.—First, A dragon's head or, pierced through the neck with a broken tilting-spear ppr. for Ware. Second, A hand holding a millrind ppr. for Hibbert.

    Motto.—Sola salus servire Deo.

The Descent is thus deduced :—

Sir James Ware, Knt. the Historian, *b.* 26 Nov. 1594, eldest son of Sir James Ware, Knt. Auditor-General of Ireland. ═ Elizabeth, dau. of Jacob Newman, of Dublin, Esq. *m.* 31 Dec. 1620; *d.* 9 June, 1651.

James Ware, Esq. Auditor-General of Ireland, *b.* 9 Aug. 1622: *d.* 6 May, 1689. ═ Barbara Stone, second wife, *m.* 24 Nov. 1667.

James Ware, Esq. son and heir, *d.* in 1755. ═ Miss Fitzgerald, of the co. of Westmeath.

Robert Ware, of Dublin, Esq. *d.* 18 July, 1779. ═ Miss Anne Thomas, of a Welsh family.

Sarah Ware, only child to leave issue, *b.* in 1751, *m.* 30 May, 1780. ═ Samuel Hibbert, of Manchester, afterwards of Clarendon House, Chorlton, Esq.

Samuel Hibbert Ware, M.D. of Edinburgh.   Other issue.

Caldwell, of Linley Wood.

James Stamford Caldwell, of Linley Wood, co. Stafford, Esq. M. A. bears the quartered Coat of Caldwell and Stamford.

    Arms.—Quarterly, first and fourth, per pale, sa. and vert, a stag's head couped ar. in chief three cold wells ppr. for Caldwell; second and third, ar. two bars az. on a canton gu. a gauntlet grasping a broken sword ppr. hilt and pomel gold, for Stamford.

    Crest.—A lion couchant ar. gorged with two bars, the upper sa. the lower vert, holding betw. the paws a cold well ppr.

    Motto.—Niti, facere, experiri.

James Caldwell, of Linley Wood, Esq. a magistrate and deputy-lieutenant for Staffordshire, Recorder of the borough of Newcastle-under-Lyme, *d.* 16 Jan. 1838. ═ Elizabeth, dau. and co-heir of Thomas Stamford, of Derby, Esq. by Hannah, his wife, eldest dau. of John Crompton, of Chorley Hall, co. Lancaster, Esq.

James Stamford Caldwell, of Linley Wood, Esq.

PLATE X.

Colquhoun, of that Ilk and Luss.

THE present Chief of the ancient house of Colquhoun, Sir JAMES COLQUHOUN, of that Ilk and Luss, co. Dumbarton, Bart. bears—

Arms.—Ar. a saltire engrailed sa.
Crest.—A hart's head gu.
Supporters.—Two greyhounds ar. collared sa.
Mottoes.—*Above the Crest*, Si je puis. *Under the Arms*, Cnock Elachan, being the war cry of the clan.

The Arms of the Colquhouns are stated to have originated thus :—During the reign of one of the early Kings of Scotland, when the turbulent nobles were accustomed to rebellion, and feuds and civil wars were of frequent occurrence, the castle of Dumbarton was in the hands of the insurgents, who refused, when summoned, to give it up. Colquhoun of Luss, being a steady loyalist, received a message from the King, requesting him to retake the castle, and wrote for answer, ' If 1 can.' Accordingly, after due consideration, he assembled his clansmen and retainers, for a grand stag hunt, fully armed and equipped, as was the custom at that period on such occasions, the hunt being appointed to take place somewhere in the neighbourhood of Dumbarton. The garrison were politely invited to witness the hunt, and having no suspicion that any ruse was intended, they nearly all left the castle. Colquhoun of Luss, in the mean time, taking advantage of their absence, quickly returned, and succeeded in taking the castle. In commemoration of this feat the King granted the Bearings, which have ever since been used by the Colquhouns of Luss.

Huband, of Ipsley, co. Warwick.

THIS family, originally Hubald, derived from Hugh Hubald, who held Ipsley of Osbernus at the time of the Conquest. The chief line, the Hubands of Ipsley, were created Baronets of England in 1660, but are now extinct. The male representation of the family at present vests in GEORGE HUBAND, Esq. M. A. Capt. 8th Hussars, son, by Frances, his wife, eldest daughter of Arthur Chichester Macartney, Esq. of the late Willcocks Huband, Esq. the lineal descendant of Anthony, son of Nicholas Huband, Esq. a younger son of the Ipsley family.

Arms.—Sa. three leopards' faces jessant-de-lis ar.
Crest.—A wolf passant or.
Motto.—Cave lupum.

Burnell, of Beauchieff Abbey and Winkbourne Hall.

BROUGHTON BENJAMIN PEGGE-BURNELL, of Beauchieff Abbey, co. Derby, and Winkbourne Hall, co. Notts, Esq., whose patronymic was STEADE, assumed, on inheriting the estates of his uncle, Peter Pegge Burnell, Esq. in 1839, the surname and arms of PEGGE and BURNELL. He is son of the late Thomas Steade, of Woodseats, Esq. by Miliscent, his wife, daughter of Strelley Pegge, Esq. of Beauchieff Abbey, and representative of the ancient family of STEADE, possessed of Onesacre, co. York, *temp.* Edward III.

Arms.—Quarterly, first and fourth, per fesse indented or and ar. a lion ramp. sa. a bordure gu. charged with eight plates, for BURNELL. Second and third, ar. a chev. betw. three wedges sa. for PEGGE.
Crests.—First, a lion's gamb erect and erased sa. in the paw a bunch of violets ppr. for BURNELL. Second, the sun rising in splendour, the rays alternately sa. or, and ar. for PEGGE.
Motto.—Caritas fructum habit.

SAMUEL HIBBERT WARE, M.D.
EDINBURGH.

JAMES STAMFORD CALDWELL, ESQ.
LINLEY WOOD, STAFFORDSHIRE.

SIR JAMES COLQUHOUN, BART.
OF THAT ILK AND LUSS.

HUBAND OF IPSLEY.
CO. WARWICK.

B. D. PEGGE BURNELL, ESQ.
BEAUCHIEFF ABBEY, CO. DERBY.

PLATE XI.

Chaucer.

GEOFFRY CHAUCER, of Woodstock, co. Oxon, the father of English poetry, was a citizen of London, where he was born in the year 1328. He was a gentleman, and appears to have studied at both the Universities of Cambridge and Oxford, and subsequently to have travelled abroad. His arise though is attributable to his connexion with John of Gaunt, Chaucer having married in 1360, the sister of Catherine Swynford, the mistress, afterwards wife of the prince. He first held the place of Valettus, or Yeoman to Edward III.; then that of Gentleman of the King's Privy Chamber, and subsequently, after returning from Genoa, when he was accredited to manage some public business in 1372, Comptroller of the Customs. Chaucer died at the age of seventy-two.

Arms.—Parted per pale ar. and gu. a bend counterchanged.

Crest.—A tortoise pass. ppr.

Shakespeare.

JOHN SHAKESPEARE, of Stratford-upon-Avon, co. Warwick, who, after passing through the regular gradations of municipal offices in that town, became one of its chamberlains in 1561, and bailiff or chief magistrate in 1569; obtained in the latter year a grant of arms from Robert Cooke, Clarenceux, which being lost, was confirmed by Dethick, Garter King at Arms, and Camden in 1599. The confirmation recites that " John Shakspere, now of Stratford-upon-Avon, in the county of Warwick, Gent., whose parent and grandfather, late antecessor for his faithful and approved service to the late most prudent prince, King Henry VII. was advanced and rewarded with lands and tenements given to him in those parts of Warwickshire, where they have continued for some descents in good reputation, credit," &c. John Shakespeare, who appears to have been a Wool-dealer, married Mary, dau. and co-heir of Robert Arden, of Willingcote, co. Warwick, son of Arden, Groom of the Chamber to Henry VII. who was nephew of Sir John Arden, Knt. Squire of the Body to Henry VII. and grandson of Walter Arden, by Eleanor, his wife, dau. of John Hampden, of the county of Bucks. To Mary Arden her

PLATE XI.

father, by his will, dated 24 Nov. 1556, devised " all his land in Willingcote, called Asbyes ;" and we learn from a document, dated 24 Nov. 1597, that John Shakespeare and Mary his wife were " lawfully seized in their demesne as of fee, as in the right of the said Mary, of and in one messuage, &c. in Wylmicote." By Mary Arden, who was buried at Stratford, 9 Sept. 1608, John Shakespeare, who was buried at the same place, 8 Sept. 1601, had issue, I. WILLIAM. II. Gilbert, resident at Stratford, living in 1602. III. Richard, died 1613. IV. Edmund, born in 1580, an actor, was buried in the church of St. Mary Overies, in Southwark, in 1613. I. Jone, baptized at Stratford, 15 Sept. 1558. II. Margaret, baptized at Stratford, 2 Dec. 1562, and buried there, 30 April, 1563. III. Jone, baptized at Stratford in 1569. The eldest son, the immortal WILLIAM SHAKESPEARE, was baptized at Stratford, 26 April, 1564, married (æt. eighteen years and a half) subsequent to 28 Nov. 25 Eliz. 1582, the date of his marriage-bond or licence, Anne, then æt. twenty-eight years, dau. of John Hathaway, of Shottery, near Stratford, Yeoman, who held a copyhold estate at Shottery in 1543. By Anne Hathaway, who died 6 Aug. 1623, æt. sixty-seven, the illustrious dramatist, who was buried at Stratford, 25 April, 1616, had issue,—I. SUSANNA, baptized at Stratford, 26 May, 1553, and living 26 April, 1616, married in 1607, Dr. Hall, a physician of repute at Stratford, and had issue, Elizabeth, born in 1608. II. HAMMET, baptized at Stratford, 2 Feb. 1585, and buried there, 11 Aug. 1596. III. JUDITH, twin with Hammet, baptized at Stratford, 2 Feb. 1585, married, Feb. 1616, and was living, 25 April, in the same year.

Arms.—Or, on a bend sa. a spear of the first.

Crest.—A falcon displayed ar. holding a spear in pale or.

Milton.

JOHN MILTON was of an ancient family, proprietors of Milton, near Thame, in Oxfordshire, from which the patronymic. They were Catholics, and so zealous, that the father of the bard was disinherited by his father, who held the post of Ranger of the Forest of Shotover, for becoming a Protestant, and forced in consequence to earn his livelihood in London as a Scrivener. This gentleman, who was a good classical scholar, and remarkable for his skill in music, married a lady also of ancient family, and had two sons and one daughter:—JOHN, born in Bread Street, where his father resided, 9 Dec. 1608, Christopher, who became one of the Judges of the Common Pleas, and Anne, married to Edward Phillips, Secondary at the Crown Office. Milton, the Poet, married in 1642, Mary, dau. of Richard Powel, Esq. a magistrate of the county of Oxford, died in November, 1674, when he had nearly completed his sixty-sixth year.

Arms.—Ar. an eagle displayed with two heads gu. beaked and legged sa.

PLATE XI.

Pope.

ALEXANDER POPE, a citizen of London, was born in Lombard Street, where his father was a Silk-Mercer, in May, 1688. Pope himself states that his ancestors were of gentle blood, and there is no reason to doubt the assertion. His paternal grandfather was a clergyman of the established church, the head of whose family was Pope, Earl of Down, and the Poet bore the Arms of that Nobleman. His Parents were, however, Catholics, and Pope was brought up, and continued in the ancient Faith; his mother was the daughter of "one Mr. Turner, of York, a gentleman and loyalist, and it may be presumed of some importance in his day; for of his three sons, who all entered into the service of Charles, it is thought worth while to record, that one fell in the field, another died while in the army, and the third, on the failure of the Royal Cause, went to Spain, were he rose to be a general officer."

> Of gentle blood (part shed in honour's cause,
> While yet in Britain honour had applause)
> Each parent sprang.—*Pope's Epistle to Arbuthnot.*

Pope died 30 May, 1774.

Arms.—Per pale, or and az. on a chev. betw. three griffins' heads erased, four fleurs-de-lis, all counterchanged.

Crest.—Two griffins' heads erased in dorso or and az. ducally collared, counterchanged.

Scott.

SIR WALTER SCOTT, the Author of "Waverley," was born in the College Wynd of Edinburgh, 15 August, 1771. He received his education at Mr. Leechman's Seminary, at the High School, and finally at the University of Edinburgh: he was called to the Bar, as an Advocate, 10 July, 1792. His love of literature, however, prevented his entering with energy into his profession, and he very soon relinquished the labours of the law for those more congenial to his taste. After attaining high reputation as a Poet, Scott entered upon his more brilliant career as a Novelist, by the anonymous publication of "Waverley," in 1814, and pursued it, uninterrupted by even a passing shadow, to nearly the close of his mortal pilgrimage—an event, deplored throughout the civilized world, which occurred on 21 September, 1832. His name lives with those of Shakespeare, Milton, and Pope.

PLATE XI.

Sir Walter was a descendant of the renowned Border Family of Scott of Harden, and quartered the Arms of Haliburton, as representative of HALIBURTON, of New Mains.

Arms.—Quarterly, first and fourth, or, two mullets in chief and a crescent in base az. within an orle of the second, for SCOTT; second and third, or, on a bend az. three mascles of the first, in the sinister chief point an oval buckle erect of the second for HALIBURTON.

Crest.—A female figure ppr. couped above the knees, vested gu. with az. waist and laced stomacher or, cuffs and ruffs ar. holding in the dexter hand a sun gold, and in the sinister a crescent of the fifth.

Supporters.—Dexter, a mermaid, holding in the exterior hand a mirror, ppr.; sinister, a Moor ppr. wreathed and cinctured ar. holding a torch reversed.

Motto.—*Over the Crest*, Reparabit cornua Phœbe; *under the Arms*, Watch weel.

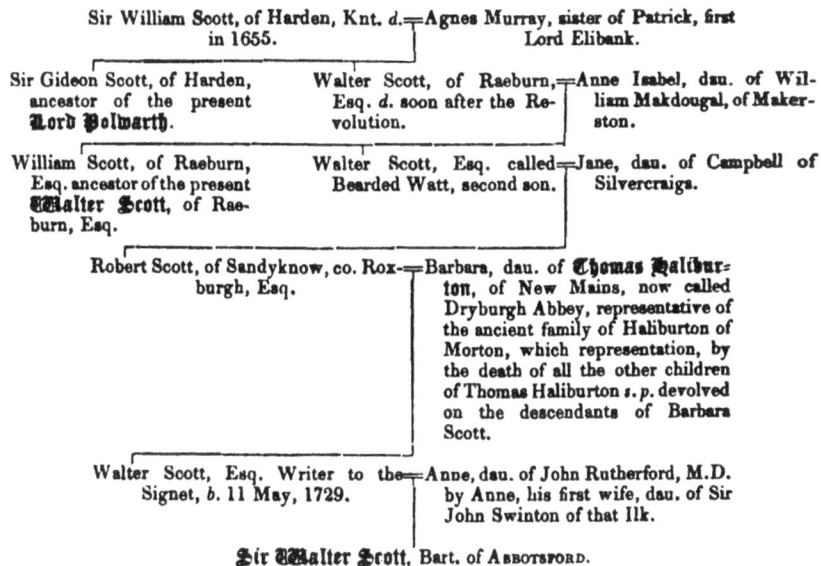

Sir William Scott, of Harden, Knt. *d.*＝Agnes Murray, sister of Patrick, first
in 1655.   Lord Elibank.

Sir Gideon Scott, of Harden, ancestor of the present **Lord Polwarth**.

Walter Scott, of Raeburn,＝Anne Isabel, dau. of William Makdougal, of Makerston.
Esq. *d.* soon after the Revolution.

William Scott, of Raeburn, Esq. ancestor of the present **Walter Scott**, of Raeburn, Esq.

Walter Scott, Esq. called＝Jane, dau. of Campbell of Silvercraigs.
Bearded Watt, second son.

Robert Scott, of Sandyknow, co. Rox-＝Barbara, dau. of **Thomas Haliburton**, of New Mains, now called Dryburgh Abbey, representative of the ancient family of Haliburton of Morton, which representation, by the death of all the other children of Thomas Haliburton *s. p.* devolved on the descendants of Barbara Scott.
burgh, Esq.

Walter Scott, Esq. Writer to the＝Anne, dau. of John Rutherford, M.D.
Signet, *b.* 11 May, 1729.   by Anne, his first wife, dau. of Sir John Swinton of that Ilk.

Sir Walter Scott, Bart. of ABBOTSFORD.

PLATE XI

Geoffrey Chaucer
Born A.D. 1328
Died A.D. 1400.

William Shakespeare
Born A.D. 1564
Died A.D. 1616.

REPARABIT CORNUA PHŒBE

WATCH WEEL

Sir Walter Scott, Bart.
ABBOTSFORD.

John Milton
Born A.D. 1608
Died A.D. 1674.

Alexander Pope
Born A.D. 1688
Died A.D. 1744.

F T Becker sc

PLATE XII.

Warter, of Cruck Meole, co. Salop.

THESE Arms, without the quartering, have been long the Bearing of the family of WARTER, originally of Warter co. York, and subsequently of Stableford, Swancok Rudge, and Cruck Meole, co. Salop; also of Staffordshire and London. They were borne in 1451 by Christopher Warter, Esq. Sheriff of London, and by Sir Willyam Warter, *temp.* Henry VIII. and were confirmed 13 Queen Anne, with the addition of the Crest, to John Warter, of the Inner Temple, Esq. Assistant to the Counsel for the affairs of the Admiralty and Navy of Great Britain.

Arms.—Quarterly, first and fourth, sa. on a chev. engr. betw. three chessrooks ar. as many crosses crosslet fitchée of the first, for WARTER. Second and third, or, on a pile az. three martlets of the field, a chief of the second, for WOOD.

Crest.—A lion ramp. sa. collared ar. holding betw. his fore-paws a chessrook of the last.

Motto.—Vi victus non coactus.

Hurt, of Alderwasley and Wirksworth, co. Derby.

THE families of Hurt, of Alderwasley and Wirksworth, in Derbyshire, bear a Coat quarterly, first, HURT; second, LOWE of Alderwasley; third, LOWE of Denby, and likewise LOWE of Alderwasley; and fourth, FAWNE of Alderwasley. The Hurts derive these Bearings from the intermarriage of Nicholas Hurt, of Castern, living in 1663, with ELIZABETH, daughter of JOHN LOWE, of Alderwasley, and sister and heir of JOHN LOWE of the same place. The Lowes had intermarried with the FAWNES, through their heiress, and thus the Coat of FAWNE.

Arms.—First, sa. a fesse betw. three cinquefoils or, for HURT; second, gu. a wolf preyant ar. for LOWE of Alderwasley; third, az. a hart trippant ar. for LOWE of Denby, and likewise for LOWE of Alderwasley; fourth, ar. a bugle horn betw. three crescents sa. each charged with a bezant, for FAWNE of Alderwasley.

Crest.—A hart passant ppr. horned, membered, and hurt in the haunch with an arrow or, feathered ar.

Motto.—Mane prædam vesperi spolium.

M'Adam, of Ballochmorrie, co. Ayr.

THE Shield and Supporters are borne by the present WILLIAM M'ADAM, of Ballochmorrie, Esq. as Chief of the ancient Scottish family of M'ADAM of Waterhead, in the Stewartry of Kirkcudbright, derived from Adam M'Gregor,

PLATE XII.

grandson of Gregor M'Gregor, Head of the Clan Gregor. Mr. M'Adam is grandson of John Loudon M'Adam, Esq. so celebrated for the improvement of the Public Roads of the kingdom, who was son of James M'Adam, of Waterhead, Esq. by Susannah, his wife, dau. of John Cochrane, of Waterside, Esq.

Arms.—Vert, three arrows paleways, points downwards, barbed and feathered, ar. The ancient Bearing, as found in the Old Tower, over the Gate of the Family Burial Ground, Tombstones, &c. was, Vert, an arrow ar. point upwards.

Crest.—The head of a red deer, erased, ppr.

Supporters.—Two naked Saracens, wreathed about the middle. ppr.

Mottoes.—*Under the Arms*, Crux mihi grata quies. *Over the Crest*, Calm.

Prytherch, of Abergole, co. Carmarthen.

Daniel Prytherch, now of Abergole, Esq. a Magistrate for Carmarthenshire, great-grandson of Rhys Prydderch, Esq. High Sheriff of that County in 1758, bears a quartered Coat, as Representative of the ancient family of Prytherch or Prydderch, originally ap Rydderch, descended, through James Prydderch, Esq. High Sheriff of Carmarthenshire in 1599, from Rhydderch ap Gwilyn, of the line of Cradoc ap Gwilyn, Lord of Tallyn; and in right of his wife, Caroline-Georgina, youngest dau. of James Dalton, Esq. by Augusta Ritso, his wife, dau. of Henry Frederick, Duke of Cumberland, impales the arms of Ritso.

Arms.—Quarterly, first and fourth, az. a stag trippant ar. collared and lined or, betw. the attires, an imperial crown ppr. Second and third, gu. on a chev. betw. three men's heads couped, in profile, ar. five guttes-de-sang.
Impaling, quarterly, first and fourth, az. semee of crosses crosslet, a lion ramp. guard. ar. for Dalton; second and third, for Ritso, ar. on a chev. betw. three boars' heads couped sa. three mullets of the first.

Crest.—A stag's head cabossed, betw. the attires an imperial crown, as in the arms.

Motto.—Duw a digon; (in English) God and enough.

Stamer, of Bath.

The Rev. William Stamer, D. D. Rector and Patron of St. Saviour's, Bath, younger son of the late Sir William Stamer, Bart. and brother of the present Sir Lovelace, bears on his paternal shield an Escutcheon of Pretence for Houlditch, in right of his wife, Eleanor-Louisa, daughter and co-heir of Richard Houlditch, Esq. of Edenham House, Hampstead.

Arms.—Quarterly, first and fourth quarterly, gu. and az. a cross erm. charged with the City Sword in the scabbard, in pale, ppr. in the first and fourth quarters, on a fesse dancettée ar. a lion passant of the second; in the second and third, three castles ar. for Stamer; second and third, gu. a lion ramp. or, on a chief of the last three martlets ppr. for Lovelace; on an escutcheon of pretence az. on a chev. or, three birds sa.

Crests.—First, a stag's head erased or, gorged with a mural crown ppr. Second, an eagle displ. ppr.

Motto.—Virtute et valore.

PLATE XII

HENRY DE GREY WARTER, ESQ.
CRUCK MEOLE, CO. SALOP.

HURT OF ALDERWASLEY & WIRKSWORTH.
CO. DERBY.

WILL^M M^C ADAM, ESQ.
BALLOCHMORRIE, CO. AYR.

DANIEL PRYTHERCH, ESQ.
ABERGOLE, CO. CAERMARTHEN

REV. WILLIAM, STAMER, D.D.
BATH.

PLATE XIII.

Middleton, of Leam, co. Derby.

Marmaduke Middleton Middleton, of Leam, Esq. High Sheriff of Derbyshire in 1808, who is son and heir of the late Rev. John Carver of Morthen, by Sarah, his wife, dau. of Thomas Allen, of Sheffield, Esq. which lady succeeded to the estates of the Middletons of Leam, assumed, upon attaining his majority, the surname and arms of Middleton.

Arms.—Quarterly, first and fourth, erm. on a saltire engr. sa. an eagle's head erased or, for Middleton. Second and third, or, upon a chev. betw. three crosses clucheé sa. a fleur-de-lis betw. two stags' heads cabossed of the first, for Carver.

Crests.—First, An eagle's head erased ar. charged on the neck with a saltire as in the arms, for Middleton. Second, A mount vert, thereon a cross cluchée or, charged in the centre with a fleur-de-lis sa. for Carver.

Motto.—Conjunctio firmat.

Gyll, of Wyrardisbury, co. Bucks.

The family of Gyll or Gill resided in Cambridgeshire, and descended from Richard Gylle or Gill, who lived in the time of King Edward I. From him derived John Gyll, who passed into Buckland, co. Hertford, about 1450, and married there. Dying in 1499, he left a son, Richard, father of John Gyll, Esq. who married Margaret, dau. and heir of George Canon, of Wyddial Hall, co. Hertford, Esq. The property was sold by the son of Sir George Gyll, Knt. about the middle of the seventeenth century. A branch of this family settled in Kent, from which proceeded George Gyll, of Boxley, grandfather of William Gyll, of Wyrardisbury House, co. Buckingham. His son, William Gyll, Esq. Captain 2nd Life Guards, married the Lady Harriet Flemyng, dau. and heir of the last Earl of Wigtoun, and left four sons and one dau. viz. Brooke Hamilton Gyll, Esq. present representative of the family, Gordon Willoughby Gyll, Esq., Hamilton Gyll, Esq., Sir Robert Gyll, and Louisa, married to Sir Jasper Atkinson, Knt. of the Royal Mint.

Arms.—Quarterly, first, Sa. two chev. ar. each charged with three mullets of the first, on a canton or, a lion pass. guard. gu. for Gyll. Second, Lozengy or and vert, a lion ramp. guard. gu. also for Gyll. Third, Ar. on a chev. engr. sa. betw. three crosses pattée, as many martlets of the first, for Canon.

Crest.—A falcon's head az. betw. two wings frettée vert.

Motto.—Virtutis gloria merces.

PLATE XIII.

Annand, of Auchter Ellon.

The Annands were seated at Auchter Ellon, co. Aberdeen, in high repute for several centuries, and on an old Monument, still to be seen in the Churchyard of Ellon, the Arms, as now borne, appear, with the date 1326. The present representative of this long descended line is ALEXANDER ANNAND, of Sutton, co. Surrey, Esq. son and heir of the late John Annand, Esq. by Helen, his wife, second dau. of Adam Smith, Esq.

Arms.—Ar. a chief and saltire gu. cantoned with two mascles in the collar and base points az. in the flanks a spot of ermine.

An Escutcheon of Pretence in right of his wife, Sophia, dau. of William Bennet, of Faversham, co. Kent, Esq. Per pale gu. and erm. a fesse embattled, counter-embattled betw. two roundles in chief and a demi lion in base, all counterchanged.

Crest.—A griffin segreant.

Supporters.—Two griffins.

Motto.—Sperabo.

Jennings, of the Shrubbery, Dover.

The Arms of the present GEORGE JENNINGS, of the Shrubbery, Esq. are :—

Az. a chev. engr. erm. betw. three golden fleeces.

Crest.—A dragon passant vair, wings or, the dexter claw resting on a shield az. charged with a golden fleece.

Motto.—Conservabo ad mortem.

Cracroft, of Hackthorn, co. Lincoln.

The family of Cracroft has been resident at Hackthorn for many centuries: the arms are recorded in the " Union of Honour," published by James York, Blacksmith, " containing the Nobility of England, and the Gentry of Lincolnshire, in the year 1640." The descent can be traced from the time of Edward III. The present representative is ROBERT CRACROFT, of Hackthorn, Esq. formerly Lieutenant-Colonel of the North Lincolnshire Militia, son and heir of the late John Cracroft, of Hackthorn, Esq. by Penelope Anne, his wife, dau. of the Rev. Charles Fleetwood Weston, Prebendary of Durham.

Arms.—Vert, on a bend dancettée ar. three martlets sa.

Crest.—A stork ppr. supporting with his dexter foot a battle-axe, staff or, head ar.

MARMADUKE, MIDDLETON, MIDDLETON, ESQ.
LEAM, CO. DERBY

GYLL OF WYDDIAL HALL.
HERTS, AND WRAYSBURY, BUCKS.

ALEXANDER, ANNAND, ESQ.
SUTTON, CO. SURREY

GEORGE, JENNINGS, ESQ.
THE SHRUBBERY, DOVER.

ROBERT, CRACROFT, ESQ.
HACKTHORN, CO. LINCOLN.

PLATE XIV.

Boyd, of Middleton Park, co. Westmeath.

THE Arms of Boyd and Mackay were confirmed to the present GEORGE
AUGUSTUS BOYD, of Middleton Park, Esq. by Letters Patent bearing date
24th August, 1837, with an augmentation of the arms of the Noble Family of
ROCHFORT, Earls of Belvedere, in consideration of a portion of the property
of the last Earl devolving upon Mr. Boyd, through his mother, Jane, Countess
of Belvedere, widow of that Nobleman in 1836. Mr. Boyd is great-grandson
of the Rev. James Boyd, Rector of Erris, co. Mayo, living in 1752. His
son, Mr. Boyd's father, Abraham Boyd, Esq. a Barrister and King's Council,
married for his second wife the above-named Jane, Countess of Belvedere,
who was dau. and eventually sole heiress of the Rev. James Mackay.

Arms.—Quarterly, first and fourth, az. a fesse chequy ar. and gu. betw. three crescents of the second, for BOYD. Second, gu. on a chev. ar. betw. three bears' heads
couped or, muzzled of the first, a roebuck's head erased ppr. betw. two hands, couped
at the wrist, each grasping a dagger, pointed to the centre, ppr. for MACKAY. Third,
Az. a lion ramp. ar. and in chief two redbreasts ppr. for ROCHFORT.

Crests.—First, out of a ducal coronet or, a hand erect, with the third and fourth
fingers folded, ppr. for BOYD. Second, a cubit arm, grasping a dagger in pale ppr. for
MACKAY. Third, a redbreast ppr. on a ducal coronet, for ROCHFORT.

Mottoes.—Under the Arms, Confido, for BOYD. Over the Crest, Manu forte, for
MACKAY.

Delaval Gray.

FRANCIS DELAVAL GRAY, Esq. of the 14th Light Dragoons, son and heir of
the late John Gray, of Hartsheath Park, co. Flint, Esq. and maternally a
descendant of the old family of Delaval, bears the quartered Coat of GRAY
and DELAVAL.

Arms.—Quarterly, first and fourth, gu. within a bordure engr. a lion ramp. ar. for
GRAY. Second and third, quarterly, first and fourth, erm. two bars vert, second and
third, ar. a fesse az. betw. an eagle displ. with two heads sa. in chief, and a lion ramp.
in base, for DELAVAL.

Crests.—First out of a mural crown a phœnix in flames ppr. for GRAY. Second, a
demi lion guard. holding in the dexter paw a dagger, all ppr. for DELAVAL.

Mottoes.—Over the Crests, Clarior e Tenebris. Under the Arms, Vixi liber et moriar.

Ferrand, of St. Ives, co. York.

MRS. FERRAND, of St. Ives, bears the quartered Coat of her late husband,
Busfeild and Atkinson quarterly, and on an Escutcheon of Pretence the arms
of Ferrand quarterly with Walker and Dale.

Arms.—Quarterly, first and fourth, sa. a chev. betw. three fleurs-de-lis or, for BUS-
FEILD. Second and third, ar. an eagle displ. with two heads sa.; on a chief or, a rose

PLATE XIV.

betw. two martlets gu. for ATKINSON. An Escutcheon of Pretence, quarterly, first, ar. on a chief gu. two crosses patonce vairé, for FERRAND; second, ar. a chev. betw. three crescents sa.; on a canton of the second a dove with an olive branch ppr. for WALKER; third, gu. on a mound of grass a swan close ppr. ducally gorged and chained or, for DALE.

Edward Dale, of Tunstal, grandson of Edward Dale, of Dalton le Dale. = Joan Shipperdson, of Merton.

George Walker, M. A. Vicar of Stockton on Tees.

George Dale, of Durham.

Edward Dale, of Stockton on Tees.

Richard Ferrand, descended from the Ferrands of Harden-Grange, Yorkshire. = Anne Walker, dau. and co-heir.

Sarah Dale, dau. and heiress. = John Ferrand, of Barnard Castle, co. Durham, Esq.

Edward Ferrand, of St. Ives, d. s. p. m. in 1837.	Walker Ferrand, of Harden-Grange, M. P. d. s. p. in 1835.	Jane	=Rev. J. B. Charlwood, B.A. of Oakhill.	Sarah. This lady, after the death of the son of her elder sister, and of her own brothers s. p. m. resumed her maiden name and arms, and is the present Mrs. Ferrand, of St. Ives.	=Currer, Fothergill Busfeild, of Cottingley Bridge, Esq.	Anne Catherine.	=Edward Surtees, of Seatonburn, co. Northumberland, Esq.
			Charles Charlwood, d. unm.				

William Edward Surtees, Esq. M. A. Barrister-at-Law.

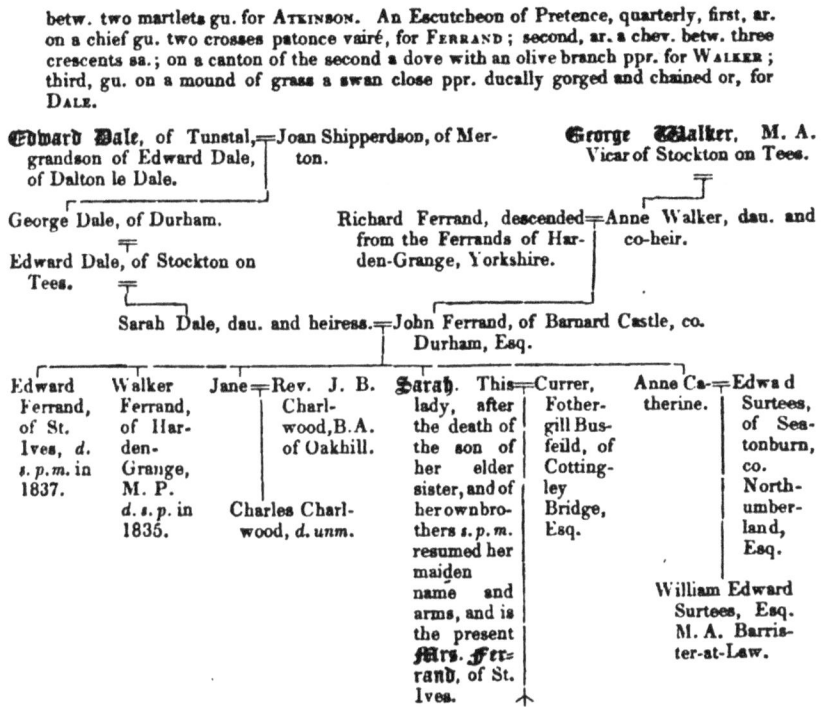

Twyning, of Bryn, co. Pembroke.

THE family, now represented by WILLIAM HENRY TWYNING, of Bryn, co. Pembroke, Esq. is one of great antiquity, and has borne its Coats of Arms for a long series of years.

Arms.—Sa. two bars betw. two stars of six points or.

Crest.—The twins, Castor and Pollux, in infancy. (The stars in the shield represent them after death.)

Motto.—Stellis aspirate gemellis.

Newman of Thornbury Park, co. Gloucester.

HENRY WENMAN NEWMAN, of Thornbury Park, Esq. bears the Arms of the extinct Baronets Newman of Fifehead-Magdalen, co. Dorset, which his father, the late Richard Newman Toll, M. D. of Thornbury Park, assumed with the name on inheriting the property and representation of the family in 1802.

Arms.—Quarterly, sa. and ar.; in the first and fourth quarters three mullets of the second, in the centre an inescutcheon gu. charged with a portcullis imperially crowned or,—an augmentation granted by King Charles I. to Colonel Newman for his distinguished conduct at the battle of Worcester.

Crest.—A swallow rising ppr.

Motto.—Lux mea Christus.

PLATE XV

Manu Forte

Contiod

GEORGE, AUGUSTUS, BOYD, ESQ.
MIDDLETON PARK, CO. WESTMEATH.

Clamor e Flammis.

Vixi liber et moriar.

FRANCIS, DELAVAL, GRAY, ESQ.
14TH LIGHT DRAGOONS.

Dick of Ferrand

MRS FERRAND,
ST IVES, CO. YORK.

Stellis aspirate Gemellis

WILLIAM, HENRY, TWYNING, ESQ.
BRTN. CO. PEMBROKE.

Lux mea Christus.

HENRY, WENMAN, NEWMAN, ESQ.
THORNBURY PARK, CO. GLOUCESTER.

PLATE XV.

—

Hamerton, of Hellifield Peel, co. York.

JAMES HAMERTON, Esq. now of Hellifield Peel, as representative of the very ancient family of Hamerton, of Hamerton and Hellifield Peel, bears a Shield of Fifteen Quarterings.

Arms.—Quarterly, first, Ar. three hammers sa. for HAMERTON. Second, Ar. a bend cottised sa. for DE KNOLL. Third, Gu. three arches ar. for DE ARCHES. Fourth, Ar. a bend engr. sa. in the sinister chief an escallop gu. for RADCLIFFE. Fifth, Ar. an eagle displayed vert. for LANGFIELD. Sixth, Ar. a bend sa. betw. an eagle, vert, and a cross moline sa. for RISHWORTH. Seventh, Ar. a chev. betw. three cinquefoils sa. for FALKINGHAM. Eighth, Sa. three pickaxes ar. for PIGOT. Ninth, quarterly, first and fourth, Ar. a garland ppr. second and third, ar. three pheons sa. for CLOTHERHAM. Tenth, Ar. a fesse gu. betw. three eagles displayed sa. for LEEDES. Eleventh, Ar. a fesse az. and a label of three points gu. for the BARON DE BIRKIN. Twelfth, Per chev. or and gu. three human hearts counterchanged, for the BARON DE CAUZ. Thirteenth, Ar. three crosses crosslet botonnée fitchée, within a bordure engr. gu. for CHISSENHALL. Fourteenth, Ar. three dungforks sa. for WORTHINGTON. Fifteenth, as first, for HAMERTON.

Crest.—A greyhound couchant, sa.

Motto.—Fixus adversa sperno.

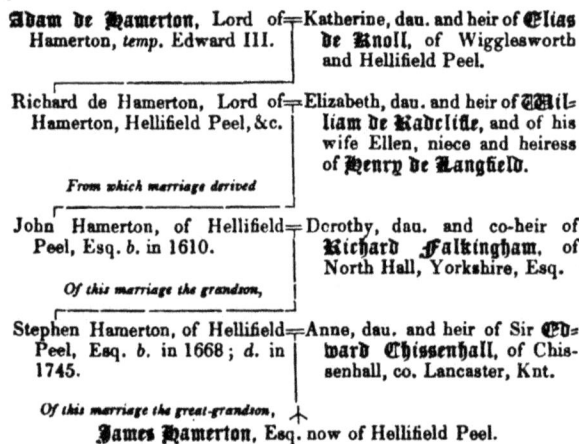

Adam de Hamerton, Lord of Hamerton, *temp.* Edward III.=Katherine, dau. and heir of Elias de Knoll, of Wigglesworth and Hellifield Peel.

Richard de Hamerton, Lord of Hamerton, Hellifield Peel, &c.=Elizabeth, dau. and heir of William de Radcliffe, and of his wife Ellen, niece and heiress of Henry de Langfield.

From which marriage derived

John Hamerton, of Hellifield Peel, Esq. *b.* in 1610.=Dorothy, dau. and co-heir of Richard Falkingham, of North Hall, Yorkshire, Esq.

Of this marriage the grandson,

Stephen Hamerton, of Hellifield Peel, Esq. *b.* in 1668; *d.* in 1745.=Anne, dau. and heir of Sir Edward Chissenhall, of Chissenhall, co. Lancaster, Knt.

Of this marriage the great-grandson,

James Hamerton, Esq. now of Hellifield Peel.

King, of Staunton Park, co. Hereford.

THE father of the present JAMES-KING KING, of Staunton Park, Esq. the Rev. James Simpkinson, M. A. Rector of St. Peter-le-Poor, Old Broad Street, London, assumed by Sign Manual, in 1837, the name and arms of KING only.

Arms.—Quarterly, ar. and az. in the second and third quarters a mullet of six points or, pierced of the field, over all a bend barry of six of the second, charged with a cinquefoil of the third, and gu.

PLATE XV.

Crest.—A lion ramp. bendy or and az. supporting two branches composed of two roses gu. and three cinquefoils vert, slipped and leaved of the first.

Motto.—Floreo in magna loenin.

William King, of Staunton Park, co. Hereford, Esq.═Eleanor Griffiths.

| James King, of Staunton Park, Esq. | Thomas King, of Court of Noke, Esq. | William King, d. unm. | Elizabeth King. ═ | Roger King-tinson, of the city of London, Esq. | William Lyne, Esq. ═ | Eleanor King. |

The Rev. James Sumpkinson, M. A.═Emma, fourth dau. of Edward Vaux, of Rector of St. Peter-Le-Poor, Old Broad Street, London, assumed the surname and arms of King in 1837. | the city of London, Esq.

| James-King King, of Staunton Park, Esq. | The Rev. Thomas King, M. A. | Five daughters. |

Spedding, of Summergrove, co. Cumberland.

THE family of Spedding came originally from Ireland, was afterwards resident for some generations in Scotland, and became settled in Cumberland about the year 1685. The present representative is JAMES SPEDDING, of Summergrove, Esq. Major of the Royal Westmoreland Militia, and a Magistrate and Deputy-Lieutenant for Cumberland, eldest son of the late James Spedding, Esq. by Elizabeth, his wife, dau. of Thomas Harrington, of Carlisle, Esq. a descendant of the ancient family of Harrington of Harrington.

Arms.—Gu. on a fesse engr. betw. three acorns slipped or, a mural crown betw. two roses of the field.

Crest.—Out of a mural crown or, a dexter arm embowed in armour, the hand grasping a scimetar, the arm charged with three acorns, one and two, and entwined by a branch of oak, all ppr.

Motto.—Utile dulci.

Plate 14

1 Hamerton.
2 De Knoll.
3 De Arches.
4 Radcliffe.
5 Langfield.
6 Riskworth.
7 Falkingham.
8 Pigot.

9 Clotherham.
10 Eccles.
11 Baron de Birkin.
12 Baron de Cauz.
13 Chissenhall.
14 Worthington.
15 Hamerton.

JAMES. HAMERTON. ESQ.
HELLIFIELD PEEL, CO. YORK,

JAMES. KING. KING. ESQ.
STAUNTON PARK, CO HEREFORD.

JAMES SPEDDING, ESQ.
SUMMERGROVE, CO. CUMBERLAND.

PLATE XVI.

Atcherley, of Marton, co. Salop.

DAVID FRANCIS JONES, Serjeant-at-Law, son of David Francis Jones, of Cymman, co. Flint, Esq. by Jane, his wife, daughter of RICHARD ATCHERLEY, Esq. assumed, by letters patent dated 21 March, 1834, in compliance with the testamentary injunction of his maternal uncle, the surname and arms of ATCHERLEY, and is the present Mr. Serjeant Atcherley of Marton, Attorney-General of the Counties Palatine of Lancaster and Durham.

The family of Atcherley of Marton has been settled in that neighbourhood at least as far back as the time of Henry VII. The direct ancestor, Sir Roger Atcherley, Knt. who was born at Stanwardine, within about a mile of Marton, served as Lord Mayor of London 3 Henry VIII.

Arms.—Gu. on a fesse engr. ar. betw. three griffins' heads erased or, as many crosses pattée fitchée sa. Serjeant Atcherley bears, in addition, an Escutcheon of Pretence, quarterly TOPPING and ROBINSON, in right of his wife, Anne Margaret, second dau. of the late James Topping, of Whatcroft Hall, co. Chester, Esq.

Crest.—A demi bustard couped gu. wings elevated or, in the beak a lily ar. slipped vert.

Motto.—Spe posteri temporis.

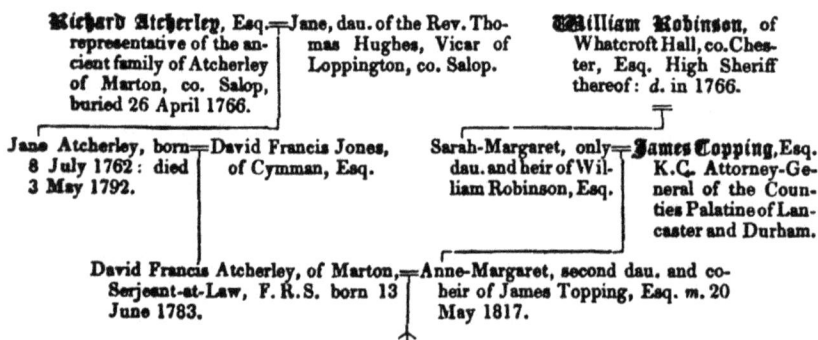

Richard Atcherley, Esq.=Jane, dau. of the Rev. Thomas Hughes, Vicar of Loppington, co. Salop.
representative of the ancient family of Atcherley of Marton, co. Salop, buried 26 April 1766.

William Robinson, of Whatcroft Hall, co. Chester, Esq. High Sheriff thereof: d. in 1766.

Jane Atcherley, born=David Francis Jones, of Cymman, Esq.
8 July 1762: died 3 May 1792.

Sarah-Margaret, only=James Topping, Esq. K.C. Attorney-General of the Counties Palatine of Lancaster and Durham.
dau. and heir of William Robinson, Esq.

David Francis Atcherley, of Marton,=Anne-Margaret, second dau. and co-heir of James Topping, Esq. m. 20 May 1817.
Serjeant-at-Law, F.R.S. born 13 June 1783.

Edwardes, of Gileston Manor.

THE Rev. JOHN EDWARDES, of Gileston Manor, co. Glamorgan, is youngest brother of the late David John Edwardes, Esq. representative of the ancient Welsh family of EDWARDES of Rhyd-y-Gôrs, co. Carmarthen.

Arms.—Quarterly, first, sa. a lion ramp. within an orle of cinquefoils or. Second, gu. a chev. or, betw. three Bowen's knots. Third, sa. three bucks' heads cabossed ar. Fourth, chequy or and sa. a fesse ar.

Crest.—A demi lion or, holding betw. the paws a Bowen's knot.

Motto.—Aspera ad virtutem est via.

PLATE XVI.

Nicolas.

Sir Nicholas Harris Nicolas, Chancellor and Knight Grand Cross of the Order of Saint Michael and Saint George, Knight of the Order of the Guelphs of Hanover, is fourth son of Captain John Harris Nicolas of the Royal Navy, by Margaret, daughter and co-heiress of John Blake, and grand-daughter and co-heiress (by Prudence, sister and heiress of William Busvargus of Busvargus, co. Cornwall, Esq.) of the Rev. John Keigwin, second son of John Keigwin of Mousehole, co. Cornwall, by Margaret, daughter of John Giffard of Brightley, co. Devon, Esq. and Joan, his wife, daughter of Sir John Wyndham, of Orchard Wyndham, ancestor of the Earls of Egremont.

Of the Families of Nicolas, Keigwin, and Busvargus, an account will be found in the fourth volume of Burke's " *History of the Commoners.*"

> **Arms.**—Ar. a fesse engr. in chief three eagles displ. Gu. quartering Harris, Blake, Keigwin, and Busvargus; and impaling Davison, viz. Gu. a stag trippant Or.
>
> **Crest.**—A fetterlock or, the fetter passing through a plume of five ostrich feathers, alternately ar. and gu.
>
> **Supporters** (as G.C.M.G.).—On either side, the Sept-Insular lion, viz. a lion guard. with wings elevated, holding in the fore-paw a book and seven arrows, with a glory round his head, all Or.
>
> **Motto.**—Patria cara carior fides.

Campbell, of Jura, co. Argyll.

Colin Campbell, of Jura and Craignish, Esq. Heritable Keeper of Craignish Castle, bears the quartered Coat of Argyll, as representative of a junior branch of the Lochnell line of the Noble House of Argyll. The Campbells of Lochnell are the latest Cadets of Argyll, and, in default of male descendants of John fourth Duke of Argyll, heirs to the titles and estates.

> **Arms.**—Quarterly, first and fourth, gyronny of eight sa. and or. Second, ar. a boar's head couped ppr. Third, ar. a galley sa. sails furled, and oars in action ppr.
>
> **Crest.**—A hand holding a spear ppr.
>
> **Motto.**—Audaces juvo.

Prior, of Rathdowney.

Andrew Redmond Prior, Esq. formerly Accountant General of the Irish Post Office, (son of Andrew Murray Prior, of Rathdowney, Esq. High Sheriff of Wicklow in 1777, by Frances, his wife, sister of Lodge Evans Morres, Viscount Frankfort de Montmorency, and grandson of John Murray, Esq. who assumed the surname and arms of Prior on succeeding to the estates of Thomas Prior, of Rathdowney, Esq. the celebrated Founder of the Royal Dublin Society,) descends from, and bears the arms of, the ancient family of Prior, which was established in Essex so far back as the time of Henry III., and became subsequently located in the counties of Oxford, Lancaster, and Cambridge.

> **Arms.**—Sa. on a bend erm. three chevronels gu. betw. four stars of eight points wavy or. In right of his wife, Katherine, youngest dau. of Sir John Call, Bart. Mr. Andrew Redmond Prior impales the arms of Call and Batty.
>
> **Crest.**—A star, as in the Arms.
>
> **Motto.**—Malo mori quam fœdari.

PLATE XV.

DAVID FRANCIS ATCHERLEY.
MARTON, CO. SALOP....SERJEANT AT LAW.

THE REV. JOHN EDWARDES.
GILESTON MANOR CO. GLAMORGAN.

SIR HARRIS NICOLAS, G.C.M.G.

COLIN CAMPBELL, ESQ.
JURA CO. ARGYLL.

ANDREW REDMOND PRIOR, ESQ.
QUEENS CO. IRELAND

PLATE XVII.

Brown, of Beilby Grange.

THESE Arms were confirmed by the Herald's College to the present WILLIAM
BROWN, of Beilby Grange, co. York, and Richmond Hill, co. Lancaster, Esq.
one of the most eminent Merchants of Liverpool, and to his brothers, George
Brown, of Baltimore, John A. Brown, of Philadelphia, and James Brown,
of New York, the four sons of the late Alexander Brown, of Baltimore, in
Maryland, North America, Esq.

Arms.—Gu. a chev. or, betw. two lions' gambs in chief ar. and four hands conjoined
in base of the second: on a chief engr. gold, an eagle displ. sa.
Crest.—A lion's gamb, erect and erased, ar. holding a hand ppr.
Motto.—Est Concordia fratrum.

Waddell, of Beach House.

GEORGE WADDELL, of Beach House, Walmer, co. Kent, Esq. bears for

Arms.—Erm. a fesse chequy ar. and az. in chief two martlets of the last.
Crest.—A lamb couchant ppr. surmounted by a demi eagle displ. or.

Lauder, of Fountain Hall, Bart.

SIR THOMAS DICK LAUDER, of Fountain Hall, co. Haddington, Bart. as lineal
male representative of the family of Lauder Tower and Bass, and, through a
female, of Dick of Braid and Grange, bears the quartered Coat of LAUDER
and DICK; and carries, on an Escutcheon of Pretence, in right of his wife,
the only child and heir of George Cumin, of Relugas, Esq. the Arms of the
ancient Family of CUMIN.

Arms.—Quarterly, first and fourth, gu. within a double tressure ar. a griffin segreant
of the last, for LAUDER. Second and third, ar. a fesse az. betw. three mullets gu. for
DICK. On an Escutcheon of Pretence the Arms of CUMIN.
Crests.—First, out of a tower ar. masoned, and portcullis down, sa. the head and
shoulders of a sentinel, in a watching posture ppr. for LAUDER. Second, a stag's head
erased ppr. attired or, for DICK.
Supporters.—Two lions ramp. ar.
Mottoes.—Below the Arms, Ut migraturus habita. Over the LAUDER Crest, Turris
prudentia Custos. Over the DICK Crest, Virtuti.

Sir Andrew Lauder, of Fountain Hall,=Isabel, only child and heir of William
  fifth Bart.   Dick, of Grange, Esq.

Sir Andrew Dick Lauder, of Fountain Hall=Elizabeth, dau. of Thomas Brown, of John-
  and Grange, died in 1820.   stonburn, Esq.

    Sir Thomas Dick Lauder, of Fountain Hall, seventh and present Bart.

PLATE XVII.

Rogers, of Yarlington.

FRANCIS ROGERS, of Yarlington, co. Somerset, Esq. descended, on strong presumptive evidence, from the Rogers's of Eastwood, co. Gloucester, quarters, with his own paternal Coat, the Arms of ROBINSON, LLOYD, and PICKERING.

Arms.—Quarterly, first, erm. three bucks trippant sa. on a chief wavy az. as many acorns slipped or, for ROGERS. Second, vert, a chev. betw. three bucks trippant or, for ROBINSON. Third, sa. three nags' heads erased ar. for LLOYD. Fourth, erm. a lion ramp. az. langued and crowned or, for PICKERING.

Crest.—A buck's head erased sa. attired or, on the neck a bendlet wavy of the last, charged with three acorns vert. in the mouth a slip of oak fructed ppr.

Motto.—Justum perficito nihil timeto.

Thomas Robinson, Esq. born at Hull 4 ᵀ Dorothy Pickering, an heiress of the
Feb. 1693, son of William Robinson, of | Pickerings of Yorkshire, m. 17 July
Kingston-upon-Hull, Esq. | 1717.

Pickering Robinson, of Rawcliffe, Esq. b. ᵀ Mary-Anne, dau. of Thomas Lloyd, Esq.
in 1726, m. 21 Aug. 1753, d. 21 June | d. 27 Oct. 1761, and was buried at the
1775. | Savannah.

Anne-Reynolds Robinson, dau. and sole ᵀ John Rogers, of Yarlington Lodge, co.
heir: and eventually heiress of her great | Somerset, Esq. only son of Thomas Ro-
uncle, Samuel Lloyd, of Friday Hill, co. | gers, of Besford Court, near Worcester,
Essex, Esq. m. 10 Nov. 1774. | Esq. by Mary Englesby, his wife. Mr.
| Rogers was High Sheriff of Somerset-
| shire in 1804. He died 28 Feb. 1821,
| aged 78.

Francis Rogers, of Yarlington, co. So- ᵀ Catherine-Elizabeth, eldest dau. of Benja-
merset, Esq. b. in 1784, m. in 1815. | min Bickley, of Ettingshall Lodge, co.
PRESENT HEAD OF THE FAMILY. | Stafford, Esq.

Thomas Englesby Rogers, B.A. eldest son   Other issue.
and heir.

Hughes, of Ely House.

ROBERT HUGHES, of Ely House, near Wexford, Esq. a Magistrate for the County, son of the late Abraham Hughes, Esq. by Jane, his wife, youngest daughter of Colonel Robert Clifford, of Cromwellsfort, represents an ancient Welsh family, and bears their Arms. The first Settler in Ireland was ABRAHAM HUGHES, a gentleman of Cambrian descent, who accompanied Cromwell to Ireland, and acquired, by marriage, the estates of Ballytrent and St. Margaret's.

Arms.—Or, on a chev. sa. betw. three griffins' heads erased gu. as many mullets pierced of the field.

Crest.—A griffin's head erased gu.

Motto.—Verus amor patriæ.

PLATE. XVII

WILLIAM BROWN, ESQ
BEILBY GRANGE, CO. YORK

GEORGE WADDELL, ESQ
BEACH HOUSE, WALMER

SIR THOMAS DICK LAUDER, BART
FOUNTAIN HALL.

FRANCIS ROGERS, ESQ
YARLINGTON, CO. SOMERSET.

ROBERT HUGHES, ESQ
ELY HOUSE, WEXFORD.

PLATE XVIII.

———

Davies, of Eton House.

OWEN DAVIES, of Eton House, co. Kent, Esq. of the Family of DAVIES of GWYSANEY, bears a Shield of Sixteen Quarterings.

Arms.—Quarterly :—

    I. Gu. on a bend ar. a lion pass. sa. for DAVIES of GWYSANEY.

    II. Quarterly, first and fourth, Ar. three boars' head couped sa. langued gu. tusked or, for CADWGAN AP ELYSTAN ; second and third, Gu. a lion ramp. reguard. or, for ELYSTAN GLODRYDD.

    III. Per bend sinister, erm. and ermines, over all a lion ramp. or, for TUDOR TREVOR.

    IV. Sa. a chev. betw. three fleurs-de-lis ar. for COLLWYN AP TANGNO.

    V. Quarterly, first and fourth, Gu. on a chev. betw. three goats' heads erased or, three trefoils slipped vert, for ITHEL VELYN ; second and third, Az. a lion pass. or, for LLEWELYN AURDORCHOG.

    VI. Or, a lion ramp. az. for CADWGAN, LORD OF NANNAU.

    VII. Quarterly, first and fourth, Gu. a chev. or, a chief erm. for Sir GRIFFITH LLOYD ; second, Gu. a chev. erm. betw. three Englishmen's dead heads couped in profile ppr. for EDNYFED VYCHAN ; third, Gu. a Saracen's head erased at the neck ppr. wreathed about the temple sa. and ar. for MARCHUDD AP CYNAN.

    VIII. Vert, a lion ramp. or, for HAYNES.

    IX. Ar. a cinquefoil az. for MUTTON of LLANERCH.

    X. Per pale sa. and ar. semée of cross crosslets counterchanged of the field, thereon an eagle displ. with two heads or, the whole within a bordure engrailed of the last, for Sir HAMO VAUGHAN.

    XI. Ar. a lion ramp. sa. debruised by a bend compony or and az. for BURLEY of MALE-HURST.

    XII. Sa. three towers embattled ar. for DE TOUR of SHREWSBURY.

    XIII. Az. three preeds (small lamperns) haurient in pale ar. for PRIDE of SHREWS-BURY.

    XIV. Gu. seven lozenges vairé, three, three, and one, for Sir JOHN DE BURGH.

    XV. Or, a lion ramp. gu. armed and langued of the first, for Sir JOHN AP WILLIAM, Lord of Mawddwy.

    XVI. Quarterly, first and fourth, Two bars gu. fretty or ; second and third, Gu. a fess betw. six pears erect or, leaved vert, both for CLOPTON.

Crest.—A lion's head erased quarterly ar. and sa. langued gu.

Motto.—Heb Dduw heb ddym Dduw a digon.

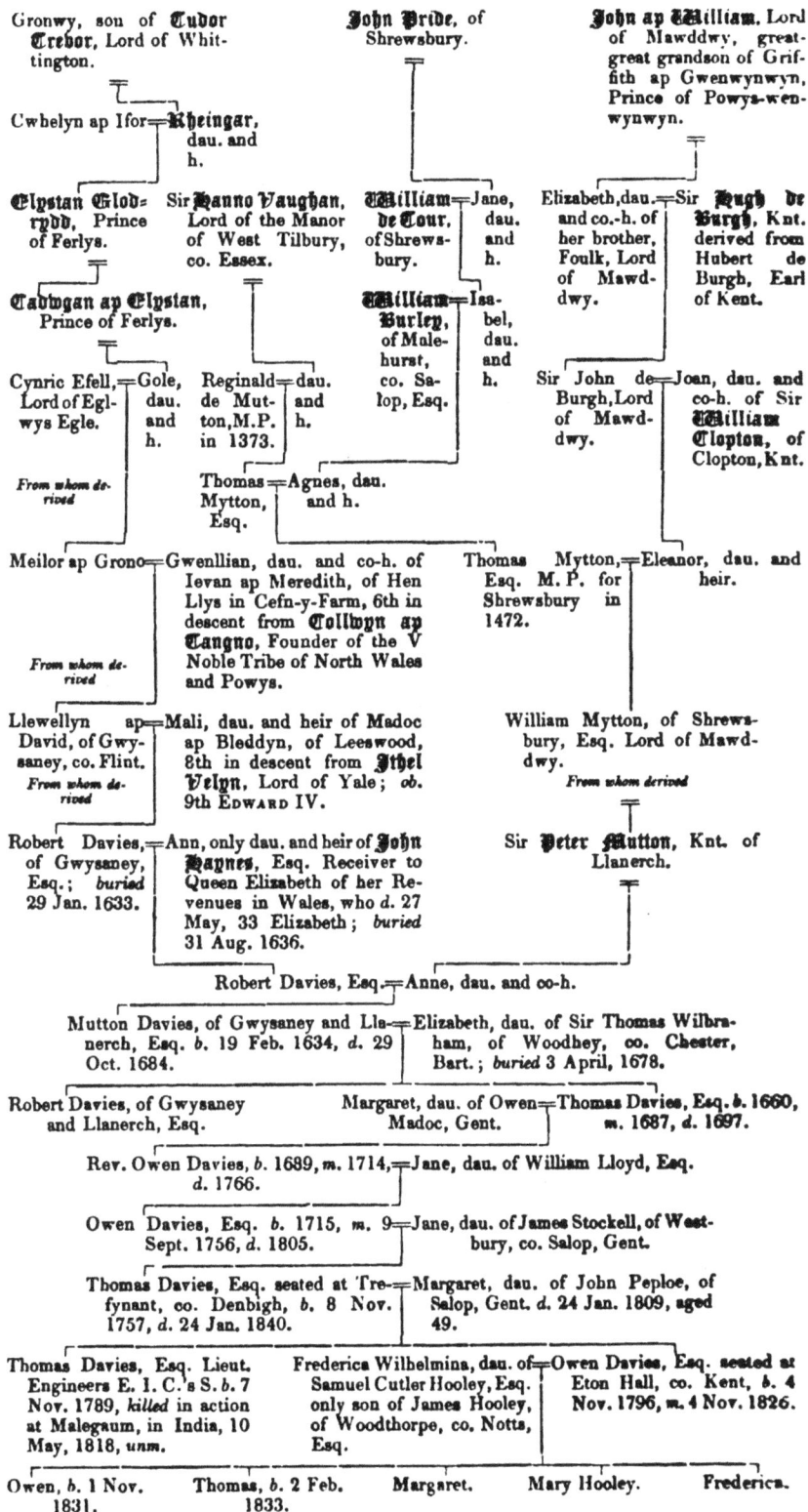

PLATE XVIII.

Gronwy, son of **Tudor Trevor**, Lord of Whittington.

John Pride, of Shrewsbury.

John ap William, Lord of Mawddwy, great-great grandson of Griffith ap Gwenwynwyn, Prince of Powys-wenwynwyn.

Cwbelyn ap Ifor = **Rheingar**, dau. and h.

Elystan Gloddrydd, Prince of Ferlys. = Sir **Hanno Vaughan**, Lord of the Manor of West Tilbury, co. Essex.

William de Cour, of Shrewsbury. = Jane, dau. and h.

Elizabeth, dau. and co-h. of her brother, Foulk, Lord of Mawddwy. = Sir **Hugh de Burgh**, Knt. derived from Hubert de Burgh, Earl of Kent.

Cadwgan ap Elystan, Prince of Ferlys.

William Burley, of Malehurst, co. Salop, Esq. = Isabel, dau. and h.

Cynric Efell, Lord of Eglwys Egle. = Gole, dau. and h.

Reginald de Mutton, M.P. in 1373. = dau. and h.

Sir John de Burgh, Lord of Mawddwy. = Joan, dau. and co-h. of Sir **William Clopton**, of Clopton, Knt.

From whom derived

Thomas Mytton, Esq. = Agnes, dau. and h.

Meilor ap Grono = Gwenllian, dau. and co-h. of Ievan ap Meredith, of Hen Llys in Cefn-y-Farm, 6th in descent from **Collwyn ap Tangno**, Founder of the V Noble Tribe of North Wales and Powys.

Thomas Mytton, Esq. M.P. for Shrewsbury in 1472. = Eleanor, dau. and heir.

From whom derived

Llewellyn ap David, of Gwysaney, co. Flint. = Mali, dau. and heir of Madoc ap Bleddyn, of Leeswood, 8th in descent from **Ithel Velyn**, Lord of Yale; *ob.* 9th EDWARD IV.

William Mytton, of Shrewsbury, Esq. Lord of Mawddwy.

From whom derived

From whom derived

Robert Davies, of Gwysaney, Esq.; *buried* 29 Jan. 1633. = Ann, only dau. and heir of **John Haynes**, Esq. Receiver to Queen Elizabeth of her Revenues in Wales, who d. 27 May, 33 Elizabeth; *buried* 31 Aug. 1636.

Sir **Peter Mutton**, Knt. of Llanerch.

Robert Davies, Esq. = Anne, dau. and co-h.

Mutton Davies, of Gwysaney and Llanerch, Esq. *b.* 19 Feb. 1634, *d.* 29 Oct. 1684. = Elizabeth, dau. of Sir Thomas Wilbraham, of Woodhey, co. Chester, Bart.; *buried* 3 April, 1678.

Robert Davies, of Gwysaney and Llanerch, Esq.

Margaret, dau. of Owen Madoc, Gent. = Thomas Davies, Esq. *b.* 1660, *m.* 1687, *d.* 1697.

Rev. Owen Davies, *b.* 1689, *m.* 1714, *d.* 1766. = Jane, dau. of William Lloyd, Esq.

Owen Davies, Esq. *b.* 1715, *m.* 9 Sept. 1756, *d.* 1805. = Jane, dau. of James Stockell, of Westbury, co. Salop, Gent.

Thomas Davies, Esq. seated at Trefynant, co. Denbigh, *b.* 8 Nov. 1757, *d.* 24 Jan. 1840. = Margaret, dau. of John Peploe, of Salop, Gent. d. 24 Jan. 1809, aged 49.

Thomas Davies, Esq. Lieut. Engineers E. I. C.'s S. *b.* 7 Nov. 1789, *killed* in action at Malegaum, in India, 10 May, 1818, *unm.*

Frederica Wilhelmina, dau. of Samuel Cutler Hooley, Esq. only son of James Hooley, of Woodthorpe, co. Notts, Esq. = Owen Davies, Esq. seated at Eton Hall, co. Kent, *b.* 4 Nov. 1796, *m.* 4 Nov. 1826.

Owen, *b.* 1 Nov. 1831.

Thomas, *b.* 2 Feb. 1833.

Margaret.

Mary Hooley.

Frederica.

PLATE XVIII.

Gabb, of Monmouthshire.

THE present Representative of the Family, the Rev. JAMES ASHE GABB,
Rector of Shire Newton, bears his Paternal Arms, quartered with those of
ASHE, being descended maternally from D'Esse, D'Essecourt, or Ashe, a
Family which was established in England at the Conquest, and from which
derived the Ashes of Clyst Fornyson, Heytesbury, Freshfield, Langley, &c.
In right of his wife, Mary Anne, daughter of FREDERICK SECRETAN, of Arcadia
House, Esq. Mr. Gabb impales the Arms of SECRETAN.

  Arms.—Quarterly, first and fourth, Barry of six or and az. an inescutcheon or, on a
  chief of the second a pile of the first, charged with three pales, also of the second, for
  GABB. Second and third, Ar. two chev. sa. for ASHE.

  Crest.—Out of a ducal coronet a harpy, wings expanded and ducally gorged.

  Motto.—Nullius in verba.

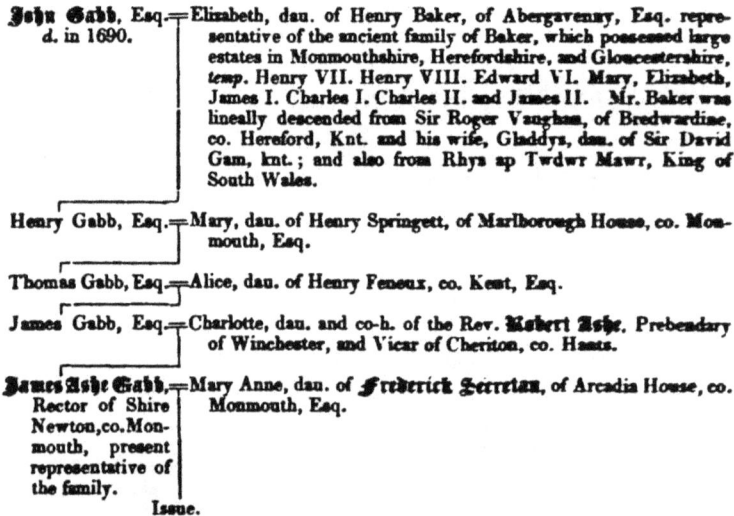

John Gabb, Esq.=Elizabeth, dau. of Henry Baker, of Abergavenny, Esq. repre-
d. in 1690.   sentative of the ancient family of Baker, which possessed large
                 estates in Monmouthshire, Herefordshire, and Gloucestershire,
                 temp. Henry VII. Henry VIII. Edward VI. Mary, Elizabeth,
                 James I. Charles I. Charles II. and James II. Mr. Baker was
                 lineally descended from Sir Roger Vaughan, of Bredwardine,
                 co. Hereford, Knt. and his wife, Gladdys, dau. of Sir David
                 Gam, knt.; and also from Rhys ap Twdwr Mawr, King of
                 South Wales.

Henry Gabb, Esq.=Mary, dau. of Henry Springett, of Marlborough House, co. Mon-
                 mouth, Esq.

Thomas Gabb, Esq.=Alice, dau. of Henry Feneux, co. Kent, Esq.

James Gabb, Esq.=Charlotte, dau. and co-h. of the Rev. Robert Ashe, Prebendary
                 of Winchester, and Vicar of Cheriton, co. Hants.

James Ashe Gabb,=Mary Anne, dau. of Frederick Secretan, of Arcadia House, co.
Rector of Shire   Monmouth, Esq.
Newton, co. Mon-
mouth, present
representative of
the family.
        Issue.

Carlyon, of Tregrehan.

EDWARD CARLYON, of Tregrehan, co. Cornwall, and Greenaway, co. Devon,
Esq. Lieutenant-Colonel in the Army, bears, as representative of the Car-
lyons, a Shield of Twelve Quarterings, derived from intermarriages with the
Families of HAWKINS, SCOBELL, TREDENHAM, &c.

  Arms.—Quarterly :—
    I. Sa. a plate between three castles ar. each charged with a cross crosslet gu. for
       CARLYON.
    II. Ar. on a saltire sa. five fleurs-de-lis of the field, for HAWKINS.
    III. Per pale ar. and gu. three fleurs-de-lis and a label in chief counterchanged, for
       SCOBELL.
    IV. Ar. seven lozenges in bend gu. for TREDENHAM.
    V. Gu. a fesse, and in chief three lozenges erm. for TIRREL.

PLATE XVIII.

VI. Ar. within a bordure gu. three wiverns in pale vert, for EXYS.

VII. Or. a chev. sa. in chief two cinquefoils, and in base a mullet of the second, for KILLOWE.

VIII. Ar. three battle-axes ppr. for GWAVAS.

IX. CARLYON, as first quarter.

X. Or. a lion ramp. gu. for POMEROY.

XI. Ar. a fesse vairé between two lions pass. guard. sa. for HOOKER.

XII. As first.

Crest.—A demi lion ramp. gu. ducally crowned or, collared ar. holding between his paws a bezant.

Motto.—Turris tutissima Virtus.

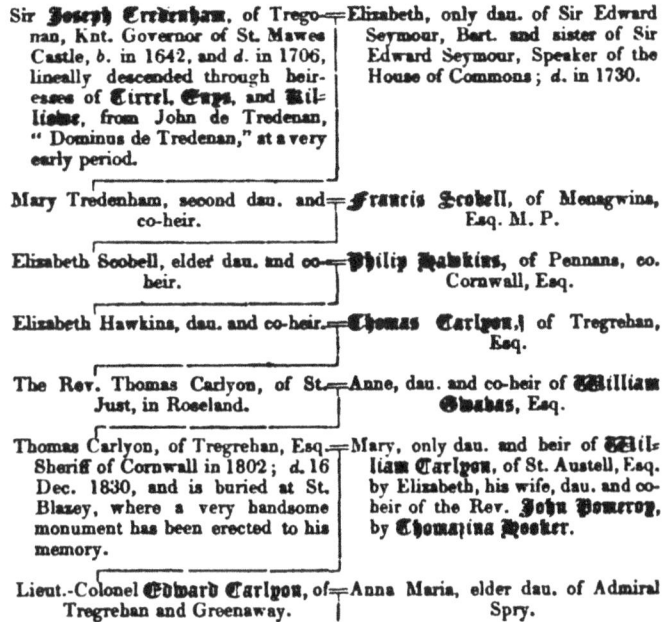

Sir **Joseph Tredenham**, of Tregonan, Knt. Governor of St. Mawes Castle, *b.* in 1642, and *d.* in 1706, lineally descended through heiresses of **Cirrel**, **Eups**, and **Killiow**, from John de Tredenan, " Dominus de Tredenan," at a very early period.	Elizabeth, only dau. of Sir Edward Seymour, Bart. and sister of Sir Edward Seymour, Speaker of the House of Commons; *d.* in 1730.
Mary Tredenham, second dau. and co-heir.	**Francis Scobell**, of Menagwins, Esq. M. P.
Elizabeth Scobell, elder dau. and co-heir.	**Philip Hawkins**, of Pennans, co. Cornwall, Esq.
Elizabeth Hawkins, dau. and co-heir.	**Thomas Carlyon,** of Tregrehan, Esq.
The Rev. Thomas Carlyon, of St. Just, in Roseland.	Anne, dau. and co-heir of **William Gwavas**, Esq.
Thomas Carlyon, of Tregrehan, Esq. Sheriff of Cornwall in 1802; *d.* 16 Dec. 1830, and is buried at St. Blazey, where a very handsome monument has been erected to his memory.	Mary, only dau. and heir of **William Carlyon**, of St. Austell, Esq. by Elizabeth, his wife, dau. and co-heir of the Rev. **John Pomeroy**, by **Thomasina Hooker**.
Lieut.-Colonel **Edward Carlyon**, of Tregrehan and Greenaway.	Anna Maria, elder dau. of Admiral Spry.

PLATE XVIII

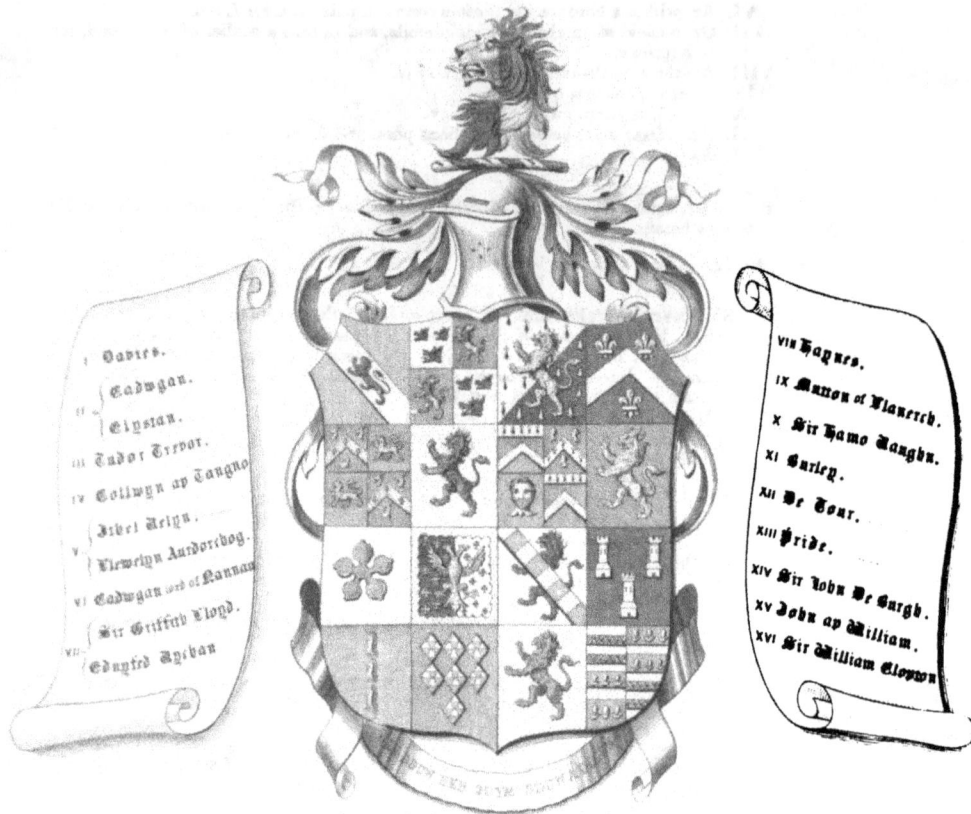

OWEN DAVIES, ESQ.
OF THE HOUSE OF GWYSANEY.

Left scroll:
i Davies.
ii Cadwgan.
ii Elystan.
iii Tudor Trevor.
iv Collwyn ap Tangno.
v Jthel Urien.
v Llewelyn Aurdorchog.
vi Cadwgan lord of Nannau.
vii Sir Griffith Lloyd.
Edynfed Vychan.

Right scroll:
viii Haques.
ix Manton of Flanerch.
x Sir Hamo Vaughn.
xi Curley.
xii De Tour.
xiii Pride.
xiv Sir John De Sargh.
xv John ap William.
xvi Sir William Clowyn.

REV. JAMES ASHE GABB.
SHIRE NEWTON, CO. MONMOUTH.

LT. COLˡ. CARLYON.
TREGREHAN, CO. CORNWALL.

PLATE XIX.

——

Anderson, of Jesmond House.

THE Andersons of Jesmond House, co. Northumberland, were settled in Newcastle from the time of Elizabeth until about the year 1620. The late JOHN ANDERSON, of Jesmond House, Esq. who died in 1829, left, with three daughters, four sons, THOMAS, now of Jesmond House; MATTHEW, of Jesmond College, J. P.; JAMES-CROSBY, who died in 1837; and JOHN, of Coxlodge, near Newcastle, J. P.

Arms.—Vert, three bucks lodged or.

Crest.—A buck lodged, holding in his mouth an acorn leaved, and wounded in the breast by an arrow.

Motto.—Nil desperandum Auspice Deo.

Sutton, of Elton.

GEORGE WILLIAM SUTTON, now of Elton Hall, co. Durham, Esq. (whose patronymic is Hutchinson) assumed the surname and arms of Sutton in 1822. He quarters the Ensigns of Sleigh and Bathurst, as representative, through his great-grandmother, Mary, of the Arkendale branch of the ancient Kentish family of Bathurst, whose chief is EARL BATHURST.

Arms.—Quarterly, first and fourth, gu. a tower or, thereon a stork ar. for SUTTON. Second, gu. a chev. betw. three owls ar. beaked and legged or, for SLEIGH. Third, sa. two bars erm. in chief three crosses formée or, for BATHURST.

Crest.—On a mount vert, a stork ppr. charged on the breast with a cross pattée gu. the dexter claw supporting a rose of the last, surmounted of another ar.

Motto.—Fidelis usque ad mortem.

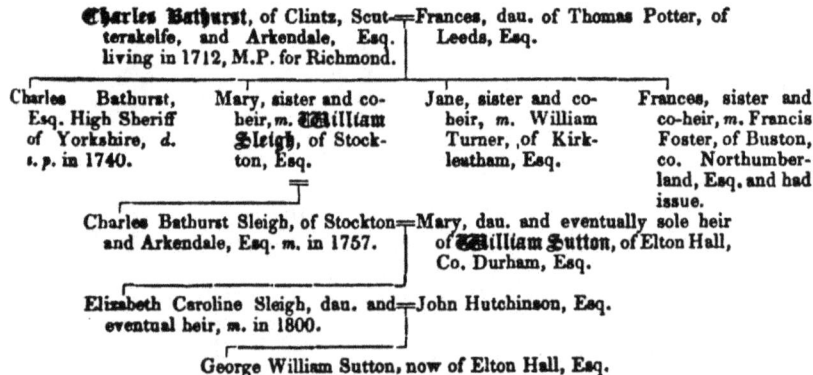

Charles Bathurst, of Clints, Scutterakelfe, and Arkendale, Esq. living in 1712, M.P. for Richmond. =Frances, dau. of Thomas Potter, of Leeds, Esq.			
Charles Bathurst, Esq. High Sheriff of Yorkshire, d. s. p. in 1740.	Mary, sister and co-heir, m. William Sleigh, of Stockton, Esq.	Jane, sister and co-heir, m. William Turner, of Kirkleatham, Esq.	Frances, sister and co-heir, m. Francis Foster, of Buston, co. Northumberland, Esq. and had issue.

Charles Bathurst Sleigh, of Stockton and Arkendale, Esq. m. in 1757.=Mary, dau. and eventually sole heir of William Sutton, of Elton Hall, Co. Durham, Esq.

Elizabeth Caroline Sleigh, dau. and eventual heir, m. in 1800.=John Hutchinson, Esq.

George William Sutton, now of Elton Hall, Esq.

Boyd, of Merton Hall.

EDWARD BOYD, of Merton Hall, co. Wigton, Esq. a Deputy-Lieutenant of that shire and of Kirkcudbright, as Representative of the Boyds of Merton Hall, derived, in direct descent, from William Boyd, Abbot of Kilwinning,

PLATE XIX.

younger brother of Sir Thomas Boyd, ancestor of the Boyds, Earls of Kilmarnock, bears the ancient Coat, Crest, and Supporters of that Noble family.

Arms.—Az. a fesse chequy ar. and gu.

Crest.—A dexter hand, couped at the wrist, erect, pointing with the thumb and the next two fingers, the others turning down.

Supporters.—Two squirrels ppr.

Motto.—Confido.

Sir Thomas Boyd, of Kilmarnock, one of=Joanna, dau. of John Montgomery, of Ardrossan. the Hostages for the Ransom of King James I. in 1424.

Sir Thomas Boyd, of Kilmarnock, ancestor of the Boyds Earls of Kilmarnock, the last of whom, bearing the title, suffered on Tower Hill in 1745, for his participation in the rising of that memorable year.

William Boyd, Abbot of Kilwinning, who received a dispensation from Rome. King James III. gave him a Charter confirming the grants of the Crown to that Abbey, and erecting the lands into a Regality. His representative is the present **Edward Boyd**, of Merton Hall, Esq.

Duckett, of Duckett's Grove.

JOHN DAWSON DUCKETT, of Duckett's Grove, co. Carlow, Esq. bears numerous Quarterings, derived from the intermarriages of his ancestors from very early times. He is eldest son of the late William Duckett, of Duckett's Grove, Esq. by Elizabeth, his wife, dau. and co-heir of John Dawson Coates, of Dawson Court, co. Dublin, Esq., and representative of Thomas Duckett, Esq. the first settler in Ireland, son, by his third wife, of JAMES DUCKETT, of Grayrigg, co. Westmoreland, Esq. twelfth in lineal descent from Richard Duckett, Lord of the Manor of Fillingham in 1205. A younger branch of the family, bearing the same Arms, was of Hartham House, co. Wilts, and is now represented by SIR GEORGE DUCKETT, Bart.

Arms.—Quarterly, first and fourth, sa. a saltire ar. charged with a crescent gu. for DUCKETT. Second and third, az. a chev. erm. betw. three arrows or, barbed and feathered ar.; on a chief of the last as many birds sa.; a canton gu. charged with a mullet of the third, for DAWSON.

Crests.—First, out of a ducal coronet or, a plume of five ostrich feathers ar. for DUCKETT. Second, a cat's head full faced and erased near the shoulders ar. spotted sa. holding in the mouth a rat of the last, for DAWSON.

Motto.—Spectemur agendo.

Harbin, of Newton House.

THESE Arms and Crest were granted in 1618 to ROBERT HARBIN, of Newton House, co. Somerset, Esq. and are now borne by his descendant, GEORGE HARBIN, of Newton House, Esq. who is great-grandson, by Abigail, his wife, daughter and heir of Richard Swayne, of Gunville, co. Dorset, Esq. of Wyndham Harbin, of Newton, Esq. who was son and heir, by Elizabeth, his wife, daughter of Sir Francis Wyndham, of Trent, co. Somerset, Bart. of William Harbin, Esq. fourth in descent from Robert Harbin, of Weeke, co. Dorset, and of Newton, co. Somerset, Esq. born in 1526.

Arms.—Az. a saltire voided betw. four spears' heads erect or.

Crest.—A hand and arm, vested, ppr. holding a spur or.

PLATE XIX.

THOMAS ANDERSON, ESQ.
JESMOND HOUSE, CO. NORTHUMBERLAND.

GEORGE WILLIAM SUTTON, ESQ.
ELTON HALL, CO. DURHAM.

EDWARD BOYD, ESQ.
MERTON HALL, CO. WIGTON.

JOHN DAWSON DUCKETT, ESQ.
DUCKETTS GROVE, CO. CARLOW

GEORGE HARBIN, ESQ.
NEWTON HOUSE, CO. SOMERSET.

PLATE XX.

Galton.

THESE Arms are borne by SAMUEL TERTIUS GALTON, of Duddeston House, co. Warwick, HUBERT JOHN BARCLAY GALTON, of Warley Hall, co. Salop, and JOHN HOWARD GALTON, of Hadzor House, Esqrs. sons of the late Samuel Galton of Duddeston, Esq. by Lucy, his wife, eldest daughter of Robert Barclay, of Ury, co. Kincardine, Esq. M. P.

    Arms.—Erm. on a fesse engr. gu. betw. six fleurs-de-lis of the second, an eagle's head erased ar. betw. two bezants.

    Crest.—On a mount vert an eagle erm. looking up at the sun or, its claws resting on a fleur-de-lis gu.

    Motto.—Gaudet luce videri.

Adams, of Middleton Hall.

EDWARD HAMLIN ADAMS, of Middleton Hall, co. Carmarthen, Esq. High Sheriff of that county in 1832, and Knight of the Shire in Parliament in 1833-4, is son of the late William Adams, Esq. by Elizabeth Anne, his wife, daughter of Thomas Coxeter, Esq. grandson of Thomas Adams, Esq. by Margaret his wife, daughter of Thomas Maxwell, great-great-grandson of Carlaveroche, Earl of Nithsdale, and great-grandson of William Adams, Esq. by Frances, his wife, daughter of Thomas Walrond, Esq. and Lady Frances Hackett, his wife, daughter of Sir Jonathan Atkins, Knt. Governor of Barbadoes from 1674 to 1680.

    Arms.—Ar. on a cross gu. five mullets or.

    Crest.—Out of a ducal coronet or, a demi lion affrontée gu.

    Motto.—Aspire, persevere, and indulge not.

Bythesea, of the Hill, Freshford.

SAMUEL WILLIAM BYTHESEA, of The Hill, Freshford, co. Somerset, Esq. bears a Shield of Eight Quarterings, and impales, in right of his wife, Mary-Agnes-Bythesea, younger daughter of the late Charles Brome, of Malling House, West Malling, co. Kent, Esq. the Arms of BROME, HODGES, and SANDFORD.

    Arms.—Quarterly :—

      I. Ar. on a chev. engr. betw. three crabs, the claws towards the dexter gu. the Roman fasces erect, surmounting two swords in saltire, and encircled by a chaplet or, for BYTHESEA.

      II. Ar. a chev. engr. gu. for CHIVERS.

      III. Quarterly, Per fesse dancettée gu. and or, for BROMLEY.

      IV. Ar. on a chev. gu. five bezants, all within a bordure engr. of the second, for CHITTLETON.

      V. Ar. on a fesse sa. betw. six fleurs-de-lis gu. three cross crosslets or, for CLIFTON.

      VI. Gu. on a chev. ar. three roses gu. for BROCK.

      VII. Ar. a bend or; on a chief ar. a saltire engr. gu. betw. two Cornish choughs ppr.

      VIII. Sa. a lion ramp. betw. six cross crosslets ar. all betw. two flaunches erm. for LONG.

PLATE XX.

Crest.—An eagle displ. ar. on the breast the Roman fasces erect surmounting two swords in saltire, and encircled by a chaplet ppr. each wing charged with a cross crosslet fitchée gu.

Motto.—Mutare vel timere sperno.

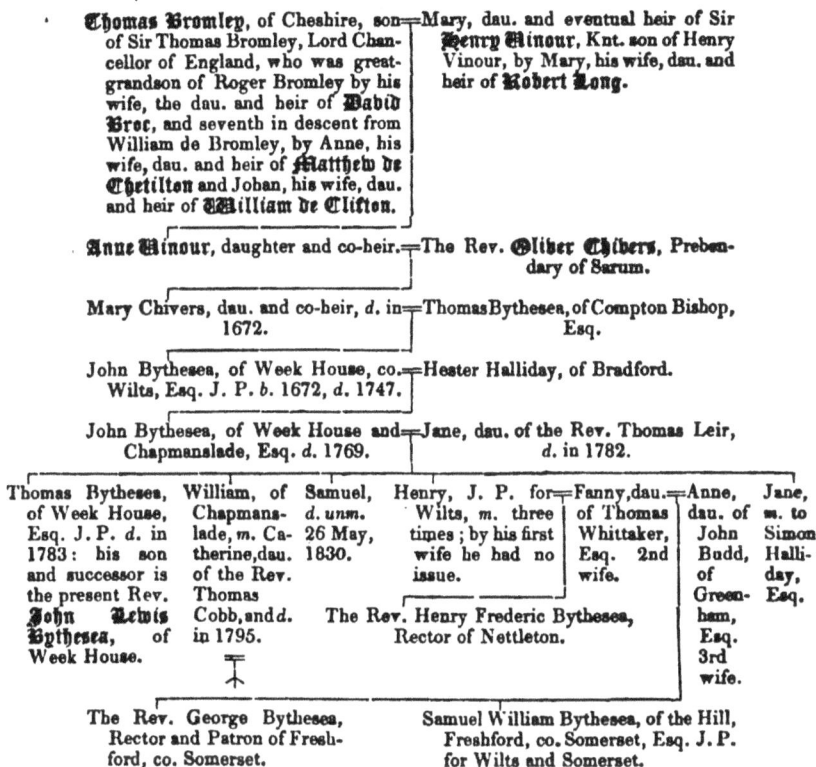

| Thomas Bromley, of Cheshire, son of Sir Thomas Bromley, Lord Chancellor of England, who was great-grandson of Roger Bromley by his wife, the dau. and heir of David Brec, and seventh in descent from William de Bromley, by Anne, his wife, dau. and heir of Matthew de Chetilton and Joban, his wife, dau. and heir of William de Clifton. | = | Mary, dau. and eventual heir of Sir Henry Vinour, Knt. son of Henry Vinour, by Mary, his wife, dau. and heir of Robert Long. |

Anne Vinour, daughter and co-heir.=The Rev. Oliver Chivers, Prebendary of Sarum.

Mary Chivers, dau. and co-heir, d. in 1672.=Thomas Bythesea, of Compton Bishop, Esq.

John Bythesea, of Week House, co. Wilts, Esq. J. P. b. 1672, d. 1747.=Hester Halliday, of Bradford.

John Bythesea, of Week House and Chapmanslade, Esq. d. 1769.=Jane, dau. of the Rev. Thomas Leir, d. in 1782.

| Thomas Bythesea, of Week House, Esq. J. P. d. in 1783: his son and successor is the present Rev. John Lewis Bythesea, of Week House. | William, of Chapmanslade, m. Catherine, dau. of the Rev. Thomas Cobb, and d. in 1795. | Samuel, d. unm. 26 May, 1830. | Henry, J. P. for Wilts, m. three times; by his first wife he had no issue. | =Fanny, dau. of Thomas Whittaker, Esq. 2nd wife. | =Anne, dau. of John Budd, of Greenham, Esq. 3rd wife. | Jane, m. to Simon Halliday, Esq. |

The Rev. Henry Frederic Bythesea, Rector of Nettleton.

The Rev. George Bythesea, Rector and Patron of Freshford, co. Somerset.

Samuel William Bythesea, of the Hill, Freshford, co. Somerset, Esq. J. P. for Wilts and Somerset.

Michell, of Forcett Hall.

John Michell, of Glassell, co. Kincardine, and Forcett Hall, co. York, Esq. bears for

Arms.—Per chev. gu. and sa. a chev. betw. three swans ar.

Crest.—On a mount ppr. a swan ar.

Motto.—Ferar unus et idem.

Colt, of Gartsherrie.

The Family of Colt was established in Scotland by Blais-Coult, who fled from France during the persecution of the Huguenots, and became Professor in the College of St. Andrews. His great-great-grandson, Sir Robert Colt, an eminent Lawyer, was Solicitor to James VII. The representation of the Family now vests in John Hamilton Colt, of Garthsherrie, co. Lanark, Esq.

Arms.—Ar. a stag's head erased gu. betw. the attires a pheon az.

Crest.—A dexter naked arm embowed, holding in the hand an arrow in bend sinister ppr.

Motto.—Transfigam.

PLATE XX.

JOHN HOWARD GALTON, ESQ.
HADZOR HOUSE, CO. WORCESTER.

EDWARD HAMLIN ADAMS, ESQ.
MIDDLETON HALL, CO. CARMARTHEN.

SAMUEL WILLIAM BYTHESEA, ESQ.
THE HILL FRESHFORD, CO. SOMERSET.

JOHN MICHELL, ESQ.
FORCETT HALL, CO. YORK.

JOHN HAMILTON COLT, ESQ.
GARTHSHERRIE, CO. LANARK.

PLATE XXI.

HIS ROYAL HIGHNESS

Albert-Edward, Prince of Wales, K.G.

BORN AT BUCKINGHAM PALACE 9 NOVEMBER, 1841.

THE Prince of Wales, as heir-apparent to the Crown, bears the Royal Arms, differenced by a Label of three points, and an Escutcheon of Pretence for SAXONY, viz. Barry of ten sa. and ar. a bend treflé vert. His Royal Highness has likewise the Royal Supporters and Crest, differenced by a similar Label of three points. The Prince of Wales's Badge or Cognizance, is a Plume of three white ostrich feathers issuing through the rim of the Royal Coronet, with the motto, ICH DIEN, on a scroll entwined at the bottom of the feathers.

"The Prince of Wales having been victorious at the battle of Crescy, was presented with the Helmet of John of Luxemberg, King of Bohemia, who was slain in that celebrated field. This Helmet being ornamented with three ostrich feathers, and bearing the German motto, ICH DIEN (I serve), allusive to the said King, who served in person as an auxiliary, the Black Prince henceforward bore the feathers and motto, and they became the ensigns of the Princes of Wales."—BURKE's *General Armory.*

His Royal Highness
Albert Edward, Prince of Wales. K.G.

PLATE XXII.

Byam, of Antigua.

The Rev. Richard Burgh Byam, Vicar of Kew and Petersham, co. Surrey, and Edward Samuel Byam, Esq. bear a coat quarterly of six, which has been allowed and is recorded in the College of Arms. They are sons, by Mary, his wife, only daughter of the Rev. Richard Burgh, of Mount Bruis, co. Tipperary, of William Byam, Esq. Captain 68th Regiment, third son of William Byam, of Byams in Antigua, and of Westbourne House, Paddington, co. Middlesex, Esq. Colonel in the Army, and member of the Privy Council of Antigua, who was second son of Edward Byam, Esq. Governor of the Leeward Islands, and President of the Council of Antigua, by his second wife, which Edward was second son of William Byam, Esq. Governor of Surinam.

Arms.—Quarterly, first and sixth, ar. three dragons' heads erased vert, each holding in its mouth a dexter hand erased ppr. dropping blood, for Byam. Second, sa. a chev. betw. three spears' heads erect ar. pointed gu. for Caradoc Vraich-Vras. Third, gu. a lion ramp. reguard. or, for Elystan Glodrydd. Fourth, gu. a tower tripple-turreted ar. for Powel, Prince of Caerleon. Fifth, vert, a chev. betw. three wolves' heads erased or, for Elvarch, Lord of Penrose and Brythlyn, co. Glamorgan.

Crests.—First, a squirrel pass. or, collared and chained vert. Second, a dragon's head erased vert, langued gu. holding in its paws a hand ppr. dropping blood.

Motto.—Claris dextera factis. " Y Gwin yn-erbyn y Byd," is the Motto borne by Edward Samuel Byam, Esq.

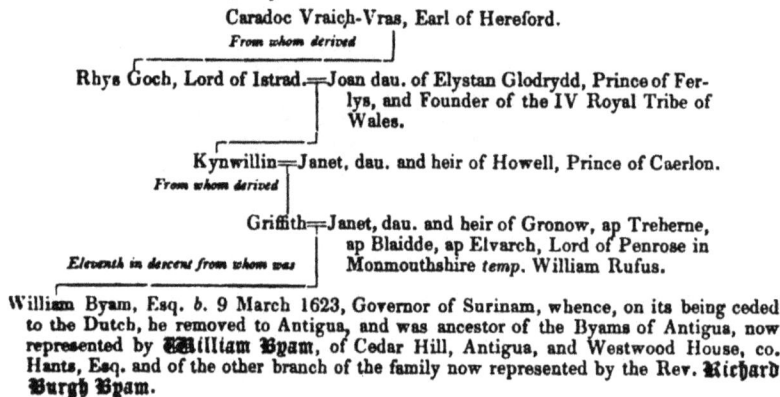

Caradoc Vraich-Vras, Earl of Hereford.
From whom derived

Rhys Goch, Lord of Istrad.⸺Joan dau. of Elystan Glodrydd, Prince of Ferlys, and Founder of the IV Royal Tribe of Wales.

Kynwillin⸺Janet, dau. and heir of Howell, Prince of Caerlon.
From whom derived

Griffith⸺Janet, dau. and heir of Gronow, ap Treherne, ap Blaidde, ap Elvarch, Lord of Penrose in Monmouthshire temp. William Rufus.
Eleventh in descent from whom was

William Byam, Esq. b. 9 March 1623, Governor of Surinam, whence, on its being ceded to the Dutch, he removed to Antigua, and was ancestor of the Byams of Antigua, now represented by William Byam, of Cedar Hill, Antigua, and Westwood House, co. Hants, Esq. and of the other branch of the family now represented by the Rev. Richard Burgh Byam.

Mellor.

Charles Mellor, of Grove Terrace, Chiswick, co. Middlesex, Esq. eldest son of the late Charles Mellor, of Frith Hall, co. Leicester, Esq. bears for

Arms.—Ar. three blackbirds ppr.: on an Escutcheon of Pretence the Arms of Wilkinson.

Crest.—A stag's head erased ppr.

Motto.—Fidelité est de Dieu.

Charles Mellor, Esq. eldest son of the late Charles Mellor, of Frith Hall, co. Leicester, Esq.⸺Frances, dau. and co-heir of Stephen Wilkinson, Esq. third son of John Wilkinson, of Hilcote Hall, co. Derby, Esq.

| 1. Charles Stephen, of Llanwrst, m. Eliza, dau. of the Rev. Mr. Ryle, and has issue. | 2. James, Major 20th Native Infantry, m. Anna Maria, dau. of Dr. Hughes of Dublin, and has issue. | 3. Stephen Wilkinson, in Holy orders. 4. Abel, E.I.C. Civil Service. 5. Abijah, in Holy orders. | 1. Sabina, m. to John Cross Starkey, Esq .of Wrenbury Hall, co. Chester, and d. s. p. | 2. Frances, m. to Capt. Winter, E. I.C.S. and has issue. | 3. Maria. 4. Harriet. |

PLATE XXII.

Burrard, of Walhampton, co. Hants, Bart.

THE present REV. SIR GEORGE BURRARD, of Walhampton, Bart. succeeded as third Baronet upon the decease of his brother, the late Admiral Sir HARRY BURRARD NEALE, G.C.B., G.C.M.G.; and in 1839 had granted, by Royal Warrant, the Supporters of his said brother, to descend to his heirs for ever with the title.

Arms.—Ar. a lion ramp. and in chief two dexter hands gu. over all a fesse or, charged with two lions ramp. counter-ramp. supporting between them a hand couped, all of the second.

Crests.—First, a dexter arm embowed, in armour, holding in the hand a sword, all ppr. Second, a naval crown or, therefrom issuant a cubit arm erect, encircled by a branch of oak ppr. the hand grasping a trident in bend sinister, the points downwards gold.

Supporters.—On either side a lion reguard. ar. standing upon an anchor ppr. supporting a trident erect or, gorged with a naval crown, therefrom a chain reflexed over the back az.

Motto.—Persevere.

Ponsonby, of Hale Hall, co. Cumberland.

MILES PONSONBY, of Hale Hall, Esq. is son and heir of the late John Ponsonby, Esq. who changed his paternal name and arms of Fisher for those of Ponsonby, in right of his wife, Dorothy, daughter and heir of Miles Ponsonby, of Hale Hall, Esq. Representative of the senior line of the great and ancient family of Ponsonby, a junior branch of which was ennobled in Ireland under the title of Bessborough.

Arms.—Gu. a chev. betw. three combs ar.

Crest.—On a ducal coronet three arrows, one in pale, and two in saltire, the points downwards, entwined by a serpent ppr.

Motto.—Pro Rege, Lege, Grege.

Bund, of Wick House, co. Worcester.

THOMAS HENRY BUND, of Wick House, co. Worcester, Esq. bears quarterly with his Paternal Coat of BUND, the Ensigns of PARSONS and JOHNSON, and on an Escutcheon of Pretence those of WILMOT, in right of his wife, Anne, daughter and only surviving child and heir of the Rev. Pynson Wilmot, Vicar of Halesowen, co. Salop.

Arms.—Quarterly, first and fourth, gu. three eagles' legs erased, a la quise, or, for BUND. Second, az. a chev. erm. betw. three trefoils ar. for PARSONS. Third, ar. a fesse lozengy, betw. three lions' heads erased gu. for JOHNSON.

Escutcheon of Pretence.—Ar. on a fesse gu. betw. three eagles' heads sa. as many escallops of the field.

Crest.—An eagle's head erased or.

William Bund, Esq. eldest son and heir⹁Mary, dau. and heiress of John Parsons, of Thomas Bund, Esq. of Overbury, co. Worcester, Esq.

Thomas Bund, Esq.⹁Susannah, youngest dau. of Benjamin Johnson, of Worcester, Esq.

Thomas Henry Bund, of Wick House, Esq. who m. 16 Nov. 1802, Anne, dau. and only surviving child of the Rev. Pynson Wilmot, Vicar of Halesowen, co. Salop.

PLATE. CX.

THE REV. RICHARD BURGH BYAM.
VICAR OF KEW & PETERSHAM CO. SURREY.

CHARLES MELLOR, ESQ.

THE REV. SIR GEORGE BURRARD, BART.
WALHAMPTON, HANTS.

MILES PONSONBY, ESQ.
HALE HALL, CO. CUMBERLAND.

THOMAS HENRY BUND, ESQ.
WICK HOUSE, CO. WORCESTER.

PLATE XXIII.

Hughes, of Gwerclas, county of Merioneth,
Subsequently of Pen-y-Clawdd,
co. Denbigh.

WILLIAM HUGHES, Esq. Representative in the Male Line of the HUGHES's of Gwerclas, Barons of Kymmer-yn-Edeirnion, bears a Shield of Sixteen Quarterings.

Arms.—Quarterly :—

I. Ar. a lion ramp. sa. armed and langued gu. (the Royal Arms of Powys), for HUGHES of GWERCLAS.

II. Az. a wolf passant ppr. for CILIN AP Y BLAIDD RHUDD, Lord of Gest.

III. Or, a lion ramp. gu. for MADOC AP GWENWYNWYN, Lord of Mawddwy.

IV. Ar. three boars' heads couped sa. langued gu. tusked or, for CADWGAN, son of ELYSTAN GLODRYDD, Prince of Fferlys.

V. Gu. a lion ramp. reguardant or, for ELYSTAN GLODRYDD.

VI. Per bend sinister ermine and ermines, over all a lion ramp. or, for TUDOR TREVOR, Lord of Hereford.

VII. Ar. a lion ramp. sa. armed and langued gu. for the " LADY OF CROGEN."

VIII. Or, a lion ramp. az. for HOWEL AP MEURIG, Lord of Nannau.

IX. Ermine, a saltire gu. with a crescent for difference, for ROGERS of BRYNTANGOR.

X. Paly of eight ar. and gu. over all a lion ramp. sa. armed and langued gu. for TUDOR, LORD OF GWYDDELWERN, brother of Owen Glendower.

XI. Gu. a lion ramp. within a bordure indented or, for THOMAS AP LLEWELLYN, LORD OF SOUTH WALES, Representative of the Sovereigns of South Wales.

XII. Az. an eagle displayed or, for PHILIP AP IVOR, LORD OF ISCOED.

XIII. Quarterly, or and gu. four lions pass. guard. counterchanged, for LLEWELLYN AP GRIFFITH, PRINCE OF NORTH WALES.

XIV. Vert, three eagles displayed in fesse or. for OWEN GWYNEDD, PRINCE OF NORTH WALES.

XV. Gu. three lioncels pass. in pale ar. armed az. for GRIFFITH AP CYNAN, KING OF NORTH WALES.

XVI. Ar. betw. four Cornish choughs ppr. armed gu. a cross flory engr. sa. for WYNN OF PEN-Y-CLAWDD.

Crest.—A demi lion ramp. sa. armed and langued gu. issuing out of a ducal coronet or.

Supporters.—Dexter, a lion sa. as in the Arms ; sinister, a dragon, gu.

Motto.—Kymmer-yn-Edeirnion.

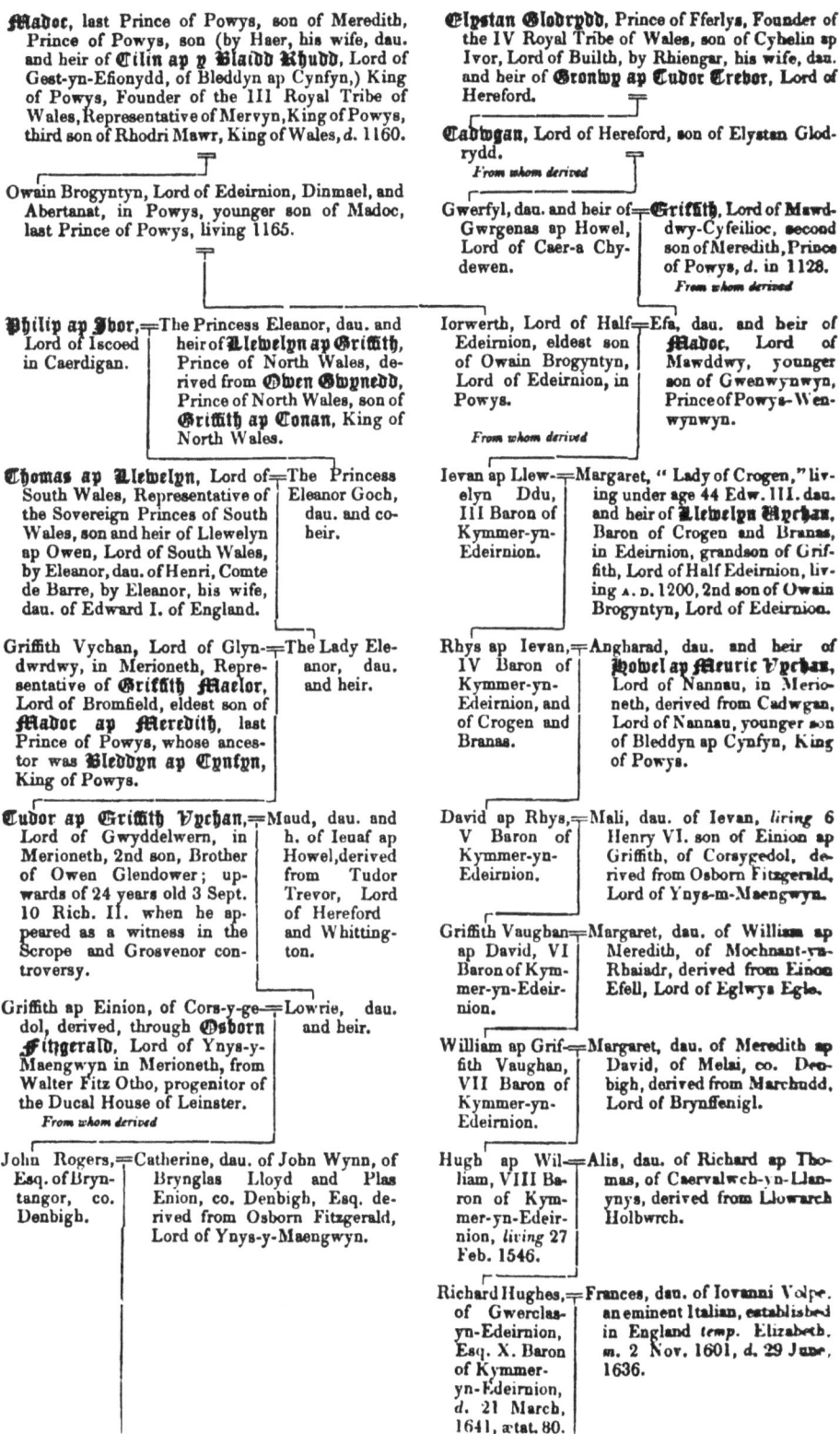

PLATE XXIII.

Madoc, last Prince of Powys, son of Meredith, Prince of Powys, son (by Haer, his wife, dau. and heir of **Cilin ap y Blaidd Rhudd**, Lord of Gest-yn-Efionydd, of Bleddyn ap Cynfyn,) King of Powys, Founder of the III Royal Tribe of Wales, Representative of Mervyn, King of Powys, third son of Rhodri Mawr, King of Wales, d. 1160.

Owain Brogyntyn, Lord of Edeirnion, Dinmael, and Abertanat, in Powys, younger son of Madoc, last Prince of Powys, living 1165.

Philip ap Ivor,=The Princess Eleanor, dau. and Lord of Iscoed in Caerdigan. | heir of **Llewelyn ap Griffith**, Prince of North Wales, derived from **Owen Gwynedd**, Prince of North Wales, son of **Griffith ap Conan**, King of North Wales.

Thomas ap Llewelyn, Lord of=The Princess South Wales, Representative of | Eleanor Goch, the Sovereign Princes of South | dau. and co-Wales, son and heir of Llewelyn | heir. ap Owen, Lord of South Wales, by Eleanor, dau. of Henri, Comte de Barre, by Eleanor, his wife, dau. of Edward I. of England.

Griffith Vychan, Lord of Glyn-=The Lady Ele-dwrdwy, in Merioneth, Repre-|anor, dau. sentative of **Griffith Maelor**, | and heir. Lord of Bromfield, eldest son of **Madoc ap Meredith**, last Prince of Powys, whose ancestor was **Bleddyn ap Cynfyn**, King of Powys.

Tudor ap Griffith Vychan,=Maud, dau. and Lord of Gwyddelwern, in | h. of Ieuaf ap Merioneth, 2nd son, Brother | Howel, derived of Owen Glendower; up-|from Tudor wards of 24 years old 3 Sept. | Trevor, Lord 10 Rich. II. when he ap-|of Hereford peared as a witness in the | and Whitting-Scrope and Grosvenor con-|ton. troversy.

Griffith ap Einion, of Cors-y-ge-=Lowrie, dau. dol, derived, through **Osborn** | and heir. **Fitzgerald**, Lord of Ynys-y-Maengwyn in Merioneth, from Walter Fitz Otho, progenitor of the Ducal House of Leinster.
From whom derived

John Rogers,=Catherine, dau. of John Wynn, of Esq. of Bryn-|Brynglas Lloyd and Plas tangor, co. |Enion, co. Denbigh, Esq. de-Denbigh. |rived from Osborn Fitzgerald, Lord of Ynys-y-Maengwyn.

a

Elystan Glodrydd, Prince of Fferlys, Founder of the IV Royal Tribe of Wales, son of Cybelin ap Ivor, Lord of Builth, by Rhiengar, his wife, dau. and heir of **Gronwy ap Tudor Trevor**, Lord of Hereford.

Cadwgan, Lord of Hereford, son of Elystan Glodrydd.
From whom derived

Gwerfyl, dau. and heir of=**Griffith**, Lord of Mawd-Gwrgenas ap Howel, | dwy-Cyfeilioc, second Lord of Caer-a Chy-| son of Meredith, Prince dewen. | of Powys, d. in 1128.
From whom derived

Iorwerth, Lord of Half-=Efa, dau. and heir of Edeirnion, eldest son | **Madoc**, Lord of of Owain Brogyntyn, | Mawddwy, younger Lord of Edeirnion, in | son of Gwenwynwyn, Powys. | Prince of Powys-Wen-wynwyn.
From whom derived

Ievan ap Llew-=Margaret, " Lady of Crogen," liv-elyn Ddu, | ing under age 44 Edw. III. dau. III Baron of | and heir of **Llewelyn Vychan**, Kymmer-yn-|Baron of Crogen and Branas, Edeirnion. | in Edeirnion, grandson of Grif-fith, Lord of Half Edeirnion, liv-ing A. D. 1200, 2nd son of Owain Brogyntyn, Lord of Edeirnion.

Rhys ap Ievan,=Angharad, dau. and heir of IV Baron of | **Howel ap Meuric Vychan**, Kymmer-yn-|Lord of Nannau, in Merio-Edeirnion, and | neth, derived from Cadwgan, of Crogen and | Lord of Nannau, younger son Branas. | of Bleddyn ap Cynfyn, King of Powys.

David ap Rhys,=Mali, dau. of Ievan, *living 6* V Baron of | Henry VI. son of Einion ap Kymmer-yn-|Griffith, of Corsygedol, de-Edeirnion. | rived from Osborn Fitzgerald, Lord of Ynys-m-Maengwyn.

Griffith Vaughan=Margaret, dau. of William ap ap David, VI | Meredith, of Mochnant-yn-Baron of Kym-|Rhaiadr, derived from Einion mer-yn-Edeir-|Efell, Lord of Eglwys Egle. nion.

William ap Grif-=Margaret, dau. of Meredith ap fith Vaughan, | David, of Melai, co. Den-VII Baron of | bigh, derived from Marchudd, Kymmer-yn-|Lord of Brynffenigl. Edeirnion.

Hugh ap Wil-=Alis, dau. of Richard ap Tho-liam, VIII Ba-|mas, of Caervalwch-yn-Llan-ron of Kym-|ynys, derived from Llowarch mer-yn-Edeir-|Holbwrch. nion, *living 27 Feb.* 1546.

Richard Hughes,=Frances, dau. of Iovanni Volpe, of Gwerclas-|an eminent Italian, established yn-Edeirnion, | in England *temp.* Elizabeth, Esq. X. Baron | m. 2 Nov. 1601, d. 29 June, of Kymmer-|1636. yn-Edeirnion, d. 21 March, 1641, ætat. 80.

b

PLATE XXIII.

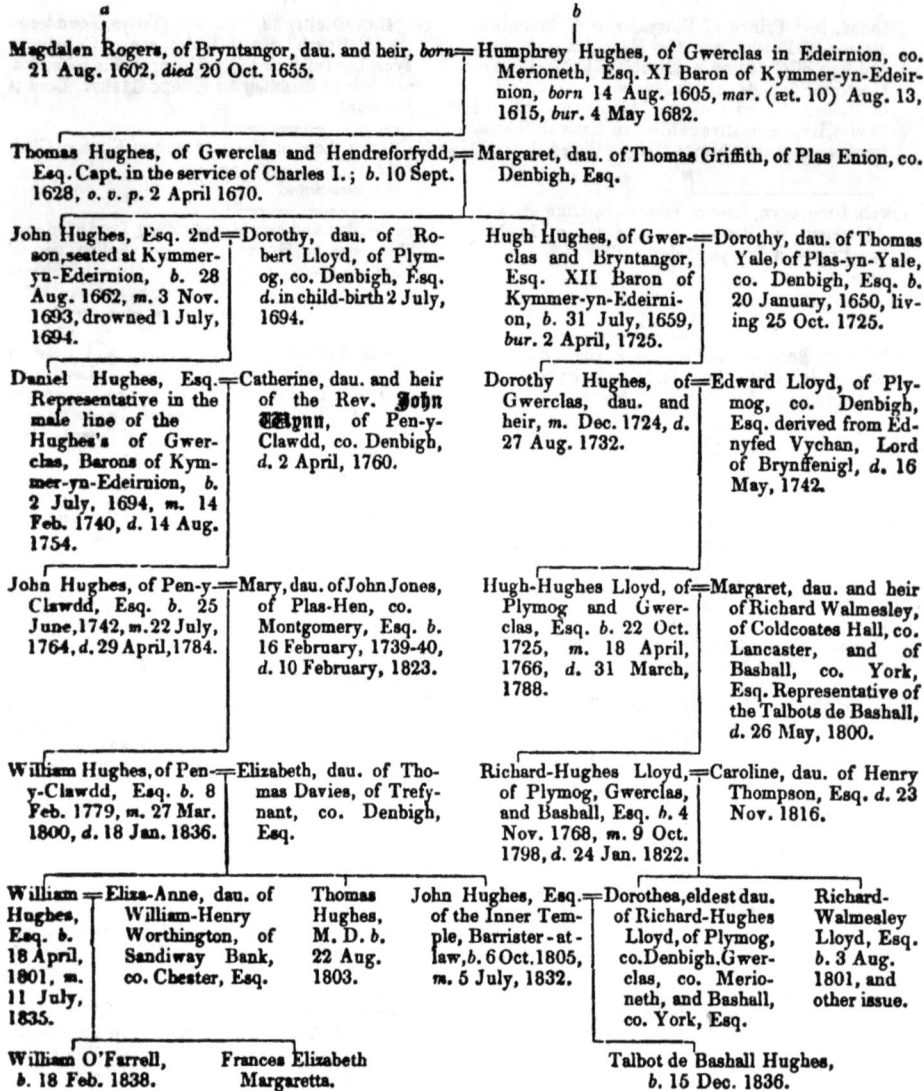

a — *b*

Magdalen Rogers, of Bryntangor, dau. and heir, *born* == Humphrey Hughes, of Gwerclas in Edeirnion, co.
21 Aug. 1602, *died* 20 Oct. 1655. Merioneth, Esq. XI Baron of Kymmer-yn-Edeir-
nion, *born* 14 Aug. 1605, *mar.* (æt. 10) Aug. 13,
1615, *bur.* 4 May 1682.

Thomas Hughes, of Gwerclas and Hendreforfydd, == Margaret, dau. of Thomas Griffith, of Plas Enion, co.
Esq. Capt. in the service of Charles I.; *b.* 10 Sept. Denbigh, Esq.
1628, *o. v. p.* 2 April 1670.

John Hughes, Esq. 2nd == Dorothy, dau. of Ro- | Hugh Hughes, of Gwer- == Dorothy, dau. of Thomas
son, seated at Kymmer- bert Lloyd, of Plym- clas and Bryntangor, Yale, of Plas-yn-Yale,
yn-Edeirnion, *b.* 28 og, co. Denbigh, Esq. Esq. XII Baron of co. Denbigh, Esq. *b.*
Aug. 1662, *m.* 3 Nov. *d.* in child-birth 2 July, Kymmer-yn-Edeirni- 20 January, 1650, liv-
1693, drowned 1 July, 1694. on, *b.* 31 July, 1659, ing 25 Oct. 1725.
1694. *bur.* 2 April, 1725.

Daniel Hughes, Esq. == Catherine, dau. and heir | Dorothy Hughes, of == Edward Lloyd, of Ply-
Representative in the of the Rev. John clas, dau. and mog, co. Denbigh,
male line of the Wynn, of Pen-y- heir, *m.* Dec. 1724, *d.* Esq. derived from Ed-
Hughes's of Gwer- Clawdd, co. Denbigh, 27 Aug. 1732. nyfed Vychan, Lord
clas, Barons of Kym- *d.* 2 April, 1760. of Brynffenigl, *d.* 16
mer-yn-Edeirnion, *b.* May, 1742.
2 July, 1694, *m.* 14
Feb. 1740, *d.* 14 Aug.
1754.

John Hughes, of Pen-y- == Mary, dau. of John Jones, | Hugh-Hughes Lloyd, of == Margaret, dau. and heir
Clawdd, Esq. *b.* 25 of Plas-Hen, co. Plymog and Gwer- of Richard Walmesley,
June, 1742, *m.* 22 July, Montgomery, Esq. *b.* clas, Esq. *b.* 22 Oct. of Coldcoates Hall, co.
1764, *d.* 29 April, 1784. 16 February, 1739-40, 1725, *m.* 18 April, Lancaster, and of
d. 10 February, 1823. 1766, *d.* 31 March, Bashall, co. York,
1788. Esq. Representative of
the Talbots de Bashall,
d. 26 May, 1800.

William Hughes, of Pen- == Elizabeth, dau. of Tho- | Richard-Hughes Lloyd, == Caroline, dau. of Henry
y-Clawdd, Esq. *b.* 8 mas Davies, of Trefy- of Plymog, Gwerclas, Thompson, Esq. *d.* 23
Feb. 1779, *m.* 27 Mar. nant, co. Denbigh, and Bashall, Esq. *b.* 4 Nov. 1816.
1800, *d.* 18 Jan. 1836. Esq. Nov. 1768, *m.* 9 Oct.
1798, *d.* 24 Jan. 1822.

William == Eliza-Anne, dau. of | Thomas | John Hughes, Esq. == Dorothea, eldest dau. | Richard-
Hughes, William-Henry Hughes, of the Inner Tem- of Richard-Hughes Walmesley
Esq. *b.* Worthington, of M.D. *b.* ple, Barrister-at- Lloyd, of Plymog, Lloyd, Esq.
18 April, Sandiway Bank, 22 Aug. law, *b.* 6 Oct. 1805, co. Denbigh. Gwer- *b.* 3 Aug.
1801, *m.* co. Chester, Esq. 1803. *m.* 5 July, 1832. clas, co. Merio- 1801, and
11 July, neth, and Bashall, other issue.
1835. co. York, Esq.

William O'Farrell, Frances Elizabeth | Talbot de Bashall Hughes,
b. 18 Feb. 1838. Margaretta. *b.* 15 Dec. 1836.

PLATE XXIII.

Parr, of Lythwood, co. Salop.

THOMAS PARR, of Lythwood Hall, co. Salop, Esq. bears the ancient Coat of the PARRS of Kendal, and, on an Escutcheon of Pretence, the Arms of WALTER, in right of his wife, Katherine, daughter and co-heir of the late Robert Walter, Esq. Captain R. N. The Parrs of Lythwood descend from a younger branch of the family of Parr of Kendal, whose Representative *temp.* Henry VIII. was William Parr, the celebrated Marquess of Northampton, brother of Queen Katherine Parr.

Arms.—Ar. two bars az. a bordure engr. sa. a crescent for difference, an escutcheon of pretence, ar. guttée de sang, two swords in saltire gu. over all a lion ramp. sa. for WALTER.

Crest.—A female's head couped below the shoulders, full faced ppr. vested az. on her head a wreath of roses, alternately ar. and gu.

Motto.—Amour avec Loyaulté.

Hemsworth, of Shropham Hall, co. Norfolk.

HENRY D'ESTERRE HEMSWORTH, of Shropham Hall, co. Norfolk, Esq. a Magistrate for the Counties of Norfolk and Suffolk, and a Deputy Lieutenant of the former, is second son of the late Thomas Hemsworth, of Abbeyville, co. Tipperary, Esq. by Mary, his wife, daughter of Henry D'Esterre, of Rosmaugher, co. Clare, Esq. In right of his wife, Jane Maria, daughter and co-heir of General James Hethersett, he bears on an Escutcheon of Pretence the Arms of HETHERSETT. The Hemsworths, settled in Ireland since the middle of the seventeenth century, were originally of Hemsworth, co. York.

Arms.—Per saltire ar. and or, a leopard's face sa. On an escutcheon of pretence the Arms of HETHERSETT.

Crest.—A dexter arm embowed in armour, the gauntlet grasping a sword ppr. hilt and pomel or, transfixing a leopard's face sa.

Motto.—Manus hæc inimica tyrannis.

PLATE XVIII

WILLIAM HUGHES, ESQ.

MALE REPRESENTATIVE OF THE HUGHES'S OF GWERCLAS, BARONS OF KYMMER-YN-EDEIRNION.

HENRY D'ESTERRE HEMSWORTH, ESQ.

SHROPHAM HALL, CO. NORFOLK.

THOMAS PARR, ESQ.

LYTHWOOD HALL, CO. SALOP.

PLATE XXIV.

Fiske-Harrison, of Copford Hall, co. Essex.

FISKE GOODEVE FISKE-HARRISON, of Copford Hall, Esq. assumed his additional Surname and Arms of FISKE on succeeding to the family estate of his mother, Sarah-Thomas, only child of the Rev. John Fiske, of Thorpe Morieux, co. Suffolk, by his wife, the dau. and heir of the late Samuel Thomas, of Lavenham, Esq.

Arms.—Quarterly, first and fourth, Az. two bars erm. betw. six estoiles, three, two, and one, ar. Second and third, Ar. three crescents barry undée az. and gu.
Crest.—A stork, wings expanded, ar. beaked and membered or.
Motto.—Ferendo et feriendo.

Gregson, of Murton and Burdon, co. Durham.

JOHN GREGSON, of Murton and Burdon, co. Durham, Esq. M. A. Barrister-at-law, bears the Quartered Coat of GREGSON and ALLGOOD, as son and heir of the late John Gregson, of Murton, Burdon, and Durham, Esq. by Elizabeth, his wife, only dau. and heir of Lancelot Allgood, Esq. The Family of Gregson derives from John Gregson, living in 1537, who came from Barton, co. Lincoln, and purchased the estate of Murton from Lord Lumley.

Arms.—Quarterly, first and fourth, Ar. a saltire gu. a canton chequy or and az. for GREGSON. Second and third, Ar. a cross engr. gu. betw. four mullets az. on a chief or three damask roses of the second, seeded gold, barbed vert, for ALLGOOD.
Crest.—An arm couped at the elbow, vested, bendy wavy of six, and environed round the wrist with a ribbon, ar. and gu. holding in the hand ppr. a battleaxe or, handle sa.

Croft, of Cowling Hall, co. York,
and Dodbington, co. Kent, Bart.

SIR JOHN CROFT, Bart. Knight Commander of the Tower and Sword, D.C.L. F.R.S. is son and heir of the late John Croft, Esq. by Henrietta-Maria, his wife, dau. and co-heir of the Rev. James Tunstall, D.D. and grandson (by Lucy, his wife, dau. and heir of Henry Thompson, Esq.) of Thomas Croft, of London, Esq. who was second son of Stephen Croft, of Stillington, Esq. the Representative of an ancient Yorkshire Family, of which was Sir Christopher Croft, Knt. who, when Lord Mayor of York, in 1641, entertained King CHARLES I. in his own house.

The present SIR JOHN CROFT was appointed Commissioner, in conjunction with the Portuguese Judge, Senhor João Gaudencio Torres, to distribute the Parliamentary Grant to the Portuguese Sufferers in the year 1811 (*vide* Report of Parliamentary Grant, 6 July, 1814), and in 1815, was constituted Chargé des Affaires at Lisbon. The Supporters, borne by Sir John, were granted by Royal License in April, 1834, in consideration of his eminent Services while attached to the British Mission at Lisbon in 1811 and 1812, (*vide* Parliamentary Report, Southey's Peninsular War, vol. iii. p. 189, and Gurwood's Despatches of the Duke of Wellington, new edition, vol. iii. p. 652,) and as Chargé des Affaires there in 1815.

Arms.—Quarterly, first and fourth quarterly, per fesse indented or and gu. in the first quarter a lion pass. guard. of the second, for CROFT. Second and third, sa. three combs ar. for TUNSTALL. Impaling (in right of his wife, Anne-Knox, dau. of the Rev. John Radcliffe, Rector of Limehouse, descended from the ancient and noble family of Radcliffe), Ar. two bends engr. sa. a canton gu.
Crests.—First, a lion pass. guard. or, supporting a shield charged with the arms of St. George (granted by King Charles I. to Sir Christopher Croft, Lord Mayor of York). Second, a lion pass. guard. per pale, indented gu. and erminois, the dexter fore-paw resting on an escutcheon ar. charged with a representation of the star of the Order of the Tower and Sword ppr.
Supporters.—On the dexter side, a lion guard. or, gorged with a wreath of laurel vert, therefrom pendent an escutcheon gu. charged with a tower gold; and on the

PLATE XXIV.

sinister, a bull sa. horned, crined, hoofed, and gorged with a ducal crown or, therefrom pendent an escutcheon ar. charged with the Star of the Order of the Tower and Sword ppr.

Mottoes.—*Under the Arms and over the first Crest*, Esse quam videri. *Over the second Crest*, Valor E Lealdale.

Shipperdson, of Piddinghall Garth, co. Durham.

EDWARD SHIPPERDSON, of Piddinghall Garth and Murton, Esq. High Sheriff of the County of Durham, Representative of a Family which is traceable among the Records of Halmot Court, Bishop Wearmouth, to the time of EDWARD III. bears a Shield of Six Quarterings.

Arms.—Quarterly, first and sixth, sa. on a bend ar. three lozenges az. each charged with a planetary sun in its glory, for SHIPPERDSON. Second, per bend nebulée or and sa. a lion ramp. counterchanged, for SYMPSON. Third, az. six annulets or, three, two, and one, for MUSGRAVE. Fourth, gu. a sword in pale ar. hilted or, in base a serpent nowed ppr. and on a chief of the third two doves close, beaked and legged of the first, for KIRSHAW. Fifth, ar. a chev. sa. betw. three fountains ppr. for SYKES.

Crest.—A hand issuing out of a cloud and grasping a sword ppr.

Motto.—Nubem eripium.

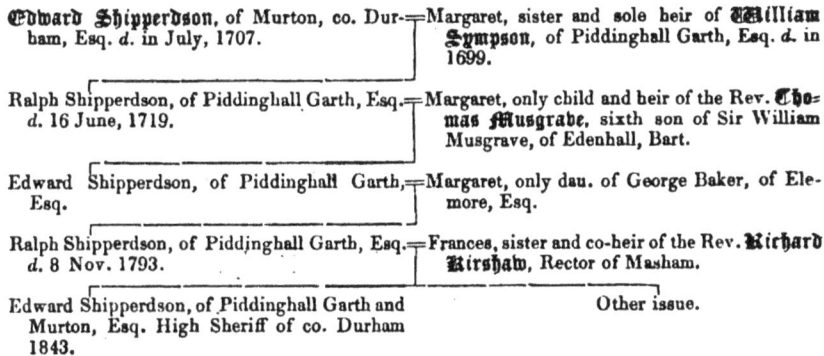

Edward Shipperdson, of Murton, co. Durham, Esq. *d.* in July, 1707. = Margaret, sister and sole heir of **William Sympson**, of Piddinghall Garth, Esq. *d.* in 1699.

Ralph Shipperdson, of Piddinghall Garth, Esq. *d.* 16 June, 1719. = Margaret, only child and heir of the Rev. **Thomas Musgrave**, sixth son of Sir William Musgrave, of Edenhall, Bart.

Edward Shipperdson, of Piddinghall Garth, Esq. = Margaret, only dau. of George Baker, of Elemore, Esq.

Ralph Shipperdson, of Piddinghall Garth, Esq. *d.* 8 Nov. 1793. = Frances, sister and co-heir of the Rev. **Richard Kirshaw**, Rector of Masham.

Edward Shipperdson, of Piddinghall Garth and Murton, Esq. High Sheriff of co. Durham 1843.　　　Other issue.

Parkhouse, of Eastfield Lodge, co. Hants.

GEORGE PARKHOUSE, of Eastfield Lodge, co. Hants, Esq. Representative of a junior branch of the Devonshire Family of the same name, impales, with his own Arms, the Quartered Coat of ARMSTRONG of Gallen, in right of his wife, Fanny, sister of Sir Andrew Armstrong, of Gallen, King's County, Bart. M.P.

Arms.—Per chev. embattled vert and ar. in chief two bucks trippant ppr. each gorged with a collar or, in base a cross flory of the first; impaling, quarterly, first and fourth, ar. issuing from the sinister side a dexter arm habited gu. the hand grasping the trunk of an oak tree, eradicated and broken at the top, ppr. Second and third, ar. three pallets az.

Crest.—A buck ppr. charged on the body with three mullets az. the dexter foreleg resting on a cross flory, as in the Arms.

Motto.—The Cross our Stay.

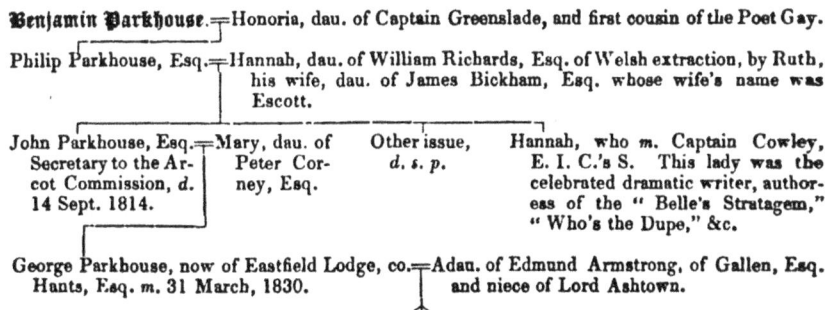

Benjamin Parkhouse. = Honoria, dau. of Captain Greenslade, and first cousin of the Poet Gay.

Philip Parkhouse, Esq. = Hannah, dau. of William Richards, Esq. of Welsh extraction, by Ruth, his wife, dau. of James Bickham, Esq. whose wife's name was Escott.

John Parkhouse, Esq. Secretary to the Arcot Commission, *d.* 14 Sept. 1814. = Mary, dau. of Peter Corney, Esq.　　Other issue, *d. s. p.*　　Hannah, who *m.* Captain Cowley, E. I. C.'s S. This lady was the celebrated dramatic writer, authoress of the " Belle's Stratagem," " Who's the Dupe," &c.

George Parkhouse, now of Eastfield Lodge, co. Hants, Esq. *m.* 31 March, 1830. = A dau. of Edmund Armstrong, of Gallen, Esq. and niece of Lord Ashtown.

FISKE GOODEVE FISKE HARRISON, ESQ.
COPFORD HALL, CO ESSEX

JOHN GREGSON, ESQ.
MURTON & BURDON, CO DURHAM

SIR JOHN CROFT, BART. D.C.L. F.R.S.
KNT. COMMANDER OF THE TOWER & SWORD

EDWARD SHIPPERDSON, ESQ.
PIDDINGHALL GARTH, CO DURHAM

GEORGE PARKHOUSE, ESQ.
EASTFIELD LODGE, HANTS

PLATE XXV.

Jones, of Llanarth Court, co. Monmouth.

JOHN JONES, of Llanarth Court, co. Monmouth, Esq. Representative of the senior branch of the great House of Herbert, derived immediately from HOWEL, third son of William ap Jenkin, *alias* Herbert, Lord of Gwarindee, living *temp.* EDWARD III. bears a Shield of Twenty Quarterings.

Arms.—Quarterly :—

I. Per pale az. and gu. three lions ramp. ar. for JONES.

II. Or, two ravens in pale ppr. in chief a label of two points az. for CORBET.

III. Gu. two bends or and ar. for MILO FITZ-WALTER, Earl of Hereford.

IV. Gu. five fusils conjoined in fesse or, for BERNARD NEWMARCH, Lord of Breck-nock.

V. Ar. on a chief gu. a label of five points or, for WILLIAM DE VIVONIA.

VI. Az. three escallops or, for WILLIAM MALLET, Lord of Cory Mallet.

VII. Per pale or and vert, a lion ramp. gu. a canton vairé or and of the third, being the Arms of FERRERS, for MARSHALL, Earl of Pembroke.

VIII. Gu. a bend lozengy or, for MARSHALL, ancient.

IX. Ar. on a chief az. three crosses patée, fitchée at the foot, of the field, for RICHARD STRONGBOW, Earl of Pembroke.

X. Or, three chev. gu. a label of five points az. for GILBERT DE CLARE, Earl of Pembroke.

XI. Gu. three lions pass. ar. for GIFFARD, Earl of Buckingham.

XII. Sa. three wheatsheaves ar. for MACMOROUGH, King of Leinster.

XIII. Ar. on a cross gu. five mullets or, for BLETHIN BROADSPEARE, Lord of Llanllowell.

XIV. Per pale az. and sa. three fleurs de lis ar. for GWARINDDY, Lord of Llandilo.

XV. Sa. on a chev. betw. three bucks' heads cabossed ar. as many bugles stringed sa. for HUNTLEY, Lord of Treowen.

XVI. Or, a maunch gu. for HASTINGS.

XVII. Chequy or and sa. on a fesse gu. three leopards' faces jessant de lis gold, for WALLIS, Lord of Llanarth.

XVIII. Ar. a griffin segreant sa. for MORGAN of Penllwyn.

XIX. Sa. a fesse or, betw. three swans ar. membered gu. for WYBORNE, of Hawkswell.

XX. Az. on a fesse cottised or, three leopards' faces gu. for LEE, of Lanfoist.

Crest.—A Moorish woman's head, with long hair tied at the end by a button, a wreath about the head or and gu.

Motto.—Asgre lân diogel ei pherchen.

PLATE III.

Peter de Fitz....... younger ...... of Herbert .... from Charle-magne, Emperor of the West. =

Herbert Fitz-Peter, ... came over at the Conquest with the first William, and was Chamber-lain to William Rufus.

Sir Robert Corbet, ... in Normandy.

Herbert Fitz-Herbert, ... Lord of .... Chamber-lain and Treasurer to King Henry I. and King Stephen.

Gilbert, sur-named ...., Earl of Arca, in Normandy. =

Walter Gif-fard, Earl of Buckingham, came to England with Wil-liam the Con-queror. = Agnes, dau. of Gerard Flaistell, sister of William, Bishop of Evereux.

Richard Fitz-Gilbert, came to England with William, and was at the battle of Hastings—called Lac Richard. = Robais, dau. and heir.

Gilbert de Clare, Lar Gilbert went with his mother Walter. = Adelisa, dau. of the Earl of Clere-mont.

Walter de Clare, conquered Ne-ther Gwent, in Wales, and founded Tintern Abbey, d. s. p.

Richard Fitz-Gilbert, Earl of Clare, an-cestor of the Earls of Glou-cester and Hertford. = Gilbert de Clare, 2nd son, Earl of Pembroke, Lord of Chep-stow and Rag-land Castles in Monmouth-shire, d. A. D. 1149. = Elizabeth de Beaumont, dau. of Robert, first Earl of Lei-cester.

Richard de Clare, surnamed Strongbow, Earl of Pem-broke and Sengzil, Marshall of England, Lord of Chep-stow and Ragland. = The Princess Eva, dau. and h. of Dermot Mac Morrough, the last King of Leinster.

Isabel de Clare, only dau. and heir. = William Marshall, Earl of Pembroke, d. A. D. 1219, buried in the Temple Church.

Sibyl, one of the daughters and co-heirs. = William de Ferrers, Earl Ferrers and Earl of Derby, d. A. D. 1254.

..... Fitz-..... Earl of Bereford, Constable of England, Lord of the Castles of Abergaven-ny and Bre-con and the Fo-rest of Deane. = Sibil, dau. and heir of Ber-..... and Sibil Lord of Brecknock.

Herbert Fitz-Herbert, Lord of the Forest of Dene, and lived in the Castle of St. Michael's in the Forest, d. 1205. = Lucy, third dau. and co-heiress.

2nd wife. Isabel, dau. and cobeir of Wil-liam de Braose, and widow of David Llew-ellen, Prince of Wales. = Peter Fitz-Her-bert, Baron of Berstople, Lord of Blenlleven-ny Castle in Breconshire, one of the Ba-rons in Magna Charta, d. 1235. = 1st wife. Alice, dau. of Robert Fitz-Roger, a great Baron in Northum-berland, Lord of Warkworth and Claver-ing.

Hugh de Vivonia, Seneschal of Poi-tou, Aquitain, and Guienne. = Mabell, eldest dau. and co-h. of Wil-liam Mallet, Lord of Corry Mallet, co. Somerset.

Maud de Ferrers, co-heir of her mother. = William de Vivonia, sur-named de Fortibus, Lord of Chewton, co. Somer-set.

Reginald Fitz-Peter, Lord of Blenllevenny Castle, Breconshire. = Joan de Vivonia, eldest dau. and co-heir.

John Fitz-Reginald, summoned to Par-liament as a Baron 1294. | Reginald Fitz-Regi-nald. | Peter Fitz-Reginald, Lord of Chewton. = Alice, dau. and heir of Ble-thin Broadspeer, Lord of Llanllowell, in Monmouth-shire.

Herbert Fitz-Peter = Margaret, dau. of Sir John Walsh, Knt.

Adam Fitz-Herbert, Lord of Llanllowen and Betesley. = Christian, dau. and h. of Gwarin Ddu.

a   b

PLATE XXV.

a   b

| John ap Adam, Lord of Llanllowell. | John Herbert, alias Jenkin, Lord of Werndee, near Abergavenny. = Gwenllian, dau. of Sir Aaron ap Bledri, Knt. | Sir Walter Huntley, of Treowen, near Monmouth, Knt. = Dau. and co-h. of Hastings. | Sir Robert Wallis, Knt. Lord of Llanarth. |

William ap Jenkin, alias = Gwenllian, daughter of Herbert, Lord Werndee, lived at Perthir, near Monmouth.   Howell Ichan, Esq.

Sir Thomas Huntley, of Treowen, Knt. = A dau. of Gwndaw of the Forest.

Sir Thomas Wallis, of Llanarth, Knt.

William Wallis, of Llanarth, Esq.

| John. | David. | Howell. = Maud. dau. of Howell ap Rhys. | Thomas ap Gwillim. = Maud, dau. and heir of Sir John Morley, Knt. | Thomas Huntley, of Treowen, Esq. = Alice, dau. and heir. |

Jenkin ap Howell. = Constance, dau. of Roger Vychan ap Walter Sais.

Sir William ap Thomas, Knt.

John Tomelin, or Huntley. = Margaret, dau. of John Thomas ap Adam Herbert.

David ap Jenkin, slain at Banbury, fighting = Margaret, dau. and co-heir. under the standard of his cousin, the Earl of Pembroke.
From whom descended

Sir Philip Jones, of Treowen, Knt. was in = Elizabeth, dau. of Sir Edward Morgan, of Ragland Castle when destroyed by Sir Llantarnam Abbey, co. Monmouth, Esq. Thomas Fairfax ; d. 1660.
From whom derived

John Jones, of Llanarth Court and Treowen, Esq. d. 1755. = Florence, sister and heir of Henry Morgan, of Penllwyn, co. Monmouth, Esq.

Philip Jones, of Llanarth Court, Treowen, and Penllwyn, Esq. d. May, 1782. = Catherine, youngest sister and co-heir of John Wyborne, of Hawkwell Place, co. Kent, Esq.

John Jones, of Lanarth Court, &c. Esq. = Mary, eldest dau. and co-heir of Richard Lee, of Llanfoist House, co. Monmouth, Esq.

John Jones, of Llanarth Court, &c. Esq. = Lady Harriett Plunkett, only dau. of Arthur James, eighth Earl of Fingall, K. P.

| John Jones, Esq. | Arthur Jones, 23rd R. W. Fusileers. Edmund Philip. Gerald Herbert. | Frances Mary. Mary Louisa. |

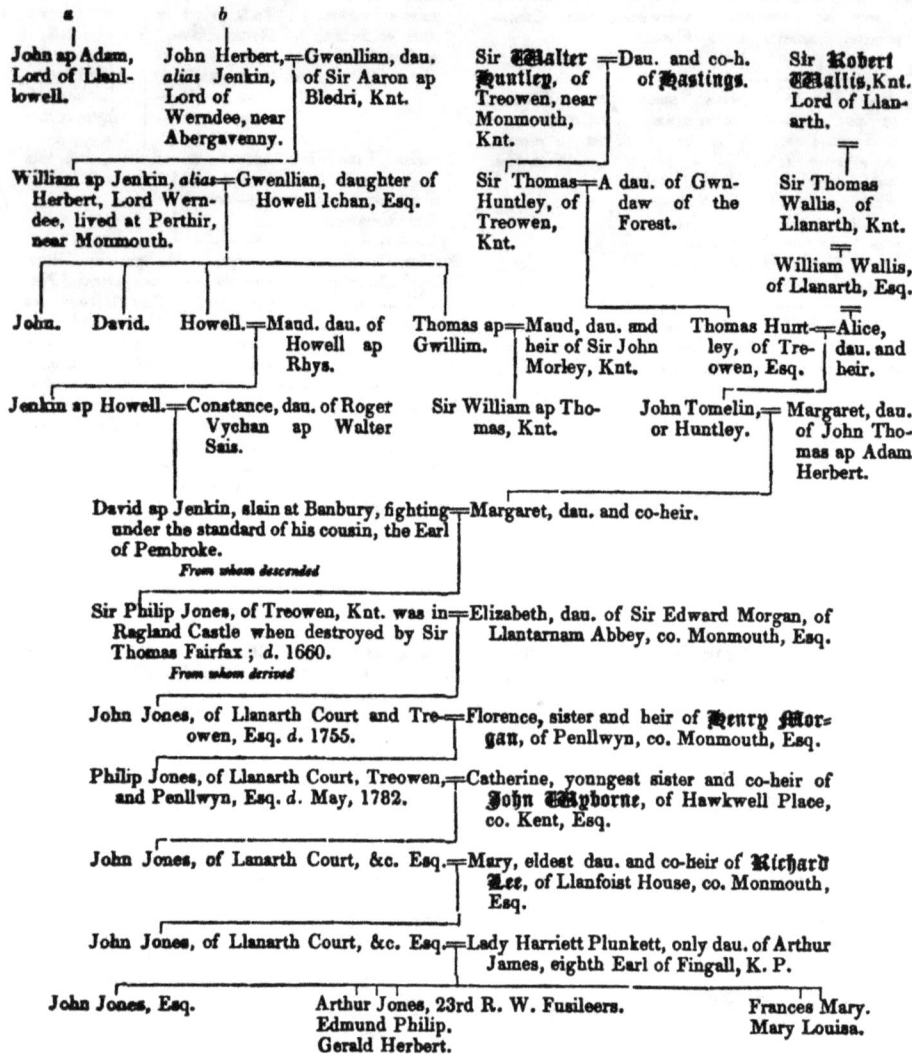

Leathes, of Herringfleet Hall, co. Suffolk.

THE present JOHN FRANCIS LEATHES, of Herringfleet Hall, Esq. is grandson of Cartaret Mussenden, Esq. M.P. who took the name and Arms of Leathes, as heir to his maternal uncle, William Leathes, Esq. many years Minister at the Courts of Brussels and the Hague. The family of Mussenden came over with William the Conqueror, and became possessed of the Lordship of Mussenden, or, as it is now written, Missenden, in the county of Buckingham, about that period. Sir William de Mussenden was Grand Admiral of England *temp.* Henry I. and founder of the Abbey of Missenden.

Arms.—Quarterly, first and fourth, az. on a bend, betw. three fleurs-de-lis or, as many mullets pierced gu. for LEATHES. Second and third, or, a cross engr. gu. ; in the dexter canton a Cornish chough ppr. beaked and legged as the second, for MUSSENDEN.

Crests.—First, a demi griffin segreant or, armed and langued gu. for LEATHES. Second, a dove, with an olive branch in its beak, all ppr. for MUSSENDEN.

Mottoes.—In ardua virtus, for LEATHES ; and *over the* MUSSENDEN *Crest*, Tending to peace.

PLATE XXV.

John Mussenden, son of John Mussen—╤**Jane**, dau. of **Adam Leathes**, of Agbat-
den, Vicar-General of the Diocese of   resk, co. Antrim: *d.* in 1736.
Down and Connor, *d.* in 1700.

Cartaret Mussenden, Esq. who took the╤Loveday, dau. of J. Garrod, of the county
name and arms of LEATHES. He was   of Lincoln, Esq.
M.P. for Harwich and Sudbury, and *d.*
in 1787.

George Leathes, of Herringfleet Hall. co.╤Mary, dau. of W. Moore, of Worcester,
Suffolk: *d.* in 1817.   Esq.

1. George-Augustus, LieutCol. 96th Regiment: *d. unm.* 1808.	2. John Francis, now of Herringfleet Hall.	3. Henry-Mussenden, of Guild House, Thorpe, co. Norfolk.	4. Frederick, in Holy orders, Rector of Wickhampton and Ringsfield.	5. Edward, of Normanstone, co. Suffolk.	1. Louisa Mary. 2. Harriet Elizabeth.

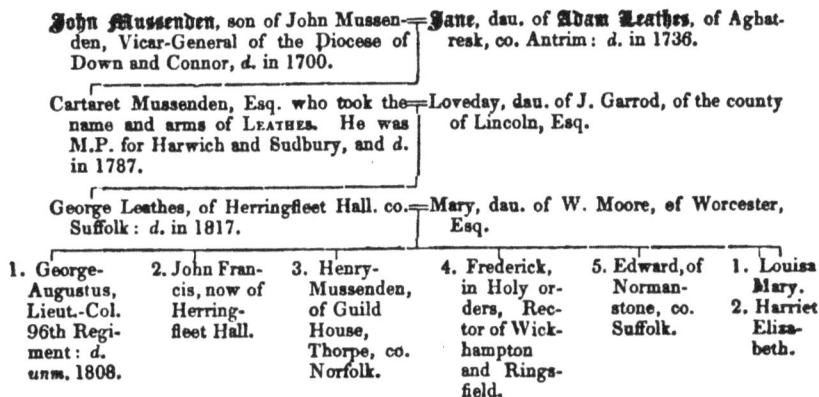

Clarke, of Welton Place, co. Northampton.

THE various branches of the stock of Clarke, Clerk, or Clerke, in Northampton-
shire and the adjoining counties, refer their common origin to the ancient family
of that name situated in Warwickshire as far back as the time of Edward I.

Richard Trevor Clarke, of Welton Place, Esq. bears a Coat of Six Quarterings, viz. CLARKE, ADAMS, PLOMER, PLOMER-CLARKE, CHILD, and TYMMS.

Arms.—Quarterly, first, ar. on a bend gu. betw. three torteaux as many swans ar. for
CLARKE. Second, erm. three cats-a-mountain pass. in pale az. for ADAMS. Third, per
chev. flory counterflory ar. and gu. three martlets counterchanged, for PLOMER. Fourth,
PLOMER and CLARKE quarterly, for PLOMER-CLARKE. Fifth, gu. a chev. erm. betw.
three martlets, for CHILD. Sixth, per chev. engr. or and az. three fleurs-de-lis counterchanged, for TYMMS.

Crest.—A swan rising ar. ducally gorged and chained or.

Motto.—Erectus non elatus.

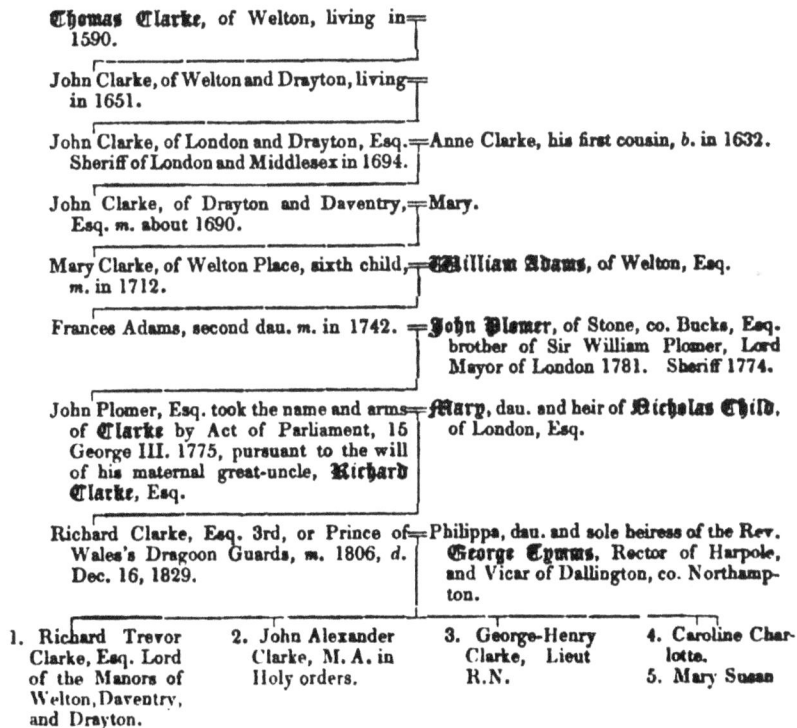

Thomas Clarke, of Welton, living in╤
1590.

John Clarke, of Welton and Drayton, living╤
in 1651.

John Clarke, of London and Drayton, Esq.╤Anne Clarke, his first cousin, *b.* in 1632.
Sheriff of London and Middlesex in 1694.

John Clarke, of Drayton and Daventry,╤Mary.
Esq. *m.* about 1690.

Mary Clarke, of Welton Place, sixth child,╤**William Adams**, of Welton, Esq.
m. in 1712.

Frances Adams, second dau. *m.* in 1742.╤**John Plomer**, of Stone, co. Bucks, Esq.
    brother of Sir William Plomer, Lord
    Mayor of London 1781. Sheriff 1774.

John Plomer, Esq. took the name and arms╤**Mary**, dau. and heir of **Nicholas Child**,
of **Clarke** by Act of Parliament, 15   of London, Esq.
George III. 1775, pursuant to the will
of his maternal great-uncle, **Richard
Clarke**, Esq.

Richard Clarke, Esq. 3rd, or Prince of╤Philippa, dau. and sole heiress of the Rev.
Wales's Dragoon Guards, *m.* 1806, *d.*   **George Tymms**, Rector of Harpole,
Dec. 16, 1829.   and Vicar of Dallington, co. Northamp-
    ton.

1. Richard Trevor Clarke, Esq. Lord of the Manors of Welton, Daventry, and Drayton.	2. John Alexander Clarke, M.A. in Holy orders.	3. George-Henry Clarke, Lieut R.N.	4. Caroline Charlotte. 5. Mary Susan

PLATE XXV

JOHN JONES, ESQ.
LLANARTH COURT, CO. MONMOUTH.

i Jones.
ii Corbet.
iii Milo Fitzwalter.
iv Bernard Newmarch.
v William de Broria.
vi William Mallet.
vii Marshal & Ferrers.
viii Marshal (Ancient).
ix Stronghow.
x De Clare.

xi Gifford.
xii Mac Morrough.
xiii Blethin Broadspear
xiv Gwarinddy.
xv Huntley.
xvi Hastings.
xvii Wallis.
xviii Morgan.
xix Glyborne.
xx Vee.

JOHN FRANCIS LEATHES, ESQ.
HERRINGFLEET HALL, CO. SUFFOLK.

RICHARD TREVOR CLARKE, ESQ.
WELTON PLACE, CO. NORTHAMPTON

PLATE XXVI.

Bigg-Wither, of Manydown, co. Hants.

The Rev. Lovelace Bigg-Wither, of Manydown and Tangier Park, as Representative of the ancient Families of Bigg and Wither, bears a shield of twenty-three quarterings. He is grandson of Lovelace Bigg, of Chilton Follyatt, co. Wilts, Esq. who assumed, upon inheriting the Wither estates, the surname and arms of that family.

Arms :—

I. Quarterly, first and fourth, ar. a chev. gu. betw. three crescents sa. for Wither. Second and third, per pale erm. and az. a lion pass. gu. ducally crowned or, within a bordure engr. of the third, charged with eight fleurs-de-lis of the fourth, for Bigg.

II. Per pale erm. and az. a lion pass. gu. ducally crowned or, within a bordure engr. of the third, charged with eight fleurs-de-lis of the fourth, for Bigg.

III. Az. a saltire betw. four escallops or, for Wade.

IV. Per bend indented or and az. a pelican in her piety, betw. two fleurs-de-lis bendwise in each compartment, all counterchanged.

V. Ar. a chev. gu. betw. three crescents sa. for Wither.

VI. Or, a lion ramp. double headed az. vulned in the shoulder, for Mason.

VII. Ar. a fesse az. betw. three crescents gu. for Risley.

VIII. Erm. a chief sa. thereon a greyhound pass. ar. for Murden.

IX. Chequy ar. and gu. on a bend sa. three mullets of the first, for Bekering.

X. Ar. a lion ramp. queue fourchée gu. for Havering.

XI. Az. two bendlets and a chief ar. for Newbald.

XII. Ar. three pellets, two and one, for Delaborne.

XIII. Or, on a bend sa. cotised gu. three mullets ar. for Hawton.

XIV. Az. a cross engr. or, an ermine spot in the first and fourth quarters, for Osborne.

XV. Gu. semée of crosses crosslet fitchée ar. three crescents or, for Derehurst.

XVI. Gu. three eagles displ. ar. a label az. for Newnham.

XVII. Ar. three torteaux, two and one, for Halberke.

XVIII. Sa. ten billets, four, three, two, and one, or, on a canton of the same a martlet sa. for Blundell.

XIX. Ar. on a fesse sa. betw. three mullets gu. as many escallops or, for Odingsells.

XX. Ar. two bars sa. in chief three lions' heads erased of the same, langued gu. for Geale.

XXI. Sa. a boar's head, couped, over two perpendicular spear-heads ar. for Loker.

XXII. Az. a chev. erm. betw. three hedgehogs or, for Harris.

XXIII. Lozengy ar. and vert, on a bend az. three griffins' heads erased of the first, for Young.

Crest of Wither.—A demi hare erect az. in the mouth three ears of ripe corn or.

Mottoes.—I grow and wither both together. Pro Rege, lege, grege. Nec habeo: nec careo: nec curo.

Lovelace Bigg, of Chilton Follyatt, Wilts, Esq. b. 8 Oct. 1661, son of Richard Bigg, of Haines Hill, Berks, Esq. = Dorothy, dau. and, in her issue, heir of William Wither, of Manydown, Hants, Esq. representative of Robert Wither, of Manydown, Esq. living temp. Edward III. This lady was entitled by descent to quarter Mason, Risley, Murden, Bekering, Havering, Newbald, Delaborne, Hawton, Osborne, Derehurst, Newnham, Halberke, Blundell, Odingsells, Geale, and Loker.

The Rev. Walter Bigg, Rector of Worting, Hants, and Fellow of Winchester College, b. in 1701, d. 18 June, 1772. = Jane, eldest dau. and eventual heiress of the Rev. John Harris, by Jane, his first wife, sister of Dr. Young, the Poet.

Lovelace Bigg, of Chilton Follyatt, b. 4 Aug. 1741; assumed the name and arms of Wither. = Margaret, second dau. of Bridges Blachford, of Osborne, Isle of Wight, Esq.

Harris Bigg Wither, of Manydown, Esq. b. 18 May, 1781; d. 23 March, 1833. = Anne Howe, only dau. of the late Bedingfeld Bramley Frith, Esq.

The Rev. Lovelace Bigg-Wither, of Manydown and Tangier Park, Hants.

PLATE XXVI.

Ashe, of Ashfield, co. Meath.

LIEUTENANT-COLONEL WILLIAM WELLESLEY ASHE, of Ashfield, is Representative of the ancient Devonshire family of Ashe or Esse, which was established in England *temp.* William the Conqueror; and, as such, bears a shield of six quarterings.

Arms.—Quarterly, first, ar. two chevronels sa. for ASHE. Second, vert, a lion ramp. ar. for FORNYSON. Third, gu. a cross erm. Fourth, Ar. a bend and three mullets in chief sa. Fifth, gu. a fesse vair ar. and az. betw. in chief a bezant, charged with an anchor sa. betw. two stars or, and in base three mullets, two and one, of the last, for BAILEY.

Crest.—A cockatrice or, crested, armed, &c. gu.

Mottoes.—*Above the Crest*, Fight. *Below*, Non nobis sed omnibus.

White, of Charlton Marshall, co. Dorset.

THE present SAMUEL WHITE WHITE, of Charlton Marshall, Esq. son of William Driver, Esq. by Anne, his wife, sister of the Samuel White of Charlton Marshall, assumed, upon succeeding to his uncle's estates, the surname and arms of WHITE by Royal License in 1835. The family of White derives from Thomas White, of Poole, M.P. for Borough, living in 1533.

Arms.—Az. on a fesse betw. three greyhounds courant or, collared gu. as many roses of the last, slipped ppr.

Crest.—A dexter arm, embowed, couped above the elbow, vested or, cuff ar. the hand holding by the legs an eagle volant ppr. beaked gold, betw. two roses slipped, as in the arms.

Motto.—Virtus omnia vincit.

Samuel White, of Charlton Marshall, co. Dorset, Esq. great-great-grandson of Capt. Samuel White, and Edith, his wife, heiress of John Watson, of Charlton, Esq.: *d.* in 1791. = Ann Thomson, niece of Sir Peter Thomson, of Poole, co. Dorset, F.R.S. and F.A.S. High Sheriff of Surrey in 1745, and M.P. for St. Alban's.

Samuel White, of Charlton Marshall, Esq. *m.* Ann Linthorne, and *d. s. p.* in 1822, aged 62.

Ann White. = William Driver, Esq.

Samuel White White, of Charlton Marshall, co. Dorset, Esq.

PLATE XLVI.

PRO REGE LEGE GREGE

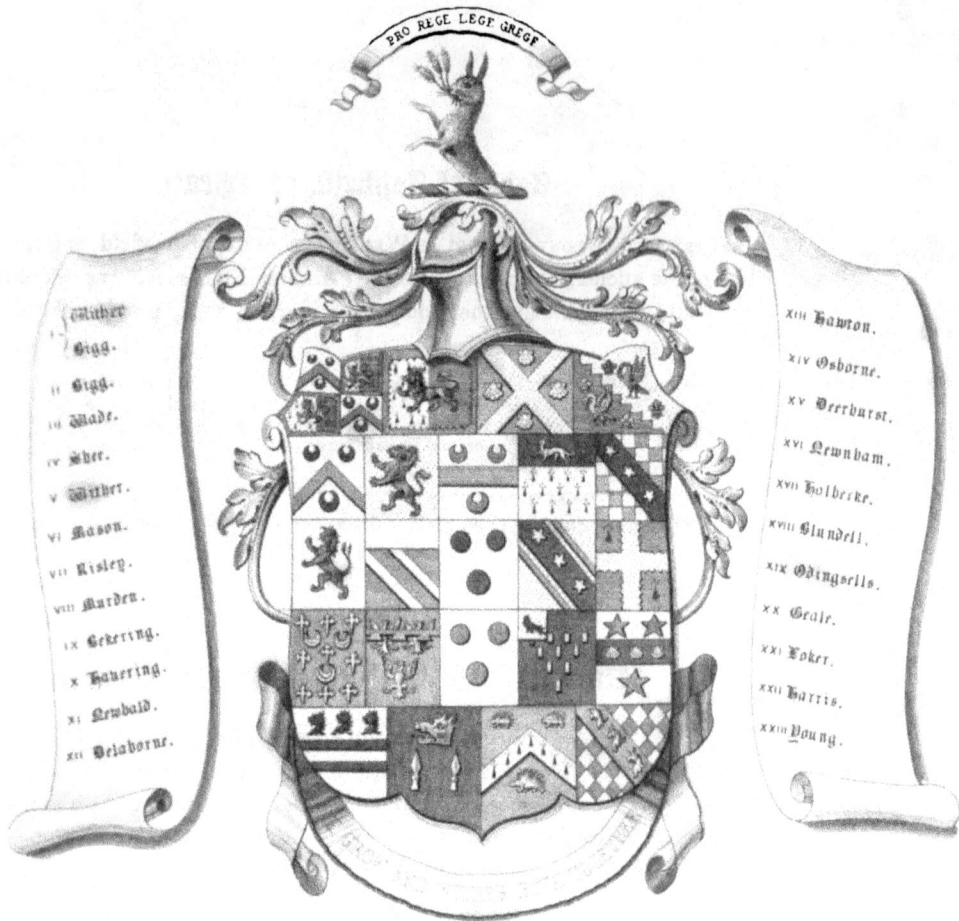

THE REV. LOVELACE BIGG-WITHER, M. A.
OF MANYDOWN & TANGIER PARK, HANTS.

LIEU. COL. WILL^M WELLESLEY ASHE.
ASHFIELD, CO. MEATH.

SAMUEL WHITE WHITE, ESQ.
CHARLTON MARSHALL, CO. DORSET.

PLATE XXVII.

Tooke.

WILLIAM TOOKE, of Russell Square, Esq. F.R.S. Vice-President of the Society of Arts, &c. descends from the ancient family of Toke or Tooke, of Bere, co. Kent.

Mr. William Tooke, and his elder brother, Thomas Tooke, of Spring Gardens, Esq. F.R.S. are the only sons of the late Rev. William Tooke, F.R.S. author of " The Life of Catherine II.," and of other valuable works relating to Russia; by Elizabeth, his wife, daughter of Thomas Eyton, of Llangynhafal, co. Denbigh, Esq. a descendant of the ancient Flintshire family of Eyton of Leeswood.

Arms.—Per chev. sa. and ar. three griffins' heads erased, counterchanged, impaling in right of his wife, Amelia, dau. of Samuel Shaen, of Crix, parish of Hatfield Peverell, co. Essex, Esq. the Arms of SHAEN, viz. Or, three piles issuant from the chief gu. within a bordure engr. erm.

Crest.—A griffin's head erased, per chev. sa. and ar. holding in the mouth a tuck sword ppr. pomelled or.

Motto.—Militia Mea Multiplex.

Higgins, of Trafalgar Park, Co. Mayo.

CHARLES FITZGERALD HIGGINS, of Trafalgar Park, Esq. quarters in right of his mother the arms of Ouseley. Paternally he derives from the very ancient Irish family of Higgins or O'Higgins, descended from Hyginus, 3rd son of Milesius Prince of Biscay.

Arms.—Quarterly, first and fourth, ar. guttée sa. on a fesse of the second three towers, double turretted or, for HIGGINS. Second and third, or, a chev. sa. betw. three holly leaves vert, a chief of the second, for OUSELEY.

Crest.—Out of a tower, double turretted, sa. a demi griffin ar. holding in the dexter paw a dagger of the last, hilt and pomel or.

Motto.—Pro Patrià.

Fitzgerald Higgins, of Westport, co. Mayo, Esq. a magistrate for that county and for the county of Galway, b. 6 Jan. 1789, m. 22 Feb. 1811.	=	Mary, only child of William Ouseley, of Rushbrook, co. Mayo, Esq. (of the family of the Right Hon. Sir Gore Ouseley, Bart.) by Marianne, his wife, sister of the late M. G. Prendergast, of Ballyfair, Esq. M.P. for Galway.		
Charles Fitzgerald Higgins, of Trafalgar Park, co. Mayo, Esq. J. P. m. Amelia Vertue, only dau. of Sir Richard Paul Jodrell, of Sall Park, co. Norfolk, Bart.	George-Gore-Ouseley Higgins, Esq. late civil service Jamaica, a magistrate for the county of Mayo.	Margaret.	Mary.	Ellen-King.

PLATE XXVII.

Chapman, of Whitby Strand, co. York.

THOMAS CHAPMAN, of Whitby, and of Montagu Place, Bryanston Square, London, Esq. Justice of the Peace for the county of Middlesex, eldest son of the late Edward Chapman, of Whitby, Justice of the Peace, and Deputy Lieutenant of the North-Riding of Yorkshire, Esq., by Martha, his wife, daughter and co-heir of Thomas Holt, Esq., quarters Temple, Sheppey, Everton, Heritage, Gaskin, Holt, and Stockton; and impales the arms of HANSON, in right of his wife, Maria-Louisa, youngest daughter of the late John Hanson, of The Rookery, Woodford, and of Great Bromley Hall, co. Essex, Esq.

Arms.—Quarterly, first, per chev. ar. and gu. a crescent counterchanged, for CHAPMAN. Second, ar. two bars sa. each charged with three martlets or, for TEMPLE. Third, az. a cross or, fretty gu. for SHEPPEY. Fourth, ar. on a fesse sa. three mullets of the field, for EVERTON. Fifth, ar. on a pale sa. a demi lucy erect, couped or, for GASKIN, having on a canton ar. three blackbirds ppr. for MELLAR. Sixth, vert, three trunks of trees raguly and erased ar. for STOCKTON. Impaling or, a chev. chequy ar. and az. betw. three martlets sa. for HANSON.

Crest.—An arm, embowed, habited in mail ppr. cuffed ar. holding in the hand ppr. a broken tilting spear or, enfiled with a chaplet vert.

Motto.—Crescit sub pondere virtus.

William Chapman, = Mary, dau. and heir of William Temple, Esq. formerly
of Whitby, co. York, | of Sheriff Hutton and Temple Sewerby, son of the Rev.
Esq. b. 19 April 1646, | Thomas Temple, D.D. Vicar of Battersea in 1634, who
d. in 1720. | was second son of Sir William Temple, Knt. Provost of
| Trinity College, Dublin, and uncle to Sir William Temple,
| Bart. the great statesman. Through this alliance with an
| heiress of Temple, the Chapmans are entitled to quarter
| Temple, Sheppey, Everton, and Heritage.

Abel Chapman, of Whitby, Esq. b. 22 Oct. = Elizabeth, dau. of John Walker, of Whitby,
1694, d. 13 Oct. 1777. | Esq.; second wife.

John Chapman, of Whitby, Esq. b. 27 = Jane, dau. of John Mellar, Esq. by Jane,
May 1732, d. 5 Jan. 1822. | dau. and co-heir of William Gaskin,
| Esq.

Edward Chapman, of Whitby, Esq. J. P. = Martha, eldest dau. and co-heir of Thomas
and D. L. of the North Riding of York- | mas Holt, of Whitby, Esq. by Esther,
shire; b. 1 Sept. 1769, d. 22 Jan. 1836. | his wife, dau. and co-heir of Isaac
| Stockton, of Hawsker Hall, co. York,
| Esq.

Thomas Chapman, of Whitby, co. York, = Maria Louisa, youngest dau. of John
and of Montagu Place, Bryanston | Hanson, of The Rookery, Woodford,
Square, London, Esq. F.R.S. and F.S.A. | and of Great Bromley Hall, co. Essex,
J. P. co. Middlesex. | Esq. J. P. and D. L. co. Middlesex, and
| High Sheriff in 1795.

Arkwright, of Willersley, co. Derby.

SIR RICHARD ARKWRIGHT, (to whom we owe the compilation and completion into a connected whole of the different parts of the invention called the Spinning Frame,) born at Preston, co. Lancaster, in 1732, obtained a grant of armorial bearings from the Heralds' College. Sir Richard, who was Sheriff of Derby-

PLATE XXVII.

shire in 1787, died in 1792, and was succeeded by his son, the late RICHARD
ARKWRIGHT, of Willersley, Esq. who died in 1843, leaving several sons and
daughters.

    Arms.—Ar. on a mount vert, a cotton tree fructed ppr. and on a chief az. betw.
two bezants, an inescutcheon of the field, charged with a bee volant ppr.

    Crest.—An eagle rising or, in the beak, pendant by a riband gu. an Escutcheon
az. thereon a hank of cotton ar.

    Motto.—Multa tuli fecique.

Gurney, of Keswick, co. Norfolk.

HUDSON GURNEY, of Keswick, Esq. F.R.S., Vice-President of the Society of
Antiquaries, bears a shield of four quarterings, viz. GURNEY, GOURNAY, WAR-
REN, and BARCLAY. The family of Gurney, or Gournay, derived its name from
the town of Gournay in Normandy, and was established in England by HUGH
DE GOURNAY, Lord of Gournay, one of the Barons of WILLIAM the Conqueror,
who had large possessions in Norfolk. The Gurneys of Keswick descend from
a younger branch of the Harpley and West Barsham line, which deduced its
lineage from MATHEW DE GOURNAY, *temp.* Henry II. who obtained from Hame-
line Plantagenet, Earl Warren, that nobleman's kinswoman, Rose, daughter of
Reginald Fitz Philip, of the House of Warren, in marriage, and with her the
Manor of Harpley. Sir John de Gurney, who was in arms against HENRY III.
at the Battles of Lewes and Evesham, attended Prince Edward to the Holy
Land, and bore for Arms " Arg. a cross engr. gu." a coat borne ever since by
the Norfolk Gurneys.

    Arms.—Quarterly, first, ar. a cross engr. gu. GURNEY. Second, paly of six or and az.
GOURNAY. Third, chequy or and az. a crescent ar. charged with a cinquefoil sa. WAR-
REN. Fourth, az. a chev. and in chief three crosses patée ar. BARCLAY.

    Crests.—First, on a chapeau gu. turned up erm. a fish paleways, ar. with its head
downward. Second, a wrestling collar or.

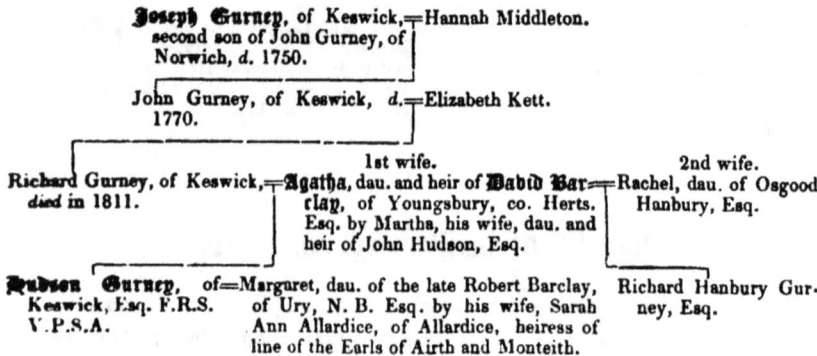

Joseph Gurney, of Keswick,═Hannah Middleton.
second son of John Gurney, of
Norwich, *d.* 1750.

John Gurney, of Keswick, *d.*═Elizabeth Kett.
1770.

                              1st wife.   2nd wife.
Richard Gurney, of Keswick,═Agatha, dau. and heir of David Bar-═Rachel, dau. of Osgood
died in 1811.   clay, of Youngsbury, co. Herts. Hanbury, Esq.
                 Esq. by Martha, his wife, dau. and
                 heir of John Hudson, Esq.

Hudson Gurney, of═Margaret, dau. of the late Robert Barclay, Richard Hanbury Gur-
Keswick, Esq. F.R.S. of Ury, N. B. Esq. by his wife, Sarah ney, Esq.
V.P.S.A.   Ann Allardice, of Allardice, heiress of
               line of the Earls of Airth and Monteith.

WILLIAM TOOKE. ESQ.
F.R.S., V.P. SOC. ARTS.

CHARLES FITZGERALD HIGGINS. ESQ.
TRAFALGAR PARK, CO. MAYO.

THOMAS CHAPMAN. ESQ. F.R.S. & F.S.A.
WHITBY, CO. YORK.

ARKWRIGHT OF WILLERSLEY.
CO. DERBY.

HUDSON GURNEY. ESQ. F.R.S. V.P.S. ANT.
KESWICK, CO. NORFOLK.

PLATE XXVIII.

Dendy, of Dorking, co. Surrey.

SAMUEL DENDY, and his brother, ARTHUR DENDY, both of Dorking, co. Surrey, Esqrs. bear a quartered Coat, viz. :

> **Arms.**—Quarterly : first and fourth, quarterly, vert and erm. a griffin segreant, betw. four escallops, three in chief and one in base, or. Second and third, quarterly, az. and or, in the first quarter a mullet of the second.
>
> **Crest.**—On a mount vert a swan ar. beaked gu. resting its dexter claw on a pheon ppr.
>
> **Motto.**—Per ardua stabilis esto.

Charnock, of Charnock, co. Lancaster.

THE family of Charnock was seated at Charnock as early as the reign of King John (*Visitation of Lancashire*). In the Harleian MSS. No. 1437, Charnock is shewn to quarter "Az. a cross moline, crowned, or," for MOLYNEUX of Crosby, ADAM CHARNOCK having married, *temp.* Edward II. Joane, daughter and co-heir of Sir Richard Molyneux, of Crosby, Knt. and to bear on an Escutcheon of Pretence, first and fourth, az. a cross moline or, for MOLYNEUX of Sefton ; second and third, ar. three boars' heads, erased and erect, sa. for BOOTH, of Barton, THOMAS CHARNOCK having married Bridget, daughter and heir of John Molyneux (brother of Sir Richard Molyneux of Sefton), by Dorothy, his wife, daughter and co-heir of John Booth, of Barton, co. Chester, Esq. The representation of the family of Charnock of Charnock now vests in SUSANNA, daughter and sole surviving heiress of Peter Brooke, of Astley, co. Lancaster, Esq. who was great-grandson of Richard Brooke, Esq. (second son of Sir Richard Brooke of Mere, Knt.) by Margaret, his wife, daughter and heir of Robert Charnock of Charnock. This lady (Susanna) married, first, Thomas Townley Parker, of Cuerden, Esq. ; and secondly, Sir Henry Philip Hoghton, of Hoghton Tower, Bart.

> **Arms.**—Quarterly, first, ar. on a bend sa. three crosses crosslet of the first, for CHARNOCK. Second, az. a cross moline, crowned, or, for MOLYNEUX of Crosby. Third, az. a cross moline or, for MOLYNEUX of Sefton. Fourth, ar. three boars' heads, erect and erased, sa. for BOOTH of Barton.
>
> **Crest.**—A lapwing or plover ppr.
>
> **Motto.**—Soies content.

Barclay-Allardice, of Urie and Allardice.

ROBERT BARCLAY-ALLARDICE, of Urie and Allardice, Esq. is male representative of the Barclays of Urie, descended from Roger de Berkeley, Lord of Berkeley Castle, co. Gloucester, before the Conquest. As heir general of Prince David Earl of Strathern, son of ROBERT II. King of Scotland ; of Malise Graham Earl of Monteith ; and of William Earl of Airth, Mr. Barclay Allardice claims the EARLDOMS of STRATHERN, MONTEITH, and AIRTH ; and his Case is still depending before the House of Lords.

PLATE XXVIII.

Arms.—Quarterly :—

I. Ar. a chev. and in chief three crosses patée ar. for BARCLAY of Urie.

II. Ar. a fesse wavy gu. betw. three boars' heads erased sa. for ALLARDICE of Allardice.

III. Quarterly, first and fourth, or, on a chief sa. three escallops of the first, for GRAHAM. Second and third, or, a fess chequy ar. and az. in chief a chev. gu. for STUART, Earls of Airth and Monteith.

IV. Or, a lion ramp. within a double tressure, flory and counter-flory gu. a label of three points ar. for PRINCE DAVID of Scotland.

Supporters.—Two wild men with clubs, ppr.

Crest.—A mitre, or.

Motto.—In cruce spero.

Long, of Preshaw, co. Hants.

" SABLE, semée of crosses crosslet, a lion ramp. ar." has been for a long series of generations the Armorial Bearing of the family of Long of Wiltshire, settled at a very remote period at Wraxall, and afterwards at Draycot, by marriage with the heiress of Cerne. The Coat bears a strong resemblance to that of the Preux family, " Sa. semée of crosses crosslet or, three lioncels ramp. ar." and supports in some degree the tradition mentioned by Camden of the origin of the Longs, from a younger son of the house of Preux, which was seated at Gidley Castle, co. Devon, soon after the Conquest. The Longs of Preshaw derive from a cadet of the Wraxall family. Their present Representative is WALTER LONG, of Preshaw, Esq. High Sheriff of Hants in 1824, who impales the Arms of Carnegie in right of his wife, Lady Mary Long, eldest daughter of William, 7th Earl of Northesk, G.C.B. Admiral of the Red.

Arms.—Sa. semée of crosses crosslet, a lion ramp. ar. impaling, for CARNEGIE, or, an eagle displ. sa. armed and membered gu. charged on the breast with a naval crown gold: over the eagle the word Trafalgar.

Crest.—Out of a ducal coronet or, a demi lion ramp. ar.

Motto.—Pieux quoique preux.

Fowle, of Wiltshire.

THIS family derives from John Fowle, of All Cannings, co. Wilts, Esq. brother of William Fowle, M.A. of Oriel College, Oxford, and Rector of All Cannings. WILLIAM, son of Thomas Fowle, of Market Lavington, co. Wilts, Esq. (by Bridget, his wife, one of the daughters and co-heirs of Richard Legge of Market Lavington aforesaid), bears the Arms here depicted, being grandson of Michael, youngest son of the above John Fowle, Esq. and grand nephew of William Fowle, Esq. formerly of Wiltshire Estate, Jamaica.

Arms.—Quarterly, first and fourth, gu. a lion pass. guard. betw. three roses or, barbed and seeded ppr. for FOWLE. Second and third, az. a stag's head caboshed ar. an annulet for difference, for LEGGE.

Crests.—First, out of a ducal coronet or, a dexter arm, in armour, embowed ppr. garnished, and holding a battle-axe in bend or, the hand ppr. for FOWLE. Second, out of a ducal coronet or, a plume of five ostrich feathers, three ar. two az. for LEGGE.

Motto.—Boutes en avant.

SAMUEL DENDY, ESQ.
DORKING, SURREY.

CHARNOCK OF CHARNOCK.
CO. LANCASTER.

ROBERT BARCLAY-ALLARDICE, ESQ.
URY AND ALLARDICE.

WALTER LONG, ESQ.
PRESHAW, HANTS.

WILLIAM FOWLE, ESQ.
CO. WILTS.

PLATE XXIX.

Mathew, of Llandaff, St. Kew, and the Leeward Islands.

For the genealogy of this ancient family, no longer (since the death of Francis Mathew, Earl and Viscount of Llandaff) to be found in the peerage, see Burke's *Landed Gentry.*

The Engraving exhibits the Arms and Quarterings of Captain George Mathew, of the Coldstream Guards, representative in Parliament for Athlone, and subsequently for Shaftesbury; who married Anne, only daughter and heir of Henry Hoare, of Stourhead, co. Wilts, Esq. (by Charlotte, daughter of Sir Edward Dering, Bart.) only son and heir of Sir Richard Colt Hoare, Bart. and of Hester, his wife, daughter of William, Lord Lyttelton and Westcote, and eventually sole heir to her mother, Mary, daughter and coheir of James Macartney, of Longford, Ireland, Esq.

The quarterings borne are very numerous, but those habitually used, are:

Arms.—

I. and VI. Quarterly, first and fourth, sa. a stork ppr. ar. within a bordure of the second, for Starkey, assumed on the marriage of Jenkyn Mathew, of Llandaff, with Lucia, sole heir of William Starkey, Esq. brother to Sir Humphrey Starkey, Lord Chief Baron of the Exchequer 10 Henry VII. Second and third, az. two mullets or, for the Barony of Van Leemput, borne from the marriage in Sept. 1682, of General Sir William Mathew, K.B. Captain General of the Leeward Islands, with the Baroness Catherine Van Leemput, heir of the historical Dutch family of that name, descended from John Van Leemput, Burgomaster of Utrecht, Plenipotentiary on behalf of the United Provinces to the Prince of Orange, by his wife Catherine de Berghes, Lady of Essendelles (niece of George de Berghes, Prince Bishop of Liege) the celebrated Heroine of Utrecht.

II. Ar. three roses purpure, seeded or, barbed vert, a chief of the second, a crescent for difference, for Sparrow.

III. and IV. Quarterly, first and fourth, or, a lion ramp. sa. armed, &c. gu. for Mathew, of Llandaff. Second and third, or, three chevrons gu. for Clare, borne from the marriage of Sir Ievan ap Meiric, Knight of the St. Sepulchre, (great grandfather of Sir David Mathew, of Llandaff, Grand Standard Bearer of England at the battle of Towton) with Cecily daughter and heir of Sir Robert de Clare, second son of Richard, Earl of Clare and Hertford, descended from the sister of King William the Conqueror.

V. Quarterly, first and fourth, gu. on a chev. or, betw. three bezants as many crosses formée fitchée sa.; second and third, gu. three men's heads affrontée ppr. for Smith, of the Leeward Islands, quartering Williams.

VI. As first.

Captain Mathew bears an Escutcheon of Pretence in right of his wife, viz.

I. and VI. Sa. an eagle displayed with two heads ar. an ermine spot on the breast, within a bordure ar. for Hoare, of Stourhead, Bart. II. Ar. on a chev. gu. three escallops or, in chief a lion passant vert. for Tully, of Wetherall Abbey. III. Or a fesse betw. three colts at speed sa. for Colt. IV. Ar. three trefoils sa. betw. two bendlets gu. for Benson. V. Macartney with Lyttelton, quartering England and France on a canton. Or, a buck trippant gu. attired ar. within a bordure gu. for Macartney. Ar. a chev. betw. three escallops sa. for Lyttelton. VI. as first, Hoare, of Barn Elms.

Crests.—First, A stork ppr. on a wreath with grass. *Motto round,* Æquam servare mentem, for Starkey. Second, On a mount vert a heathcock ppr. sa. *Motto round,* "Towton."

Motto.—Yffynno Dwy y Fydd. What God willeth shall be.

PLATE XXIX.

Meadows, of Witnesham Hall, co. Suffolk.

DANIEL CHARLES MEADOWS, of Witnesham Hall, and Great Bealings, co. Suffolk, Esq. son and heir of the late Rev. Philip Meadows, Rector of Great Bealings, senior male representative of the ancient house of Meadows, or Medows, from a junior branch of which the Earls of Manvers descend, bears his paternal Coat, quartered with BREWSTER, and impales the Arms of Wood in right of his wife, Agnes, youngest daughter of John Wood, of Melton Hall, co. Suffolk, Esq.

Peter de Medewe was seised of lands at Witnesham 34 Henry I. which are still possessed by the family.

> **Arms.**—Quarterly, first and fourth, gu. a chev. erm. betw. three pelicans vulning themselves ppr. in a canton a lion sejant, and in chief a label of three points, for MEADOWS. Second and third, sa. a chev. erm. betw. three estoiles ar. for BREWSTER, impaling az. three naked savages ambulant in fesse ppr. in their dexter hands a shield ar. charged with a cross gu. in the sinister a club, resting on their shoulders, also ppr.

> **Crest.**—A pelican vulned ppr.

> **Motto.**—Mea dos virtus.

Phillipps, of Garendon Park, and Grace Dieu Manor.

CHARLES MARCH PHILLIPPS, of Garendon Park, Esq. High Sheriff in 1825, and formerly M.P. for Leicestershire, son and heir of the late Thomas March, of More Critchell, co. Dorset, Esq. who took the surname and arms of PHILLIPPS, and subsequently assumed the Arms and Crest of Lisle, in right of his mother, SUSAN LISLE, daughter and coheiress of Charles Lisle, Esq. whose family Mr. March Phillipps represents.

> **Arms.**—Quarterly, first and fourth grand quarters,—first and fourth, sa. a chev. ar. betw. three eagles close ppr. for PHILLIPPS. Second and third quarterly, gu. and az. a cross erm. betw. four lions' heads erased or, for MARCH. Second and third grand quarters—Or, on a chief az. three lions ramp. of the field, for LISLE.

> **Crests.**—First, a demi griffin ppr. gorged or, holding a shield az. charged with a lion ramp. gold, for PHILLIPPS. Second, a demi lion ramp. ar. holding a Maltese cross or, for MARCH. Third, a stag trippant ppr. for LISLE.

> **Motto.**—Quod justum non quod utile.

Mary, only dau. of Sir **Ambrose Phillipps**, Knt. of Garendon, co. Leicester.═**Edward Lisle**, of Lincoln's Inn, Barrister at Law—of Crux Easton and Moyles Court, Hants, Esq. only son of Sir William Lisle, Knt. of Holt, co. Wilts, and Boscoville and Wootton, Isle of Wight.

Jane Lisle, second surviving dau. *mar.* 24 Aug. 1734, *d.* 1764.═**Thomas March**, of the City of London, Turkey Merchant, *d.* 1754.

Thomas March, of Garendon, and of More Critchell, co. Dorset, Esq. only surviving son and heir, *b.* 24 March, 1747, assumed by Royal Licence the additional surname and arms of **Phillipps** in pursuance of the will of his maternal cousin, Samuel Phillipps, of Garendon, Esq.═**Susan**, 2nd dau. of **Charles Lisle**, of Moyles Court, Esq. and sister and coheir of Charles Lisle, Esq. who *d.* in 1819; *mar.* Aug. 1777.

Charles March Phillipps, Esq. now of Garendon Park, and Grace Dieu Manor, *b.* 28 May, 1779.═Harriet, youngest dau. of John Ducarel, of Walford, co. Somerset, Esq. *d.* in 1813.

Ambrose Lisle March Phillipps, of Grace Dieu Manor, Esq. elder son and heir.═Laura Mary, eldest dau. of the Hon. Thomas Clifford, 4th son of Hugh, 4th Lord Clifford, of Chudleigh. | Charles Lisle, *b.* 7 March, 1812. | Augusta Jane Lisle, *m.* in 1832, to John Fitzgerald, Esq.

PLATE XVIX

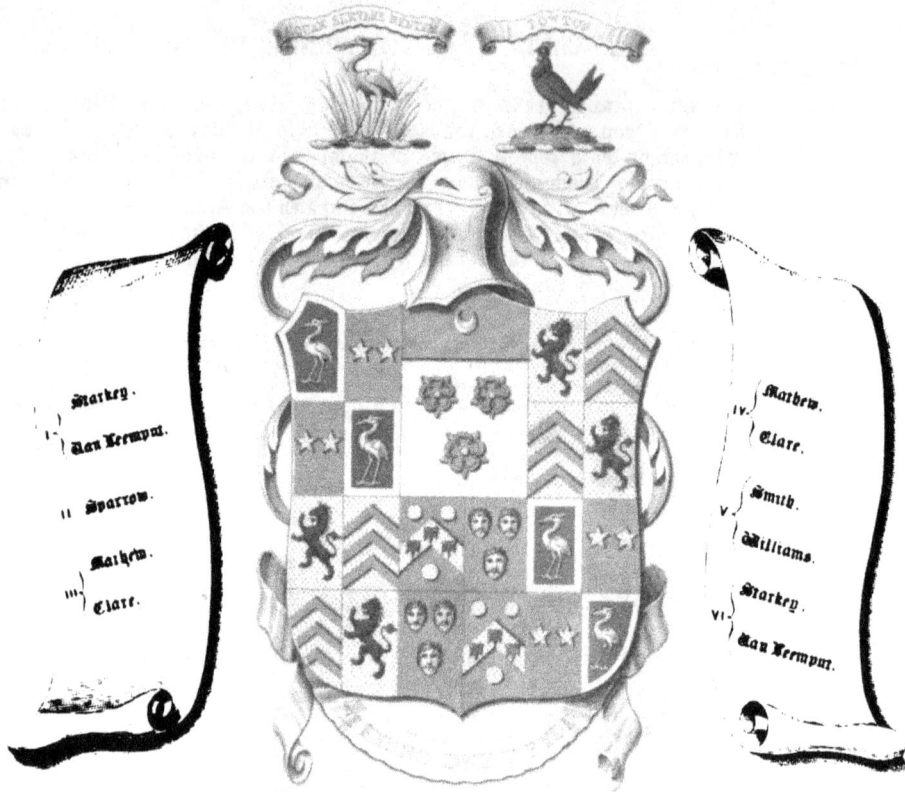

CAPTAIN GEORGE MATHEW.
COLDSTREAM GUARDS.

DANIEL CHAS MEADOWS, ESQ.
GREAT BEALINGS, CO. SUFFOLK.

AMBROSE LISLE PHILLIPPS.
GRACE DIEU MANOR CO. LEICESTER.

PLATE XXX.

Darby, of Colebrookdale, co. Salop.

FRANCIS DARBY, of Colebrookdale, Esq. elder son of the late Abraham Darby, of Colebrookdale, Esq. and grandson of Abraham Darby, Esq. by Abiah, his second wife, youngest child of Samuel Maude, of Sunderland, Esq. bears, in addition to his family Arms, an Escutcheon of Pretence in right of his wife, HANNAH, only child of JOHN GRANT, of Leighton Buzzard, Bedfordshire, Esq. The Darby family have been for many generations resident and possessed of landed property at Colebrookdale and its vicinity.

Arms.—Per chev. embattled erminois and az. three eagles displayed, each charged on the breast with an escallop, all counterchanged; an Escutcheon of Pretence for GRANT.

Crest.—In front of two crosses crosslet fitchée in saltire sa. a demi eagle displayed, couped, erm. wings az. charged on the breast with an escallop of the last.

Motto.—Ut cunque placuerit Deo.

Holford, of Weston Birt, co. Gloucester.

ROBERT STAYNER HOLFORD, of Weston Birt, Esq. High Sheriff of Gloucestershire, is representative of the Weston Birt branch of the ancient Cheshire family of Holford, of Holford. He bears a shield of four quarterings, HOLFORD, STAYNER, NUTT, and LADE.

Arms.—Quarterly, first, ar. a greyhound pass. sa. for HOLFORD; second, az. a lion pass. or, on a chief engrailed of the last three mullets sa. for STAYNER; third, per fesse az. and erm. a pale counterchanged, three pheons or, for NUTT; fourth, or, a fesse wavy betw. three escallops sa. for LADE.

Crest.—A greyhound's head, couped, sa.

Farquharson, of Invercauld, co. Aberdeen.

JAMES FARQUHARSON, of Invercauld, Esq. is only son and heir of Captain James Ross, R.N. (second son of Sir John Lockhart Ross, of Balnagowan) by Catherine, his wife, daughter and heir of JAMES FARQUHARSON, of Invercauld, Esq. undoubted CHIEF OF THE CLAN FARQUHARSON. The late Captain James Ross assumed the surname of Farquharson in consequence of his marriage, and died in 1810. The Farquharsons descend from Donald Farquharson, eldest son of Farquhar, Chamberlain of Mar, temp. Robert II. who was son of Shaw Macduff, a Scion of the Thanes of Fife.

Arms.—Quarterly, first and fourth, or, a lion ramp. gu. as the paternal Coat of FARQUHARSON; second and third, ar. a fir tree growing out of a mount in base, seeded, ppr. on a chief gu. the Banner of Scotland in bend displayed; a canton of the first charged with a dexter hand couped at the wrist, in fesse, holding a dagger point downwards ppr. The fir tree is borne from an ancient custom of carrying twigs of fir as a badge in the time of battle. The banner is commemorative of the death of Findla More, a distinguished ancestor of the family, who fell at Pinkie, bearing the Royal Standard. The hand and dagger, in the canton, records that another progenitor slew the rebel Cuming, of Stratheogie.

Crest.—A lion issuant gu. holding a sword in his dexter paw ppr. pomelled or.

Supporters.—Two wild cats ppr.

Motto.—Fide et fortitudine.

PLATE XXX.

Gillbanks, of Whitefield House, co. Cumberland.

JOSEPH GILLBANKS, of Whitefield House, Esq. a Magistrate and Deputy Lieutenant of the County, son of the late Joseph Gillbanks, Esq. owner of Scawthwaite Close, an estate possessed by his family for upwards of two centuries, went out to Jamaica in 1800, and returning in 1814, purchased considerable property in Cumberland.

Arms.—Az. five hearts in saltire or, on a chief of the second a rose gu. betw. two trefoils slipped vert.

Crest.—A stag's head or, collared.

Wells, of East Allington, co. Devon.

THE family of Wells, derived from the marriage of the Rev. NATHANIEL WELLS, Rector of East Allington, co. Devon, with Catharine, elder daughter and eventually sole heiress of THOMAS BURY, Esq. (son of Sir Thomas Bury, of Exeter, Knt.) by Dorothy, his wife, daughter and coheir of EDMUND FORTESCUE, of Fallapit, co. Devon, Esq. are entitled to the quartered Coat of WELLS, BURY, and FORTESCUE.

Arms.—Quarterly, first, or, a lion ramp. double queued sa. on a chief gu. two annulets interlaced of the field, for WELLS. Second, erm. on a bend az. a bezant betw. two fleurs-de lis or, for BURY. Third, az. a bend engr. ar. cotised or, for FORTESCUE.

Crest.—Out of an embattlement ppr. a demi lion, double queued sa. holding betw. his paws two annulets interlaced or.

Motto.—Virtute et honore.

Edmund Fortescue, of Fallapit, co. Devon, Esq. b. in 1666, Representative of the senior line of the great House of Fortescue,—Mary, dau. of Sampson Wyse, of Dittisham, d. in 1722.

1. Mary Fortescue, m. the Rt. Hon. Wm. Fortescue, of Buckland Filleigh, Master of the Rolls, and d. in 1710.

2. Elizabeth Fortescue, of Fallapit, d. unm. in 1768, aged 73.

3. Sarah Fortescue. 5. Grace Fortescue, both d. unm. the former in 1703, the latter in 1743-4.

4. Dorothy Fortescue, d. in 1733, aged 34.—Thomas Bury, Esq. son of Sir Thomas Bury, of Exeter, Knt.

Mary Fortescue, only child and heir, b. in 1710, d. s. p.—John Spooner, Esq.

Catharine Bury, elder dau. and eventually sole heir, d. in 1770.—The Rev. Nathaniel Wells, Rector of East Allington, (of the ancient Lincolnshire family of Welles, son of Samuel Welles,) of the city of Oxford.

Dorothy Bury, d. unm. in 1792.

1. Edmund Wells, b. in 1752, inherited Fallapit, &c. and assumed the surname of Fortescue.

2. Rev. Wm. Wells, Rector of East Allington, b. in 1756, d. in 1836.

3. Rev. Nathaniel Wells, b. in 1757, d. in 1806.

4. Rev. Samuel Wells, Rector of Portlemouth, and a Magistrate for Devon, b. in 1759; d. in 1839.

5. Thomas Wells, an officer of the 46th Reg. b. in 1761, d. unm. in 1784.

Six daughters.

PLATE XXX.

FRANCIS DARBY, ESQ.
COLEBROOKDALE, CO. SALOP.

ROBERT STAYNER HOLFORD, ESQ.
WESTON BIRT. CO. GLOUCESTER.

JAMES FARQUHARSON, ESQ.
INVERCAULD. CO. ABERDEEN.

JOSEPH GILLBANKS, ESQ.
WHITEFIELD HOUSE, CO. CUMBERLAND.

THE REV: SAMUEL WELLS,
RECTOR OF PORTLEMOUTH, CO. DEVON.

PLATE XXXI.

Botfield, of Morton Hall, co. Northampton.

BERIAH BOTFIELD, of Norton Hall, co. Northampton, Esq. M. P. for Ludlow, derives from, and bears the Arms of, the ancient Shropshire Family of Botfield or Botevyle, originally seated at Botevyle, near Church Stretton, of which the Marquess of Bath is the head.

      Arms.—Barry of twelve or and sa.

      Crest.—A reindeer statant or.

      Motto.—J'ay bonne cause.

Beriah Botfield, b. 28 Feb. 1702-3, son of Thomas Botfield and Abigail his wife. = Margaret, dau. of John Adams, b. 7 Oct. 1703.

Thomas Botfield, of Dawley, b. 14 Feb. 1736, d. 5 April 1801. = Margaret, only dau. of William Baker, of Bromley, co. Salop, Esq. b. 6 Dec. 1730, d. 5 Nov. 1803.

Thomas Botfield, of Hopton Court, co. Salop, Esq. b. 14 Feb. 1762, m. 14 Feb. 1800, d. 17 Jan. 1843, s. p. = Lucy, dau. of William Skelhorne, of Liverpool.

William Botfield, of Decker Hill, co. Salop, Esq. High Sheriff in 1806, b. 7 May 1766. = Lucy, dau. of John Bishton, of Kilsall, Esq. m. 14 Jan. 1794.

Beriah Botfield, Esq. b. 27 July 1768, d. 27 April 1813. = Charlotte, dau. of William Withering, M. D. of the Larches, co. Warwick.

Beriah Botfield, of Norton Hall, co. Northampton, Esq. F. R. S. M. P. for Ludlow

---

Staunton, of Longbridge, co. Warwick.

WILLIAM STAUNTON, now of Longbridge, Esq. a Magistrate and Deputy Lieutenant of Warwickshire, and formerly Captain of the First Regiment of Life Guards, eldest son of the late John Staunton, of Longbridge, Esq. High Sheriff of the county in 1801, by Maria, his wife, daughter and coheir of Edmund Crynes, of Nottingham, M. D. represents a branch of the Family of Staunton of Staunton, co. Notts, seated at Longbridge before 1450 ; and as such bears the Ensigns of that ancient Norman Family.

      Arms.—Ar. two chev. sa. within a bordure engr. of the same.

      Crest.—A fox statant ppr.

      Mottoes.—*Under the Arms,* En Dieu ma foy. *Above the Crest,* Moderata durant.

PLATE XXXI.

Atkinson, of Rehins, co. Mayo.

THE Atkinsons of Rehins were established in Ireland *temp.* Queen ELIZABETH, by Captain Charles Atkinson, a near relative of Sir Thomas Atkinson, of Yorkshire, Knt. the Representative of a very ancient House in that county. The present head of the Family is WILLIAM ATKINSON, of Rehins, Esq. a Magistrate and Deputy Lieutenant for Mayo, eldest son and heir of the late Charles Atkinson, of Rehins, Esq. by Mary, his wife, daughter and heir of George Atkinson, of Ballina, Esq.

> Arms.—Erm. on a fesse vert three fleurs-de-lis ar.
> Crest.—An eagle with two heads displayed ar.
> Motto.—Est pii Deum et Patriam delegere.

Feilden, of Witton, co. Lancaster.

JOSEPH FEILDEN, of Witton House, Esq. son of the late Henry Feilden, of Witton, Esq. and grandson of Joseph Feilden, also of Witton, Esq. by Margaret, his wife, daughter and co-heir of William Leyland, of Blackburn, Esq. descends from Randle Felden or Feilden, appointed, in the Queen's Charter dated 1567, one of the original Governors of the Blackburn Grammar School. Mr. Feilden's uncles, the younger sons of his grandfather, are JOHN FEILDEN, of Mollington, Hall, co. Chester, Esq. and WILLIAM FEILDEN, of Feniscowles, co. Lancaster, Esq. M. P.

> Arms.—Ar. on a fesse cottised az. betw. two martlets in chief sa. and in base a rose gu. barbed and seeded ppr. three lozenges or.
> Crest.—A nuthatch, perched upon a branch of hazel fructed, in the beak a rose gu. slipped vert.
> Motto.—Virtutis præmium honor.

Grantham, of Ketton Lodge, co. Rutland.

CHARLES GRANTHAM, of Ketton Lodge, Esq. Captain in the Royal Navy, son of Thomas Bennett Grantham, Esq. Captain 15th Foot, by Margaret, his wife, daughter of Captain Arthur Webber, R. N. represents the Family of Grantham of Goltho', co. Lincoln, and bears the Arms of that ancient House.

> Arms.—Erm. a griffin segreant gu.
> Crest.—A demi griffin gu.
> Motto.—Honore et amore.

WILLIAM STAUNTON, ESQ.
LONGBRIDGE, CO. WARWICK.

BERIAH BOTFIELD, ESQ. M.P.
NORTON HALL, CO. NORTHAMPTON.

WILLIAM ATKINSON, ESQ.
REHINS, CO. MAYO.

JOSEPH FEILDEN, ESQ.
WILTON, CO. LANCASTER.

CHARLES GRANTHAM, ESQ. CAP. R.N.
KETTON LODGE, CO. RUTLAND.

PLATE XXXII.

Gwynne Holford, of Buckland, co. Brecon, and Kilgwyn, co. Carmarthen.

LIEUTENANT-COLONEL GWYNNE HOLFORD, of Kilgwyn, High Sheriff of Brecon-shire in 1840, eldest son and heir of the late John Josiah Holford, of Kilgwyn, co. Carmarthen, Esq. by Jane, his wife, daughter of Charles Jackson, Esq. and grandson of Josiah Holford, of Hampstead, Esq. by Magdalen, his wife, daugh-ter of William Price, of Kilgwyn, Esq. assumed in 1831, by Royal Sign Manual, the additional surname and arms of GWYNNE, in consequence of his marriage with ANNA MARIA ELEANOR GWYNNE, grand-daughter and heir of THYNNE HOWE GWYNNE, of Buckland, Esq. second son of RODERICK GWYNNE, of Glan-brane, Esq. by ANNE, his wife, daughter and eventually co-heir of JOHN HOWE, LORD CHEDWORTH. Colonel Gwynne Holford bears, consequently, a quartered shield, first and fourth, HOLFORD; second and third, GWYNNE: and an Escut-cheon of Pretence quarterly of twenty-one Coats, comprising, with many others, the arms of MEREDITH, Prince of Powys, GRONWY AP TUDOR, EDNOWAIN, Lord of Tegaingle, HOWE, Lord Chedworth, GWYNNE, of Garth, JONES, BAR-RETT, MATHEW, &c. &c.

The GWYNNES of Glanbrane and Buckland descend from the marriage in 1405 of RHYDDERCH AP RHYS, of Llwyn Howel, (derived from Trahaern ap Einon, Lord of Cwmwd, co. Brecon,) with Gwenllian, daughter and heir of Howell ap Griffith, of Trecastle, younger brother of the renowned Sir David Gam, so distinguished at Azincourt.

Arms.—Quarterly, first and fourth, ar. on a mount vert, a greyhound pass. sa. col-lared or, for HOLFORD. Second and third, sa. a fesse cotised or, betw. two swords ar. hilts and pomels gold, the one in chief pointing upwards, the one in base downwards, for GWYNNE. An Escutcheon of Pretence quarterly of twenty-one, also for GWYNNE.

Crests.—First, from the sun in splendour or, rising from behind a hill vert, a grey-hound's head issuant sa. for HOLFORD. Second, a dexter arm ppr. issuant from a crescent ar. holding a sword erect, also ppr. pomel and hilt gold; enfiled by a boar's head or, erased and vulned ppr. for GWYNNE.

Motto.—*Over the Crest*, Vim vi repellere licet. *Under the Arms*, Toujours Fidele.

Rhydderch ap Rhys, of Llwyn Howel.═Gwenllian, dau. and heir of Howel ap Griffith, Lord of Trecastle, *m.* in 1405.

David Gwynne ap Rhydderch, of Glan-brane.═Elizabeth, dau. of Morrice ap Owen.

Rhydderch Gwynne, of Glanbrane.═Jane, dau. and co-heir of Allan Owen Barrett, of Gelliswik.

David Gwynne, of Glanbrane.═Joan dau. of John Games, of Aberbran.

Rowland Gwynne, of Glanbrane.═Gwellian, dau. of Howell John Powell.

a

PLATE XXXII.

a

Ruddr: Gwynne, of Glanbrane.═Mary, dau. of Sir Thomas Jones, Knt. of Abermarles.

Howell Gwynne, of Glanbrane.═The sole dau. and heir of Herbert Jones.

Rowland Gwynne, ═Anne, dau. of Hum-   Roderick Gwynne, ═Anne, dau. and heir of Pri-
of Glanbrane.   phrey Wyndham.   of Llanover.   thard of Bryn-y-oye.

Sackville Gwynne, of Glan-   Howell Gwynne, of═Mary, dau. and sole heir of Mar-
brane, *d. unm.* 1734.   Bryn-y-oye.   maduke Gwynne, of Garth.

Roderick Gwynne, of Glanbrane, Esq. ═The Hon. Anne Howe, second dau. of John,
heir to Sackville Gwynne, Esq.   Lord Chedworth, *m.* 14 Sept. 1748.

Sackville Gwynne, of Glan-   Thynne Howe Gwynne, of═Miss Mathew, of Lundock
brane, Esq.   Buckland, Esq.   Castle, co. Glamorgan.

Roderick Gwynne, Esq. *d. v. p.*═Elizabeth Anna Maria, dau. and co-heir of Hughes
of Tregunter.

Anna Maria Eleanor, only═James Price Holford, of Kilgwyn, Esq. Lt.-Col.
dau. and heir, *m.* in 1830.   in the Army, who has taken the additional surname
and arms of Gwynne.

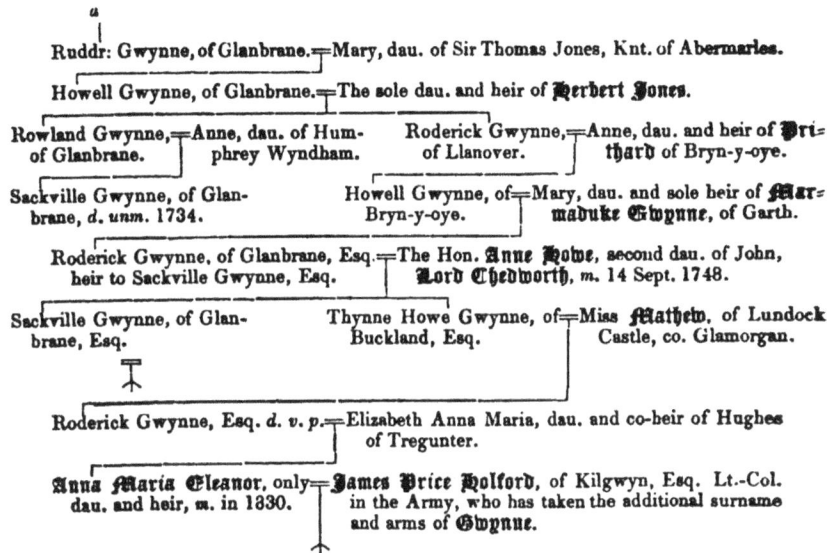

Faunce, of Sharsted, co. Kent.

THE Faunces have been settled in Kent since the time of EDWARD VI. and
Monuments still exist in the Churches of Rochester, Cliffe, High Halston,
Aylsford, &c. to different members of the family. The present Representative
is EDMUND BARRELL FAUNCE, of Sharsted, co. Kent, and Newington, co.
Surrey, Esq. eldest son of Lieutenant-Colonel Edmund Faunce, of St. Mary's
Hall, co. Kent, grandson of the Rev. Edmund Faunce, of St. Mary's Hall, and
great-grandson of Thomas Faunce, of St. Margaret's, Rochester, Esq. whose
father, Thomas Faunce, of High Halston, Esq. was elder brother of Sir ROBERT
FAUNCE, of Maidstone and Ildon, Knighted in 1660.

     Arms.—Ar. three lions ramp. sa. armed and langued gu. ducally gorged or.
     Crest.—A demi lion ramp. sa. langued and gorged as in the Arms, between two
wings ar.
     Motto.—Ne tentes aut perfice.

Higgins, of Eastnor, co. Hereford.

THE REV. JOSEPH HIGGINS, Rector of Eastnor, co. Hereford, the Representative
of an ancient Family derived immediately from the marriage, in 1561, of
Edward Higgins, Esq. with Mary, daughter of Thomas Clynton, of Castleditch,
Esq. by Margaret, his wife, daughter of Richard Tracy, of Toddington, co.
Gloucester, Esq. bears a Shield of Four Quarterings.

     Arms.—First, Paly of six or and az. on a chev. cottised erm. three crosses pattée gu.
for HIGGINS. Second, Paly of six or and az. a chev. erm. for CLYNTON. Third, Per

PLATE XXXII.

pale dancettée az. and or, for   . Fourth, Ar. on a bend sa. three griffins' heads erased or, for YONGE.

Crest.—A garb ppr. charged with two crosses pattée gu.

Motto *(allusive to the Crest).*—Patriam hinc sustinet.

Thomas Clynton, of Castleditch, co. Hereford, Esq. High Sheriff 1568 : descended from Sir John de Clinton, Knt. living 9 Edw. I. = Margery, dau. of Richard Tracy, of Toddington, co. Gloucester.

Mary Clynton, daughter and coheir. = **Edward Higgins**, living in 1563.

Thomas Higgins, of the Birchen and Eastnor. = Anne, dau of James Parry, of Ledbury, Gent. A.D. 1601.

Robert Higgins, of Eastnor, son and heir of Thomas. = Joan Machan, of English Bicknor.

Thomas Higgins, of Eastnor, son and heir of Robert. = **Dorothy**, dau. and heir of **Thomas Yonge**, of Hanley Castle, co. Worcester, descended from Sir Philip Yonge, of Taynton, co. Salop.

Thomas Higgins, of Eastnor, son and heir. = Wynifred, dau. of T. Barnes, of Longdon.

Thomas Higgins, of Eastnor, son and heir, b. 1701. = Elizabeth, dau. of Joseph Allen.

Thomas Higgins, of Eastnor, b. 1730. = Sarah, dau. of Wood, of Preston.

The Rev. **Joseph Higgins**, Rector of Eastnor and Pixley, J. P. for the counties of Hereford, Worcester, and Gloucester, b. 1770. = Mary, dau. of T. Hussey, Gent.

The Rev. Thomas Higgins, of Stoulton, co. Worcester.	Joseph Allen Higgins, of West Bank, near Ledbury.	Samuel Higgins of Berrow Court, co. Worcester.	Rev. Edward Higgins, of Bosbury House, near Ledbury.	James Higgins, *d. unm.*	Robert Higgins. William Higgins. Francis Higgins.	Three daus.

LIEU. COL. GWYNNE HOLFORD,
BUCKLAND, CO. BRECON.

EDMUND DARRELL FAUNCE, ESQ
SHARSTED, KENT.

THE REV. JOSEPH HIGGINS,
RECTOR OF LASTNOR CO. HERTFORD.

PLATE XXXIII.

Dale, of Glanvilles Wootton, co. Dorset.

JAMES CHARLES DALE, of Glanvilles Wootton, co. Dorset, Esq. M.A. High Sheriff of the county for 1843, bears a Shield of Four Quarterings. He is only son and heir, by Mary Kelloway his wife, daughter of Stephen Barton, Esq. son of Stephen Barton, of Andover, Gent. by Mary, his wife, only child of the Rev. Obadiah Bean, Rector of Shapwick, co. Dorset, of James Dale, of Glanvilles Wootton, Esq. eldest son, by Elizabeth his wife, daughter of John Ganett, of Blandford and Woolland, Esq. of Captain James Dale, High Sheriff of Dorsetshire in 1770, who purchased Glanvilles Wootton in 1767, and who was son of Thomas Dale, of Parewell, Christchurch, co. Southampton, Esq. a younger son of William Dale, of Chewton House, Hants, Esq.

Arms.—Quarterly :—
  I. Az. three bugleborns stringed.
  II. Ar. on a bend cottised three fleurs-de-lis.
  III. Barry of six ar. and az. over all a bend gu.
  IV. Ar. three boars' heads couped gu.
Crest.—A garb ppr.

Lumsden, of Pitcaple, co. Aberdeen.

HUGH LUMSDEN, of Pitcaple Castle, co. Aberdeen, Esq. a Magistrate and Deputy Lieutenant for that county, one of the Commissioners of the Northern Lighthouses, and Sheriff of the County of Sutherland, bears the Arms of the Lumsdens of Cushnie, one of the oldest families in Aberdeenshire, having possessed that and other estates there as far back as the earliest records of the County extend. Some of their Charters, still extant, bear date 24th March, 1471; others have ceased to be legible. The present Mr. Lumsden, of Pitcaple, is son of the late Harry Lumsden, of Belhelvie and Pitcaple, Esq. by his wife and cousin, Catherine, daughter of Hugh M'Veagh, Esq. and great-grandson of Alexander Lumsden, Esq. whose father William Lumsden, Esq. was fifth son of Robert Lumsden, of Cushnie, Esq. by Agnes, his wife, daughter of John Leith, of Bucharn, Esq.

Arms.—Az. a buckle or, betw. two wolves' heads in chief and an escallop in base ar.
Crest.—A naked arm grasping a sword ppr.
Motto.—Dei dono sum quod sum.

PLATE XXXIII.

Forbes-Leith, of Whitehaugh, co. Aberdeen.

THE Family of FORBES-LEITH, of Whitehaugh, represents, in the male line, the Forbes's of Tolquhon, a distinguished branch of the Noble House of Forbes, derived from the marriage of Sir JOHN FORBES (third son of Sir John Forbes, of that Ilk, Justiciar of Aberdeenshire 5 ROBERT III.) with Marjorie Preston, daughter and co-heir of HENRY PRESTON, Thane of Formartin. The late Chief, JAMES-JOHN FORBES-LEITH, of Whitehaugh, Esq. Lieutenant-Colonel East India Company's Service, married in 1827 Williamina-Helen, only child of the late gallant and distinguished Lieutenant-Colonel James Stewart, younger son of Charles Stewart, of Shambelly, Esq. and a descendant of one of the branches of the Royal House of Stewart, and left at his decease, with junior issue, a son and successor, the present JAMES FORBES-LEITH, of Whitehaugh, Esq. male heir of Forbes of Tolquhon.

Arms.—Quarterly.—
I. Az. three bears' heads couped ar. muzzled, for FORBES.
II. Or, a lion ramp. within a double treasure flory, counterflory, gu. for STEWART.
III. Ar. five lozenges conjoined in fesse sa. for LEITH.
IV. Ar. three unicorns' heads erased sa. for PRESTON.
Crests.—A stag's head attired with ten tynes ppr. for FORBES. A dove with an olive branch in its mouth ppr. for LEITH.
Supporters.—Two greyhounds ppr. collared gu.
Mottoes.—*Under the Arms*, Salus per Christum. *Above the Leith Crest*, Fidus ad extremum.

Burgoyne, of Stratford Place, London, Feltham, co. Middlesex, and Potton, co. Bedford.

THOMAS JOHN BURGOYNE, of Stratford Place, St. Mary-le-bone, descended from John, second son of Sir John Burgoyne, first Baronet, of Sutton Park, co. Bedford, and Wroxhall Abbey, co. Warwick, M.P. for Warwickshire; holds lands in Potton and Feltham; bears the Arms (Enrolled in the Herald's College, *temp.* Henry VII.) of the ancient Family of Burgoyne, to whom Sutton and Potton were given by a rhyming grant from John of Gaunt, Duke of Lancaster.

This gentleman has two sons, Thomas, and John Charles, and several daughters; he is the Trustee (with the late Right Rev. William Otter, Lord Bishop of Chichester,) of the Charities for Sutton, bequeathed by his kinsman, Montagu Burgoyne, Esq. younger son of Sir Roger Burgoyne, sixth Bart. by his wife, Lady Frances Montagu, eldest daughter of George, Earl of Halifax.

Arms.—Gu. a chev. or, betw. three talbots ar. on a chief embattled of the last, as many martlets az.
Crest.—A talbot sejant or, ears sa. and plain collared gu.

PLATE XXXIII.

Blathwayt, of Dyrham Park, co. Gloucester.

THE Blathwayts are of a very ancient origin, the first of the name having come over to England with William the Conqueror, and settled in the counties of Cumberland and Westmoreland, where they had grants of land for services rendered. The name was then spelt " Brauthwait," and it will be found in the early history of the above counties, a Richard and Robert Brauthwait having acted as Commissioners in collecting the tax levied for the support of the Parliamentary Army in the time of the Commonwealth, as will be seen on reference to the Statutes passed for that purpose in the " *Black Letter Book*," but which are now expunged from the Statutes at Large.

The present representative, GEORGE WILLIAM BLATHWAYT, Esq. of Dyrham Park, co. Gloucester, and of Langridge and Porlock, co. Somerset, a Captain (H. P.) of the First Dragoon Guards, Captain in the Bath Troop of Yeomanry, and a Magistrate for the city of Bath and counties of Somerset and Londonderry, bears a Shield of Six Quarterings, viz. BLATHWAYT, BRAYN, WYNTER, GERARD, BRUEN, and BLATHWAYT, and impales in right of wife, Mary Anne, daughter of the Rev. Thomas Agmondisham Vesey, (a branch of the De Vesci Family) the Arms of VESEY.

Arms.—Quarterly :—
      I. and VI. Or two bends engr. sa.
      II. Sa. on a fess betw. three buglehorns stringed ar. a hemp hackle gu.
      III. Sa. a fess erm. in chief a crescent ar.
      IV. Az. a lion ramp. ar. crowned or.
      V. Ar. a saltire engr. gu.
Impaling the Arms of VESEY, viz. Or on a cross sa. a patriarchal cross of the field.

Crest.—On a rock ppr. an eagle rising ar. wings az.

Motto.—Virtute et veritate.

George Wynter, Esq. youngest brother of⚊Anne, sister and co-heir of **Robert Brayn**, Sir William Wynter, of Lyndney in the   Esq. Merchant of Bristol. Forest of Dean, purchased the Dyrham estates from Sir Walter Dennis, Knt. 13 Eliz. 1571, *d.* 1581.

John Wynter, of Dyrham, Esq. Captain⚊Mary, dau. of Sir William Bruen, of Dorsetshire. R. N. *d.* 1619.

Sir George Wynter, of Dyrham, Knt. eldest⚊Mary, dau. of Edward Rogers, of Cannington, co. Somerset, Esq. son, High Sheriff of Gloucestershire 7 Charles I. 1631, *d.* 1638.

John Wynter, of Dyrham and Hinton, co.⚊**Frances**, dau. of **Thomas Gerard**, of Gloucester, Esq. eldest son, *d.* 1668. Trent, co. Somerset, Esq. descended from the ancient Lancashire family of that name.

a

PLATE XXXIII.

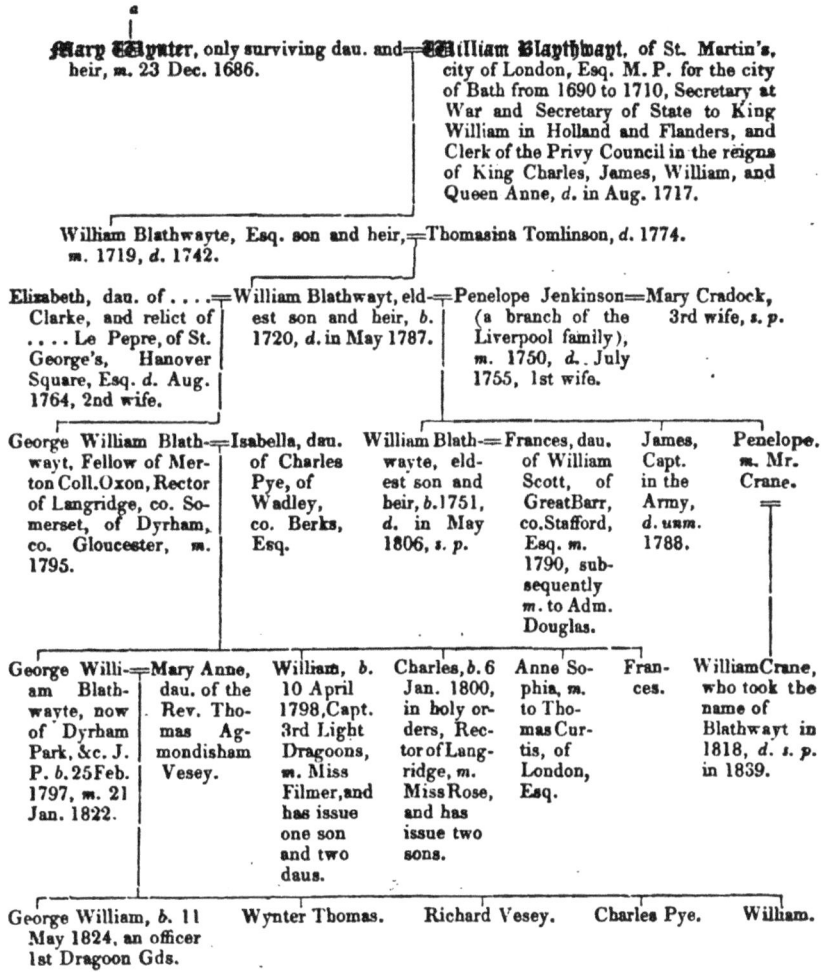

Mary Wynter, only surviving dau. and heir, *m.* 23 Dec. 1686. = **William Blathwayt**, of St. Martin's, city of London, Esq. M. P. for the city of Bath from 1690 to 1710, Secretary at War and Secretary of State to King William in Holland and Flanders, and Clerk of the Privy Council in the reigns of King Charles, James, William, and Queen Anne, *d.* in Aug. 1717.

William Blathwayte, Esq. son and heir, *m.* 1719, *d.* 1742. = Thomasina Tomlinson, *d.* 1774.

Elizabeth, dau. of .... Clarke, and relict of .... Le Pepre, of St. George's, Hanover Square, Esq. *d.* Aug. 1764, 2nd wife. = William Blathwayt, eldest son and heir, *b.* 1720, *d.* in May 1787. = Penelope Jenkinson (a branch of the Liverpool family), *m.* 1750, *d.* July 1755, 1st wife. = Mary Cradock, 3rd wife, *s. p.*

George William Blathwayt, Fellow of Merton Coll. Oxon, Rector of Langridge, co. Somerset, of Dyrham, co. Gloucester, *m.* 1795. = Isabella, dau. of Charles Pye, of Wadley, co. Berks, Esq.

William Blathwayte, eldest son and heir, *b.* 1751, *d.* in May 1806, *s. p.* = Frances, dau. of William Scott, of GreatBarr, co. Stafford, Esq. *m.* 1790, subsequently *m.* to Adm. Douglas.

James, Capt. in the Army, *d. unm.* 1788.

Penelope. *m.* Mr. Crane.

George William Blathwayte, now of Dyrham Park, &c. J. P. *b.* 25 Feb. 1797, *m.* 21 Jan. 1822. = Mary Anne, dau. of the Rev. Thomas Agmondisham Vesey.

William, *b.* 10 April 1798, Capt. 3rd Light Dragoons, *m.* Miss Filmer, and has issue one son and two daus.

Charles, *b.* 6 Jan. 1800, in holy orders, Rector of Langridge, *m.* Miss Rose, and has issue two sons.

Anne Sophia, *m.* to Thomas Curtis, of London, Esq.

Frances.

William Crane, who took the name of Blathwayt in 1818, *d. s. p.* in 1839.

George William, *b.* 11 May 1824, an officer 1st Dragoon Gds.

Wynter Thomas.

Richard Vesey.

Charles Pye.

William.

PLATE XXXII

JAMES CHARLES DALE, ESQ. A.M.
GLANVILLES WOOTTON, CO.DORSET,

HUGH LUMSDEN, ESQ.
PITCAPLE CASTLE, CO. ABERDEEN.

JAMES FORBES LEITH, ESQ
WHITEHAUGH, CO. ABERDEEN.

THOMAS JOHN BURGOYNE, ESQ.
LONDON.

GEORGE WILLIAM BLATHWAYT, ESQ.
DYRHAM PARK, CO. GLOUCESTER,

PLATE XXXIV.

Gale Braddyll, of Conishead Priory, co. Lancaster.

THOMAS RICHMOND GALE-BRADDYLL, Esq. of Conishead Priory and Bardsea
Hall, co. Lancaster, and Highead Castle, co. Cumberland, late Lieutenant-
Colonel Coldstream Guards, represents the ancient families of BRADDYLL of
Braddyll and Brockhole, GALE of Whitehaven, and RICHMOND of Highead
Castle, and bears their Arms.

 Arms.—Quarterly, first and fourth, ar. a cross lozengy vert, over all a bend chequy
erm. and az. for BRADDYLL. Second, ar. a fesse az. charged with an anchor between
two lions' heads or, between three saltires couped of the second, for GALE. Third, gu.
two bars gemelles and a chief or, for RICHMOND.

 Crests.—First, a badger passant or, for BRADDYLL. Second, a unicorn's head ppr.
charged with two pales az. over all an anchor or, for GALE. Third, a demi tiger,
platée, holding between the paws an esquire's helmet.

 Motto.—Cognoies toy mesme.

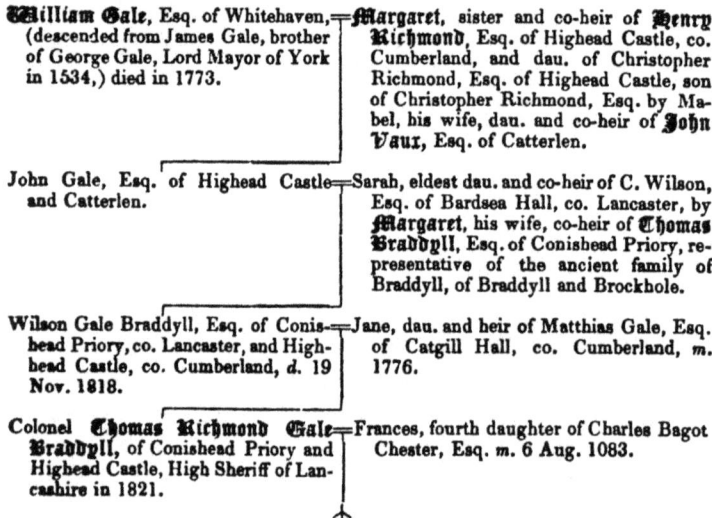

William Gale, Esq. of Whitehaven, === **Margaret**, sister and co-heir of **Henry**
(descended from James Gale, brother | **Richmond**, Esq. of Highead Castle, co.
of George Gale, Lord Mayor of York | Cumberland, and dau. of Christopher
in 1534,) died in 1773. | Richmond, Esq. of Highead Castle, son
              | of Christopher Richmond, Esq. by Ma-
              | bel, his wife, dau. and co-heir of **John**
              | **Vaux**, Esq. of Catterlen.

John Gale, Esq. of Highead Castle === Sarah, eldest dau. and co-heir of C. Wilson,
and Catterlen. | Esq. of Bardsea Hall, co. Lancaster, by
              | **Margaret**, his wife, co-heir of **Thomas**
              | **Braddyll**, Esq. of Conishead Priory, re-
              | presentative of the ancient family of
              | Braddyll, of Braddyll and Brockhole.

Wilson Gale Braddyll, Esq. of Conis- === Jane, dau. and heir of Matthias Gale, Esq.
head Priory, co. Lancaster, and High- | of Catgill Hall, co. Cumberland, *m.*
head Castle, co. Cumberland, *d.* 19 | 1776.
Nov. 1818. |

Colonel **Thomas Richmond Gale** === Frances, fourth daughter of Charles Bagot
Braddyll, of Conishead Priory and | Chester, Esq. *m.* 6 Aug. 1083.
Highead Castle, High Sheriff of Lan- |
cashire in 1821. |

Brome.

THE family of BROME of Shropshire, Hertfordshire, and Kent, was originally
seated at Brome, in the first named county. The present representative is
CHARLES JOHN BYTHESEA BROME, of Malling House, West Malling, co Kent,
Esq. son of the late Charles Brome, of Malling House, and of the Manor House,
Bishop's Stortford, co. Herts, Esq. by Cecilia, his wife, daughter of William

T. R. GALE BRADDYLL, ESQ.
CONISHED PRIORY, CO. LANCASTER.

CHARLES JOHN BYTHESEA BROME, ESQ.
MALLING HOUSE, KENT.

ALEXANDER MACKINTOSH, ESQ.
OF THAT ILK, CO. INVERNESS.

ICHABOD WRIGHT, ESQ.
MAPPERLEY, NOTTS.

THE REV. JAMES FOLLIOT,
CHESTER.

T. R. GALE DRADDYLL, ESQ
CONISBEE PRIORY, CO. LANCASTER.

CHARLES JOHN DYTHESEA BROME, ESQ
MALLING HOUSE, KENT.

ALEXANDER MACKINTOSH, ESQ.
OF THAT ILK, CO. INVERNESS.

ICHABOD WRIGHT, ESQ.
MAPPERLEY, NOTTS.

THE REV. JAMES FOLLIOT.
CHESTER.

PLATE XXXV.

Rowan, of Mount Davis, co. Antrim.

THE Rev. ROBERT WILSON ROWAN, of Mount Davis, co. Antrim, only son of John Rowan of Merville in the same county, Esq. and Eliza Honoria, his wife, eldest daughter of Alexander Macmanus, of Mount Davis, Esq. Lieutenant-Colonel of the Antrim Militia, &c. succeeded, on the death *s. p.* 4 January, 1838, of his late uncle, Alexander Bryan Macmanus, Esq. only son of the aforesaid Lieutenant-Colonel Macmanus, to a portion of the Macmanus estate, and is now the representative of that family, whose arms he quarters. (See BURKE's *Landed Gentry*.) He married, 30 September, 1824, Anna, second daughter of Joshua Minnitt, of Annabeg, co. Tipperary, Esq. by whom he has issue two sons and a daughter: John-Joshua, born 12 December, 1838; Alexander, born 24 April, 1841, and Eliza Hester.

The Rev. Mr. Rowan quarters on the paternal side the arms of STEWART and REDMOND, with those of ROWAN, and on the maternal side the arms of O'NEILL, KER, and TOBIN, with those of MACMANUS.

Jodrell, of Yeardsley, co. Chester.

YEARDSLEY, in the county of Chester, together with other lands in the adjoining townships of Desley and Rettleshulme, in the same county, were possessed, in the early part of the reign of Edward III. (as appears by several documents now existing) by William Jauderell, who served as Archer in the French wars under Edward the Black Prince (Earl of Chester), and whose great-grand-father owned lands in Derbyshire in the Manor of High Peak, A. D. 1286.

The Arms and Crest still used were borne, together with other quarterings, by his son Roger, for many years one of the four Esquires of the King's body in the reign of Richard II. and are appended in a seal to a grant of land by the said Roger dated 1401, 3 Henry IV.

The Arms of Jodrell were exemplified by Sign Manual in 1755 to John Bower, of Manchester, Esq. on his marriage with FRANCES, heiress of Yeardsley, as eldest daughter of Francis Jodrell, Esq. born in 1723, and sixteenth in lineal descent from the first of the name on record.

The grandson of this marriage, JOHN WILLIAM JODRELL, of Yeardsley, Esq. is the present Representative of the family.

Arms.—Sa. three round buckles ar.
Crest.—A cock's head and neck, couped or, wings elevated and endorsed ar. comb and wattles gu.

PLATE XXXV.

Fulford, of Great Fulford, co. Devon.

BALDWIN FULFORD, of Great Fulford, Esq. Lieut.-Col. of the Devon Militia, is the Representative of one of the most ancient and distinguished families in the County of Devon, of which was the celebrated SIR BALDWIN FULFORD, Knight of the Sepulchre, Under Admiral to Holland, Duke of Exeter, High Admiral of England, *temp.* HEN. VI. (*See* BURKE'S *Landed Gentry*.) Colonel Fulford bears a Shield of nine quarterings for the heiresses who intermarried with his ancestors.

Arms.—Quarterly, first, gu. a chev. ar. for FULFORD, second, ar. on a bend, three bears' heads erased sa. for FITZURSE; third, ar. a chev. between three moorcocks, sa. for MORETON; fourth, or, on a bend gu. three crosses formée for BELSTON; fifth, gu. three birdbolts ar. for BOZOM; sixth, ar. a lion ramp. gu. a chief az.; seventh, az. a bend erm. between three leopards' faces jessant de lys, for CANTELUPE; eighth, erm. on a cross gu. five bezants; ninth, gu. two bars and an orle of martlets ar. for CHALBONE.

Crest.—A bear's head erased sa. muzzled or.

Supporters.—Two Saracens ppr.

Walsham, of Knill Court, co. Hereford.

SIR JOHN JAMES WALSHAM, of Knill Court, Bart. bears a Shield of nine Quarterings, as a Representative of the Families of WALSHAM of Knill, Knill of Knill, Morgan of Kinnersley, Price of Pilleth, Hughes of Bodwryn, Pugh of Penrhyn, and Coytmore of Coytmore.

Arms.—Quarterly, first, sa. a cross voided or, for WALSHAM. Second, gu. crusily fitchée a lion ramp. or, for KNILL. Third, ar. three bulls' heads cabossed sa. for MORGAN. Fourth, or, a dragon ramp. vert, for PRICE, being the Coat of Cadwgan ap Elystan Glodrydd. Fifth, ar. an eagle with two heads displ. sa. for HUGHES. Sixth, gu. a chev. erm. betw. three Englishmen's heads ppr. for PUGH, being the Coat of Ednyfed Vychan. Seventh, vert, three eagles in fesse or, for OWEN GWYNEDD, Prince of North Wales. Eighth, gu. three stags' heads erased ar. for COYTMORE. Ninth, sa. a lion ramp. ar. within a bordure engr. or, for DAVID GOCH, Lord of Penmachno.

Crest.—Out of a ducal coronet or, a demi eagle with two heads displ. sa. having pendant from the neck an escutcheon ar. charged with a Saracen's head couped at the neck ppr. and wreathed round the temples az.

Motto.—Sub libertate quietem.

John Walsham, of Presteigne, co. Radnor, Esq. Representative of the very ancient family of Walsham, *d.* in 1639. *From whom, 4th in descent,* = Barbara, dau. and h. of Francis Knill, of Knill Court, co. Hereford, Esq.

Robert Coytmore, of Coytmore, derived from Yarddur ap Cyndellw, Lord of Uchaf, Chief Counsellor to Llewellyn Mawr, Prince of Wales. = Lady Bridget Bertie, only sister of Willougby, third Earl of Abingdon.

John Walsham, of Knill Court, co. Hereford, Esq. *d.* in 1734. *From whom, 3d in descent,* = Hester, elder dau. and co-h. of Sir John Morgan, of Kinnersley Castle, Bart. by Hester, his wife, dau. and co-heir of James Price, of Pilleth, co. Radnor, Esq.

Mary Coytmore, of Coytmore, only surviving child. = Edward Philip Pugh, of Penrhyn, Esq. Sheriff of Radnorshire in 1743, one of the Chiefs of that branch of the VIII Noble Tribe of Wales, from which sprang the Royal House of Tudor.

Anna Pugh, of Coytmore, 2nd dau. and in her issue sole heir. = Hugh Hughes, of Bodwryn, Esq.

John Garbett Walsham, of Knill Court, Esq. Col. of the Royal Radnor Militia. = Anna Maria, dau. and eventually sole heir of Hugh Hughes, of Bodwryn, in Anglesey, Esq.

Sir John James Walsham, Bart.

PLATE XXXV.

Gurwood.

JOHN GURWOOD, Esq. Deputy Governor of the Tower, Colonel in the Army, and Esquire to Field Marshal the Duke of Wellington, under whom he served during the whole of the Peninsular War and at Waterloo, bears the Ancient Arms of his ancestors, the Gorrewods, Comtes de Pont de Vaux en Bresse, with an honourable augmentation granted to him by the Earl Marshal for having led the successful Forlorn Hope at the assault of Ciudad Rodrigo in Spain, on the 19th of June, 1812.

Colonel Gurwood was born at Hoddesdon, co. Herts, 7th April, 1788, his progenitors having, for seven generations, resided at Barnby Moor and Langton, co. York. Jean de Gorrevod, who served with his cousin, Laurent de Gorrevod, afterwards Comte de Pont de Vaux, under the Duke of Savoy, in fighting against the French at the great battle of St. Quentin in 1557, was wounded and conveyed to Calais, then in the possession of the English. He escaped from that town previously to the surrender of it in 1558, and arrived at Kingestowne-upon Hull, in Yorkshire, where he married and settled at Barnby Moor. His son, John Gorwood, having succeeded to property at Langton, near Malton, belonging to his mother and eldest brother Henry, resided there. Colonel Gurwood is eighth in descent from the aforesaid Jean de Gorrevod. The pedigree is deduced from Guy de Gorrewood, Chevalier, Seigneur de Gorrewod in 1130; and name derived from the Château de Gorrevod, a quarter of a mile from Pont de Vaux, near the river Saone, in the country formerly called La Bresse, which, being one of the conquests of Louis XIV. was ceded to France in 1668 by the treaty of Aix la Chapelle.

Arms.—Az. a chev. or, and for honourable augmentation, the Shield of the Town of Ciudad Rodrigo with the Sword of the Governor, whom Colonel Gurwood took prisoner, being placed " in pretence."

Crest.—A unicorn's head az. maned and horned or, being placed for augmentation on a breached tower, with the words over " Follow me."

Motto.—Pour à jamais.

PLATE LXIV

THE REV. ROBERT WILSON ROWAN.
MOUNT DAVIS, CO. ANTRIM

JOHN WILLIAM JODRELL, ESQ.
OF YEARDSLEY, CO. CHESTER.

BALDWIN FULFORD ESQ
GREAT FULFORD CO. DEVON

SIR JOHN WALSHAM, BART.
KNILL COURT, CO. HEREFORD.

COL. GURWOOD, C.B.
DEPUTY GOVERNOR OF THE TOWER.

PLATE XXXVI.

Rowan, of Garry, co. Antrim.

JOHN ROWAN, of Garry and Ahoghill, co. Antrim, Esq. resident at Merville, near Belfast, High Sheriff in 1814, descended from the Scottish family of Rowan, (See BURKE's *Landed Gentry*,) bears a Shield quarterly; first and fourth, ROWAN; second, STEWART; and third, REDMOND.

Arms.—First and fourth, vert, a fesse chequy or and gu. between a trefoil slipped in chief, and in base three cross-crosslets fitchée issuant from as many crescents of the second for ROWAN; second, or, a fesse chequy ar. and az. between two sinister hands gu. all within a double tressure flory counterflory of the last, for STEWART; third, gu. three cushions ermine, for REDMOND.

Crest.—A naked arm couped at the elbow grasping a dagger ppr.

Motto.—Cresco per crucem.

The Rev. **Robert Rowan**, of Mullans, co. = **Letitia**, dau. and sole heir of **John Stew-**
Antrim, (seventh son of the Rev. John | art, of Garry, co. Antrim, Esq. by his
Rowan, of Ballynagappog, co. Down, | wife, the dau. and coheir of **Redmond**
fourth in descent from John Rowan, of | of Blaris, co. Down.
Greenhead, co. Lanark, born in 1548,) |
will, dated 1742, was proved 1769. |

John Rowan, of Mullans, Esq. High = Rose, dau. of Capt. Stewart, of Clunie in
Sheriff co. Antrim 1754. | Scotland, by Rose, his wife, dau. of
| Roger Hall, of Narrow Water, Esq.

Robert Rowan, of Mullans, Esq. High = Eliza, dau. of Hill Wilson, of Purdysburn,
Sheriff co. Antrim 1772. | co. Down, Esq.

John Rowan, now of Garry, Esq. m. 2dly. Dorothea Shaw Ogilvie, relict of Jas. Blair, of Merville, Esq.	1st. Eliza Honora, eldest dau. of Alex. McManus, of Mount Davis, co. Antrim, Esq.	Hill Wilson. Robert. James.	Charles, Comm. of Metropolitan Police.	Frederick, d. Edward. William.	1. Eliza, d. unm.	Eleanor.	John Joseph Heywood, Esq.

Rev. Robert Wilson Rowan, of Mount Davis, only child.

Meigh, of Ash Hall, co. Stafford.

THE following Ensigns were granted in May, 1840, to the present JOB MEIGH, of Ash Hall, Esq. a magistrate for the county of Stafford, son of the late Job Meigh, Esq. (See BURKE's *Landed Gentry*.)

Arms.—Gu. on a cross engrailed between four boars' heads erased ar. three blackbirds in fesse ppr. and two crosses patée fitched at the foot az.

Crest.—A lion rampant or, holding in his dexter paw a cross patée, as in the arms, the sinister paw resting on an anchor ppr. pendant therefrom by a chain or, an escocheon gu. charged with a boar's head erased ar.

Motto.—Benigno numine.

McAlester, of Loup and Kennox.

CHARLES SOMERVILLE MCALESTER, of Loup and Kennox, Esq. Lieut.-Col. Commandant of the First Regiment of Ayrshire Local Militia, and a Deputy Lieutenant of the County, Chief of the Clan Allaster of Kintyre, (known formerly as the Clan Eandubh,) claims to represent the ancient Lords of the Isles, as lineal descendant and heir male of Alexander, or Alester, eldest son of Angus Mor, Lord of the Isles and Kintyre, A. D. 1284. Alexander acquired a consi-

PLATE XXXVI.

derable addition to his territories by marriage with one of the daughters and coheiresses of Ewen de Ergadia, but having espoused the cause of Baliol in opposition to the claims of BRUCE, he was finally subdued by that Prince, imprisoned in Dundonald Castle, (where he died) and his possessions bestowed on his younger brother, ANGUS OG, who had from the beginning supported the cause of Bruce.

The present McAlester bears a quartered Coat, first and fourth, McALESTER *ancient;* second, McALESTER, *modern;* third, SOMERVILLE.

Supporters.—Two bears ramp. each pierced by an arrow.
Crests.—First, A dexter arm in armour, couped, holding a dagger, *over it the Motto,* Fortiter, for McALESTER; second, A dexter hand in pale ppr. holding a crescent ar. for SOMERVILLE; *over it the Motto,* Donec rursus impleat orbem.
Motto.—Per mare per terras.

Bailey, of Glanusk Park, co. Brecon.

JOSEPH BAILEY, of Glanusk Park, Esq. M.P. for the City of Worcester, and High Sheriff of Monmouthshire in 1823, bears the Arms of BAILEY, impaled with those of his wife, Mary-Anne, daughter of the late John Thomas Hendry Hopper, Esq. of Witton Castle, co. Durham.

Arms.—Ar. a fesse between three martlets gu. charged with as many bezants.
Impaling—Gyronny of eight sa. and erm. a tower or, for HOPPER.
Crest.—A griffin sejant erm. wings and forelegs or.
Motto.—Libertas.

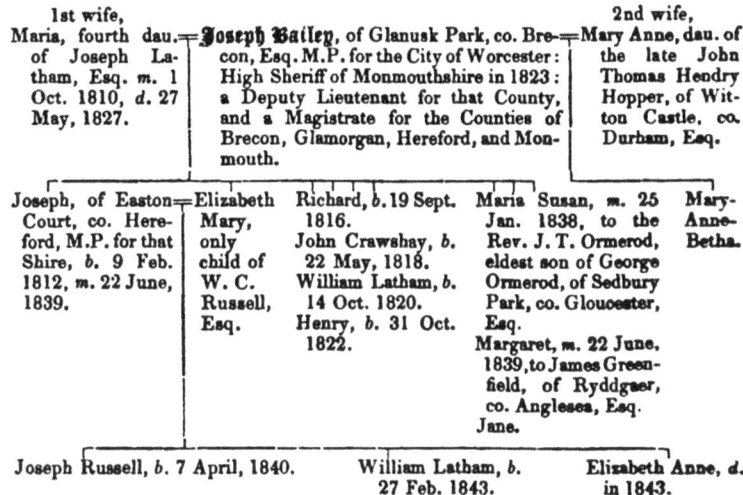

1st wife, Maria, fourth dau. of Joseph Latham, Esq. *m.* 1 Oct. 1810, *d.* 27 May, 1827.	Joseph Bailey, of Glanusk Park, co. Brecon, Esq. M.P. for the City of Worcester: High Sheriff of Monmouthshire in 1823: a Deputy Lieutenant for that County, and a Magistrate for the Counties of Brecon, Glamorgan, Hereford, and Monmouth.	2nd wife, Mary Anne, dau. of the late John Thomas Hendry Hopper, of Witton Castle, co. Durham, Esq.

Joseph, of Easton Court, co. Hereford, M.P. for that Shire, *b.* 9 Feb. 1812, *m.* 22 June, 1839.	Elizabeth Mary, only child of W. C. Russell, Esq.	Richard, *b.* 19 Sept. 1816. John Crawshay, *b.* 22 May, 1818. William Latham, *b.* 14 Oct. 1820. Henry, *b.* 31 Oct. 1822.	Maria Susan, *m.* 25 Jan. 1838, to the Rev. J. T. Ormerod, eldest son of George Ormerod, of Sedbury Park, co. Gloucester, Esq. Margaret, *m.* 22 June, 1839, to James Greenfield, of Ryddgaer, co. Anglesea, Esq. Jane.	Mary-Anne-Betha.

Joseph Russell, *b.* 7 April, 1840.	William Latham, *b.* 27 Feb. 1843.	Elizabeth Anne, *d.* in 1843.

Starkey, of Wakefield, of Thornton Lodge,
Springwood and Heaton Lodge, near Huddersfield, co. York.

THE following Arms were confirmed in 1843 to the family of Starkey of the above places, derived from John Starkey, of Huntroyd, afterwards of Padiham, third son of Edmund Starkey, of Huntroyd, co. Lancaster, Esq. by Ann, his wife, daughter of Nicholas Hancock, of Lower Higham. (See BURKE's *Landed Gentry.*)

Arms.—Ar. a bend engr. vaire between six storks sa.
Crest.—A stork ar. semée of etoiles az.
Motto.—Homo proponit Deus disponit.

PLATE XXXII

HUGH BEAVER, ESQ.
GLYN-GARTH, CO. ANGLESEY.

JOHN FARQUHARSON, ESQ.
HAUGHTON, CO. ABERDEEN.

ROBERT GRÆME, ESQ.
GARVOCK, CO. PERTH.

WILLIAM MONSELL, ESQ.
TERVOE, CO. LIMERICK.

THOMAS F. COLOGAN, ESQ.
TENERIFFE.

PLATE XXXVII.

Beaver, of Glyn Garth, co. Anglesey.

Hugh Beaver, of Glyn Garth, co. Anglesey, and of The Temple, co. Laucaster, Esq. a Magistrate for the former county, and High Sheriff in 1837, third and eldest surviving son of the late Robert Beaver, of Maesllwyn, co. Anglesey, Esq. impales the Quartered Coat of Campbell of Barcaldine, in right of his wife, Isabella Janet, third daughter of Sir Duncan Campbell, of Barcaldine, co. Argyll, Bart.

Arms.—Or, a fesse az. between three lions ramp. in chief gu. and a beaver passant in base ppr. impaling, quarterly, first and fourth, gyronny of eight or and sa. for Campbell; second, ar. a galley sa. sails unfurled, oars in action, for Lorn; third, or a fesse chequy ar. and az.

Crest.—A mount vert, thereon, in front of three arrows, one in pale and two in saltire, the pheons downwards, a beaver passant ppr.

Motto.—Industriâ et Virtute.

Hugh Beaver, of Glyn Garth, co. Angle-sey, and The Temple, co. Lancaster, Esq. High Sheriff co. Anglesey in 1837, m. 10 Oct. 1839.	Isabella-Janet, third dau. of Sir Duncan Campbell, of Barcaldine, co. Argyll, Bart.
Elizabeth-Dreghorn.	Ada-Isabella.

Farquharson, of Haughton, co. Aberdeen.

The following Arms of Farquharson of Haughton were confirmed by the Lord Lyon in 1752 to " Francis Farquharson, of Haughton, co. Aberdeen, Esq. lineally descended from William Cumming, *alias* Farquharson, Esq. who was Proprietor of the lands of Kellis, in the co. of Elgin, in 1562." The said Francis Farquharson was succeeded at his decease by the son of his sister Mary, his nephew, Alexander Ogilvie, Esq. who assumed the Surname and Arms of Farquharson. His son, the present Representative of this ancient Family, is John Farquharson, of Haughton, Esq. a Magistrate and Deputy Lieutenant of Aberdeenshire.

Arms.—Quarterly, first, or, a lion ramp. gu. armed and langued az. for Farquharson. Second and third, az. a bezant betwixt three garbs or, for Cumming. Fourth, ar. a fir tree growing out of a mount ppr. also for Farquharson.

Crest.—The sun in his glory, breaking out of a cloud ppr. In an escroll above —Illumino.

Motto.—Memor esto majorum.

PLATE XXXVII.

Graeme, of Garvock, co. Perth.

ROBERT GRÆME, of Garvock, Esq. represents the Family of Græme of Garvock, one of the most ancient and distinguished Branches of the House of Graham, being directly descended from Sir WILLIAM GRAHAM, Lord of Kincardine, who is also Ancestor of the Ducal House of Montrose by a prior marriage. He bears the Arms of Graham, within a double tressure flory and counter-flory, as being lineally descended from King ROBERT III. of Scotland, through Mary Stewart, second daughter of that monarch, who married Sir William Graham, of Kincardine. The third son of that marriage, William, obtained a grant of the Barony of Garvock from King JAMES I. his uncle, and from him the present Proprietor is directly descended. Sir William Graham, of Kincardine, was also ancestor of the GRAHAMS of Fintry, GRAHAMS of Claverhouse, Viscount of Dundee, and other distinguished Families of the name.

Arms.—Or, three piles gu. issuing from a chief sa. charged with as many escallops of the first, within a double tressure flory and counter-flory, gu.

Crest.—A lion ramp. gu.

Motto.—Noli me tangere.

Monsell, of Tervoe, co. Limerick.

WILLIAM MONSELL, of Tervoe, Esq. High Sheriff of the county of Limerick, son and heir of the late William Monsell, of Tervoe, Esq. by Olivia, his wife, eldest daughter of Sir John Allen Johnson Walsh, Bart. bears the Arms of MONSELL, impaled with those of QUIN, in right of his wife, the Lady Ann-Maria-Charlotte Wyndham Quin, only daughter of the second Earl of Dunraven. The Family of Monsell went to Ireland from the county of Somerset early in the reign of CHARLES I.

Arms.—Ar. a chev. betw. three mullets, sa. impaling, for QUIN, vert, a pegasus pass. ar. a chief or.

Crest.—A lion ramp. holding in the paws a mullet.

Motto.—Mone sale.

Cologan.

A BRANCH of the old and distinguished House of WALSH, of the county of Waterford, settled in Teneriffe, one of the Canary Islands, in or about the year 1680, and eventually succeeded to the sole Representation of the Family, its Chiefs exercising the right of nominating the Master of the Holy Ghost Hospital at Waterford, founded by their ancestor, Patrick Walsh, as far back as the year 1545, in the reign of HENRY VIII. which Monarch granted to the said Patrick

PLATE XXXVII.

this privilege as a reward for the munificent act which originated the Institution. Subsequently the male line of the Walshes became extinct, and their property and representation merged almost exclusively in the COLOGAN Family, also of Irish extraction, John Cologan, Esq. (or rather Colgan, as the name is said originally to have been written) having married one of the daughters of the first of the Walshes that settled at Teneriffe. Of this alliance, the present THOMAS F. COLOGAN, of Teneriffe, Esq. is the great grandson and representative. He bears a quartered Coat, COLOGAN, FALLON, WALSH, and GANT.

Arms.—Quarterly, first, az. a lion ramp. betw. three pheons ar. for COLOGAN. Second, az. two greyhounds erect and respectant ar. supporting between them a sword erect ppr. in the centre chief point a castle of the second, for FALLON. Third, ar. a chev. gu. betw. three pheons sa. for WALSH. Fourth, gu. a bunch of grapes ar. surmounted of a bend or, for GANT.

Crest.—A dexter arm in armour, embowed, holding a lance, transfixing a stag's head erased, all ppr.

Motto.—In Deo spes mea.

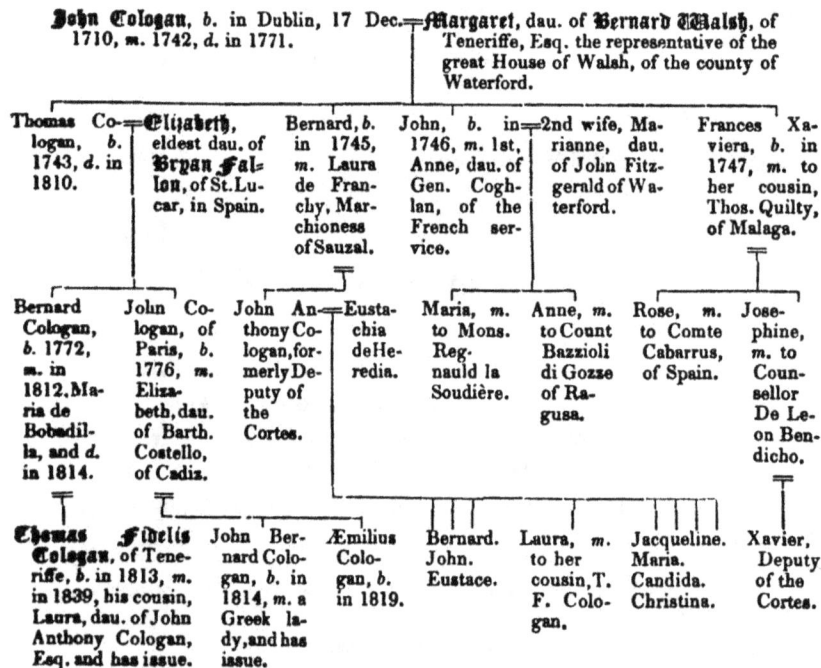

John Cologan, b. in Dublin, 17 Dec. 1710, m. 1742, d. in 1771. = Margaret, dau. of Bernard Walsh, of Teneriffe, Esq. the representative of the great House of Walsh, of the county of Waterford.

Thomas Cologan, b. 1743, d. in 1810. = Elizabeth, eldest dau. of Bryan Fallon, of St. Lucar, in Spain.

Bernard, b. in 1745, m. Laura de Franchy, Marchioness of Sauzal.

John, b. in 1746, m. 1st, Anne, dau. of Gen. Coghlan, of the French service. = 2nd wife, Marianne, dau. of John Fitzgerald of Waterford.

Frances Xaviera, b. in 1747, m. to her cousin, Thos. Quilty, of Malaga.

Bernard Cologan, b. 1772, m. in 1812. Maria de Bobadilla, and d. in 1814.

John Cologan, of Paris, b. 1776, m. Elizabeth, dau. of Barth. Costello, of Cadiz.

John Anthony Cologan, formerly Deputy of the Cortes. = Eustachia de Heredia.

Maria, m. to Mons. Regnauld la Soudière.

Anne, m. to Count Bazzioli di Gozze of Ragusa.

Rose, m. to Comte Cabarrus, of Spain.

Josephine, m. to Counsellor De Leon Bendicho.

Thomas Cologan, of Teneriffe, b. in 1813, m. in 1839, his cousin, Laura, dau. of John Anthony Cologan, Esq. and has issue.

Fidelis Cologan.

John Bernard Cologan, b. in 1814, m. a Greek lady, and has issue.

Æmilius Cologan, b. in 1819.

Bernard John Eustace.

Laura, m. to her cousin, T. F. Cologan.

Jacqueline. Maria. Candida. Christina.

Xavier, Deputy of the Cortes.

PLATE XXXVIII.

Woodd, formerly of Shine Wood, co. Salop, now of Yorkshire.

BASIL THOMAS WOODD, Esq. Justice of the Peace for the North and West Ridings of Yorkshire, eldest son and heir of Basil George Woodd, of London, Esq. and sixth in descent from Basil Woodd, Doctor of Laws and Chancellor of Rochester, who suffered severely for his devotion to the Royal Cause, bears the arms of WOODD and BALLARD quarterly, and impales DAMPIER and DIGBY in right of his wife, Charlotte-Mary, eldest daughter of the Rev. John Dampier of Colinshays, co. Somerset, by Mary-Charlotte, his wife, only child of the Hon. and Rev. Charles Digby.

Arms.—Quarterly, first and fourth, gu. three demi savages ar. holding clubs over their dexter shoulders, or, for WOODD; second and third, sa. a griffin segreant erm. for BALLARD. (George Basil Woodd, Esq. grandfather of Basil Thomas Woodd, Esq. Justice of the Peace, having married Gertrude, daughter and eventual heiress of George Ballard, of Leatherhead, Esq.)

Impaling—First and fourth, or, a lion rampant sa. on a chief gu. a label of five points ar. for DAMPIER; second and third, az. a fleur-de-lis ar. for DIGBY.

Crest.—A demi savage, as in the arms.

Motto.—Non nobis.

Pedder, of Ashton Lodge, co. Lancaster.

JAMES PEDDER, of Ashton Lodge, co Lancaster, Esq. a Magistrate and Deputy Lieutenant of the County, is son of the late Edward Pedder, of Bispham Lodge and Preston, Esq. by Margaret his wife, only daughter and heir of Richard Wilson, Gent. of Newton with Hardhom, and grandson of Edward Pedder, of Preston, Esq. by Katherine his wife, daughter of John Clayton, of Stockport, Esq. and great-grandson of Alderman Richard Pedder, Mayor of Preston in 1748 and 1756. (See BURKE's *Landed Gentry*.) Mr. Pedder impales with his paternal Arms the Coat of NEWSHAM, having married Jane, only daughter of Richard Newsham, of Preston, Esq.

Arms.—Quarterly, sa. and gu. on a bend ar. between two escallops or, a greyhound courant between two quatrefoils of the second : impaling, az. on a fesse ar. three crosses crosslet gu.

Crest.—Between two branches of olive ppr. as many lions' heads erased at the neck and addorsed, erminois, gorged with one collar gu.

Motto.—Je dis la verité.

PLATE XXXVIII.

Macpherson, of Cluny, co. Inverness.

EWEN MACPHERSON, of Cluny Macpherson, Chief of the Clan Macpherson, and Representative in the male line of the ancient Chiefs of Clan Chattan, derives in direct descent from Gallichattan Moir, *temp.* Malcolm Canmore. The hand and dagger borne in the Arms were assigned to the Macphersons for killing the last of the Cummings at Badenoch, and the cross crosslet as commemorative of one of the ancestors having made a pilgrimage to the Holy Land.

Arms.—Per fess or and az. a lymphad with her sails trussed up and oars in action, of the first; in the dexter chief point a hand couped grasping a dagger point upwards gu. in the sinister chief a cross crosslet fitchée of the last, impaling DAVIDSON.

Crest.—A cat sejant ppr.

Supporters.—Two highlandmen with steel helmets on their heads, thighs bare, their shirts tied between them, and round targets on their arms.

Motto.—Touch not the cat but a glove: in Gaelic, Na bean do'n chat gun Laimhn.

Claxson, of Oxon and Gloucestershire.

THE REV. BENJAMIN SAUNDERS CLAXSON, D.D. of Eastgate House and Wotton Lodge, Gloucester, Incumbent of St. Matthews, &c. only son of the late Benjamin Claxson, of Eastgate House, Esq. Justice of the Peace, by Susannah, his wife, only surviving daughter of Thomas Saunders, of Gloucester, Esq. bears the CLAXSON Arms quartered with the Coat of SAUNDERS, and impaled with that of EAMER, in right of his wife, Charlotte-Anne, daughter of the late Sir John Eamer, Knt. Lord Mayor of London, 1801-2, and Colonel of the Royal East London Militia. The family of Claxson have been proprietors of landed estates at Woodcote in the parish of South Stoke, co. Oxford, from the year 1651, uninterruptedly, to the present time.

Arms.—First and fourth, gu. a fess engr. paly erm. and or, between two porcupines in chief and in base a stag lodged ar. attired and hoofed of the third for CLAXSON; second and third, per chev. gu. and or, in chief two elephants' heads of the last, in base a crescent az. for SAUNDERS, impaling the quartered Coat of EAMER and ROBINSON.

Crest.—A mount vert, thereon a stag lodged ar. attired and unguled or, supporting with his dexter foot an escutcheon gu. charged with a porcupine ar.

Motto.—Sapere aude: incipe.

Lane Fox, of Bramham, co. York.

GEORGE LANE FOX, of Bramham Park, Esq. eldest son of the late James Lane Fox, Esq. M.P. who inherited the estates of his uncle George Fox, Lord Bingley, and great-grandson of Henry Fox, Esq. by the Hon. Frances Lane, his wife, sister and heir of James, Viscount Lanesborough, bears the quartered Coat of Fox and LANE.

Arms.—Quarterly, first and fourth, ar. a chev. between three foxes' heads erased gu. for Fox; second and third, ar. a lion rampant gu. within a bordure sa. on a canton of the first, a harp and crown or, for LANE.

Crests.—First, a fox passant gu. for Fox; second, out of a ducal coronet or, a griffin segreant sa

PLATE XLVII.

BASIL THOMAS WOODD, ESQ.
J.P. OF YORKSHIRE.

JAMES PEDDER, ESQ.
ASHTON LODGE, CO. LANCASTER.

EWEN MACPHERSON.
CLUNY MACPHERSON, CO. INVERNESS.

THE REV. B. SAUNDERS CLAXSON D.D.
EASTGATE HOUSE, GLOUCESTER.

GEORGE LANE FOX, ESQ.
BRAMHAM, CO. YORK.

London, Edward Churton, 26 Holles Street, Cavendish Square, 1860.

PLATE XXXIX.

Oldfield of Oldfield, co. Chester, and Peckham Cottage, co. Surrey.

THE very ancient family of Oldfield derive their descent and their earliest quartering from the marriage (*temp.* HEN. III.) of GUY OF PROVENCE with Alice, daughter of WILLIAM DE HASELWALL, of Oldfield in Cheshire. The descendant in the ninth degree from this alliance, RICHARD OLDFIELD, of Oldfield, Esq. married Margaret, daughter and heir of JAMES GROSVENOR, younger son of Ralph Grosvenor of Eaton, and their great-grandson, WILLIAM OLDFIELD, Esq. baptized in 1586, wedded Elizabeth, daughter and heir of Ralph Leftwich, of Leftwich, Esq. by whom he was great-great-great-grandfather of the present male representative of this ancient line, THOMAS BRAME OLDFIELD, of Peckham Cottage, Surrey, Esq. who quarters, by right of descent, the Arms of HASEL-WALL, GROSVENOR, and LEFTWICH.

Arms.—Quarterly, first, ar. on a bend gu. three crosses pattée fitchée of the field for OLDFIELD; second, ar. a chief az. for HASELWALL; third, az. a garb or, for GROSVENOR; fourth, ar. on a fesse dancetté az. three garbs, for LEFTWICH.

Crest.—A demi wyvern, with wings displayed ar. issuing from a ducal coronet or.

Motto.—Viresco vulnere.

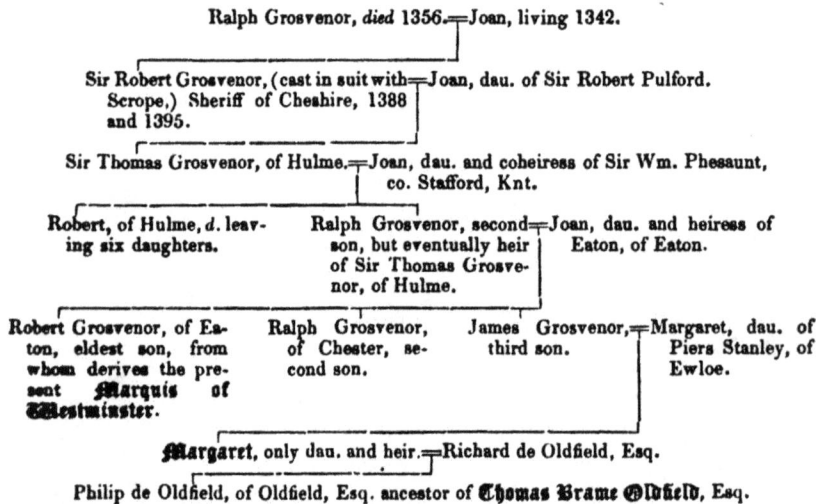

Ralph Grosvenor, *died* 1356.=Joan, living 1342.

Sir Robert Grosvenor, (cast in suit with=Joan, dau. of Sir Robert Pulford.
Scrope,) Sheriff of Cheshire, 1388
and 1395.

Sir Thomas Grosvenor, of Hulme.=Joan, dau. and coheiress of Sir Wm. Phesaunt,
co. Stafford, Knt.

Robert, of Hulme, *d.* leaving six daughters.

Ralph Grosvenor, second=Joan, dau. and heiress of
son, but eventually heir   Eaton, of Eaton.
of Sir Thomas Grosve-
nor, of Hulme.

Robert Grosvenor, of Eaton, eldest son, from whom derives the present **Marquis** of **Westminster**.

Ralph Grosvenor, of Chester, second son.

James Grosvenor,=Margaret, dau. of
third son.   Piers Stanley, of
                  Ewloe.

Margaret, only dau. and heir.=Richard de Oldfield, Esq.

Philip de Oldfield, of Oldfield, Esq. ancestor of **Thomas Brame Oldfield**, Esq.

PLATE XXXIX.

Brodie, of Lethen.

JAMES CAMPBELL BRODIE, of Lethen and Coulmony, in the counties of Moray and Nairn, Esq. descended of the Family of Brodie, of That Ilk, bears his Paternal Arms of Brodie, with part of the Arms of Campbell, of Calder (now Earls of Cawdor), of which Family he is descended by his great-grandmother, Sophia Campbell, daughter of Sir Hugh Campbell, of Calder. These Arms were confirmed by Alexander Brodie, then Lord Lyon of Scotland, to Alexander Brodie, of Lethen, paternal granduncle of the said James Campbell Brodie, and to his heirs, by grant recorded in the Lyon Office, dated 12 January 1753.

Arms.—Ar. on a chev. gu. betw. three mullets az. a galley or lymphad sa.

Crest.—A dexter hand holding a bunch of five arrows ppr.

Motto.—*Above the Crest*, Be mindful to unite.

John, Thane of Brodie, (lineally descended from Malcolm, Thane of Brodie, who lived in the time of Alexander III. 1246-1285), *d.* before 1511.

Alexander Brodie, of That Ilk, *d.* before 1540.

Thomas Brodie, of That Ilk, *d.* before 1550.

Alexander Brodie, of That Ilk, *d.* in August 1583.

David Brodie, of That Ilk, *b.* 1553, *d.* 1626.

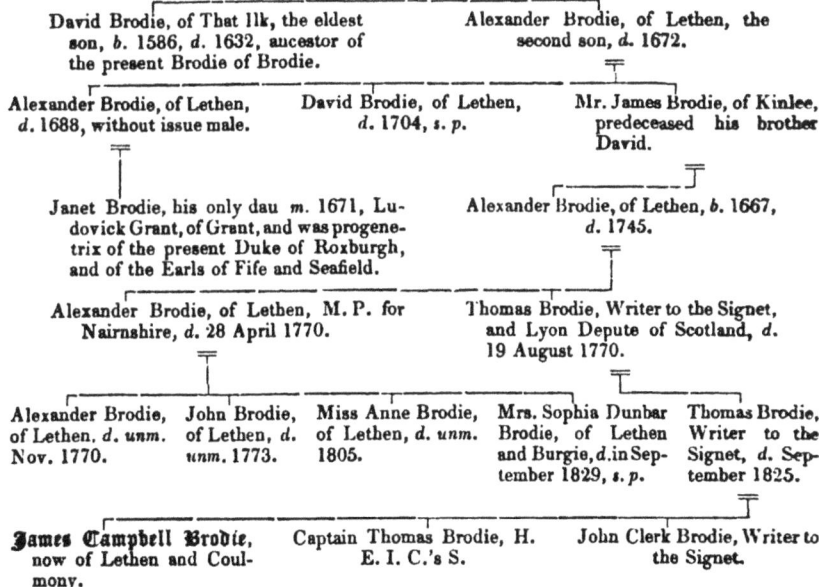

David Brodie, of That Ilk, the eldest son, *b.* 1586, *d.* 1632, ancestor of the present Brodie of Brodie.

Alexander Brodie, of Lethen, the second son, *d.* 1672.

Alexander Brodie, of Lethen, *d.* 1688, without issue male.

David Brodie, of Lethen, *d.* 1704, *s. p.*

Mr. James Brodie, of Kinlee, predeceased his brother David.

Janet Brodie, his only dau. m. 1671, Ludovick Grant, of Grant, and was progenetrix of the present Duke of Roxburgh, and of the Earls of Fife and Seafield.

Alexander Brodie, of Lethen, *b.* 1667, *d.* 1745.

Alexander Brodie, of Lethen, M. P. for Nairnshire, *d.* 28 April 1770.

Thomas Brodie, Writer to the Signet, and Lyon Depute of Scotland, *d.* 19 August 1770.

Alexander Brodie, of Lethen. *d. unm.* Nov. 1770.

John Brodie, of Lethen, *d. unm.* 1773.

Miss Anne Brodie, of Lethen, *d. unm.* 1805.

Mrs. Sophia Dunbar Brodie, of Lethen and Burgie, *d.* in September 1829, *s. p.*

Thomas Brodie, Writer to the Signet, *d.* September 1825.

James Campbell Brodie, now of Lethen and Coulmony.

Captain Thomas Brodie, H. E. I. C.'s S.

John Clerk Brodie, Writer to the Signet.

PLATE XXXIX.

Barry, of Rocklaveston Manor, co. Notts.

PENDOCK BARRY BARRY, of Rocklaveston Manor, Esq. Deputy Lieutenant for Notts, (the representative of the great house of Barry, of Tollerton, founded in England at the time of the Conquest, of which was SIR JOHN BARRY, of Tollerton, one of the Knights of the Shire in Parliament, who is mentioned in the siege of Caerlaverock, *See* BURKE's *Landed Gentry*,) bears a Shield of six quarterings.

Arms.—Quarterly, first, gu. three bars embattled ar. for BARRY ; second, ar. a fess gu. between in chief two crescents az. and in base a bugle horn of the same stringed vert, for NEALE ; third, az. semée of cross crosslets or, two barbles endorsed of the last, within a bordure engrailed gu. ; fourth, az. a stag trippant ar. for LOWE ; fifth, gu. four bars gemelle ar. a chief of the last charged with five trefoils az. three and two, for PENDOCK ; sixth, quarterly, ar. and az. a cross engrailed counterchanged, for HEYDON.

Crests.—The embattlement of a tower gu. charged with three roses in fess ar. for BARRY ; on a mount vert, a stag trippant, ppr. charged with three lozenges az. for LOWE ; and a demi pelican or, vulning herself and issuing from a castle gu. masoned ppr.

Supporters.—Two lions guardant ar. each gorged with a collar embattled gu. and thereto affixed a chain, passing between their forelegs, and reflexed over their backs or, each holding in its fore paw a flag staff, and therefrom flowing a banner gu. charged with three bars embattled ar. fringed or.

Motto.—A Rege et victoriâ.

Lomax, of Clayton Hall, co. Lancaster.

JOHN LOMAX, of Clayton Hall, co. Lancaster, Esq. son of the late Richard Grimshaw Lomax, of Clayton Hall, Esq. by Catharine, his wife, daughter and heir of Thomas Greaves, Esq. Banker, of Preston, and grandson of James Lomax, Esq. whose father, Richard Lomax, of Pilsworth, Gent. married Rebecca, daughter of Heywood, of Urmston, sole heiress of the GRIMSHAWS OF CLAYTON, bears a Shield quarterly, LOMAX, GRIMSHAWE, and CLAYTON.

Arms.—Quarterly, first and fourth, per pale or and sa. on a bend cottised erm. three escallops gu. for LOMAX. Second, ar. a griffin segreant sa. armed or, for GRIMSHAW. Third, ar. a cross sa. betw. four bezants for CLAYTON.

Crest.—Out of a mural crown a demi-lion gu. collared and holding an escallop.

Motto.—Fato prudentia major.

Weld, of Twickenham.

SAMUEL WELD, of Twickenham, co. Middlesex, and of Oxford Square, Esq. eldest son of the late William Weld, of Twickenham, Esq. and grandson of Joseph Weld, tenth in lineal descent from Richard Weld, of Rushton, third son of William Weld, of Eaton, co. Chester, bears the Arms of the ancient Family of Weld, differenced by a bordure gobonny.

Arms.—Az. a fesse nebulée erm. betw. three crescents or, all within a bordure dovetailed ar.

Crest.—A wyvern sa. bezantée, gorged with a collar, and chain reflexed over the back or, the wings expanded erm. each charged with a crescent of the first.

Motto.—Nil sine numine.

PLATE XXXIX.

THOMAS BRAME OLDFIELD, ESQ.
OLDFIELD, CO. CHESTER
& PECKHAM COTTAGE, CO. SURREY.

JAMES CAMPBELL BRODIE, ESQ.
LETHEN & COULMONY, SCOTLAND.

PENDOCK BARRY BARRY, ESQ.
ROCKLAVESTON MANOR, NOTTS.

JOHN LOMAX, ESQ.
CLAYTON HALL, CO. LANCASTER.

SAMUEL WELD, ESQ.
TWICKENHAM, MIDDLESEX.

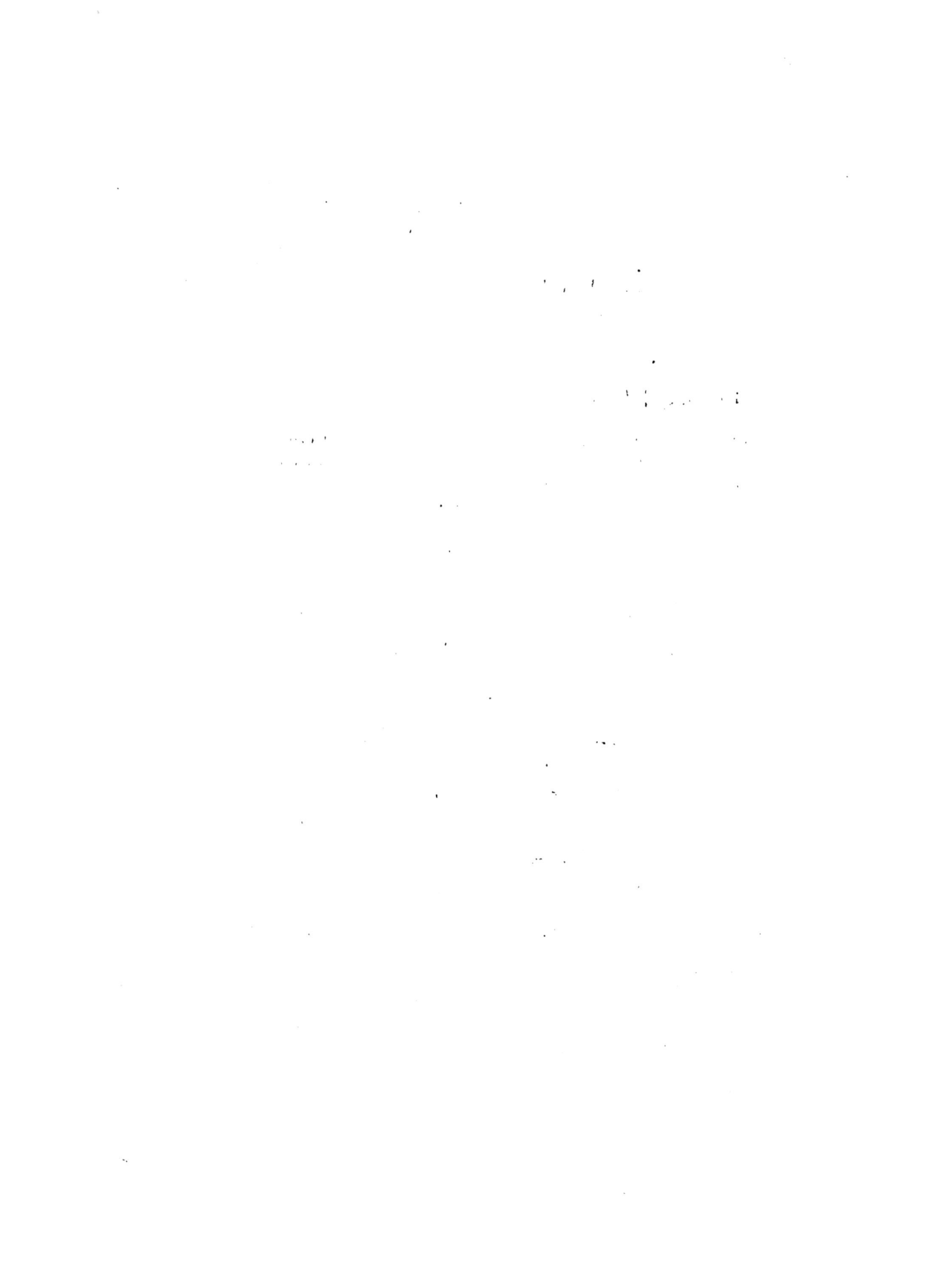

PLATE XL.

Lloyd, of Plymog, Gwerclas, and Bashall.

RICHARD-WALMESLEY LLOYD, Esq. as Representative of the Houses of LLOYD of Plymog, HUGHES of Gwerclas, WALMESLEY of Coldcoates, and TALBOT of Bashall, bears a Shield of Thirty-five Quarterings.

Arms.—Quarterly :—

    I. LLOYD OF PLYMOG. The Arms of Ednyfed Vychan, Lord of Brynffenigl, Gu. a chev. ermine betw. three dead Englishmen's heads in profile, couped and bearded ppr. two and one.

    II. LLOYD OF PLYMOG. (*Ancient*) The Arms of Marchudd ap Cynan, Lord of Brynffenigl, Gu. a Saracen's head erased at the neck ppr. wreathed about the temples sa. and ar.

    III. HWFA AP KENDRIG, Lord of Christionydol, derived from Tudor Trevor, Lord of Hereford. Per bend sinister ermine and ermines, over all a lion ramp. or, armed and langued gu.

    IV. RHYS AP GRIFFITH, derived from Llewelyn ap Ynyr o'Ial, Lord of Gelligy-ynan in Denbighland. Paly of eight or and gu. a bordure az. bezantée.

    V. DAVIES OF DENBIGH, derived from Ednowain Bendew, Lord of Tegaingl, in Flintshire. Ar. a chev. betw. three boars' heads couped sa.

    VI. HUGHES OF GWERCLAS, Barons of Kymmer-yn-Edeirnion, co. Merioneth, derived from Owain Brogyntyn, Lord of Edeirnion, Dinmael, and Abertanat, son of Madoc ap Meredith, last Prince of Powys. The Royal Arms of Powys, Ar. a lion ramp. sa. armed and langued gu.

    VII. MADOC, Lord of Mawddwy in Merionethshire, son of Gwenwynwyn, Prince of Powys-Wenwynwyn. The Arms of Bleddyn ap Cynfyn, King of Powys, Or, a lion ramp. gu.

    VIII. CADWGAN, Prince of Fferlys, son of Elystan Glodrydd. Ar. three boars' heads couped sa. langed gu. tusked or.

    IX. ELYSTAN GLODRYDD, Prince of Fferlys, Founder of the IV Royal Tribe of Wales. Gu. a lion ramp. reguardant or.

    X. MARGARET, BARONESS OF CROGEN AND BRANAS, dau. and h. of Ievan ap Llewelyn, Baron of Crogen and Branas, co. Merioneth, derived from Owain Brogyntyn, Lord of Edeirnion, Dinmael, and Abertanat. Ar. a lion ramp. sa. armed and langued gu.

    XI. HOWEL AP MEURIC, Lord of Nannau, co. Merioneth, derived from Cadwgan, Lord of Nannau, son of Bleddyn ap Cynfyn, King of Powys. Or, a lion ramp. az.

    XII. ROGERS OF BRYNTANGOR, derived, through Osborne Fitzgerald, Lord of Ynys-y-Maengwyn in Merionethshire, from Walter Fitz-Otho, progenitor of the Ducal House of Leinster. Erm. a saltire gu. with a crescent for difference.

PLATE XL.

xiii. TUDOR, Lord of Gwyddelwern, co. Merioneth, (brother of Owen Glendower), younger son of Griffith Vychan, Lord of Glyndwrdwy, co. Merioneth, derived from Griffith Maelor, Lord of Bromfield, eldest son of Madoc, ap Meredith, last Prince of Powys. The Arms of Griffith Maelor, Paly of eight ar. and gu. over all a lion ramp. sa. armed and langued gu.

xiv. THOMAS AP LLEWELYN, Lord of South Wales, representative of the Sovereign Princes of South Wales. The Royal Arms of South Wales, Or a lion ramp. within a bordure indented or.

xv. PHILIP AP IVOR, Lord of Iscoed in Caerdigan. Az. an eagle displ. or.

xvi. LLEWELYN AP GRIFFITH, Prince of North Wales. Quarterly, or and gu. four lions pass. guard. counterchanged.

xvii. OWEN GWYNEDD, Prince of North Wales. Vert, three eagles displayed in fesse or.

xviii. GRIFFITH AP CYNAN, King of North Wales. Gu. three lionels pass. in pale ar.

xix. WALMESLEY OF COLDCOATES, co. Lancaster. Gu. on a chief ermine two hurts.

xx. FERRERS OF BASHALL, co. York, derived from William de Ferrers, VII Earl of Derby, and Margaret his wife, dau. and co-h. of Roger de Quinci, II Earl of Winchester. The Arms of De Quinci, assumed by the Ferrers's Earls of Derby, Gu. seven mascles voided or, three, three, and one.

xxi. WILLIAM DE FERRERS, VI Earl of Derby, derived from William de Ferrers, III Earl of Derby, and Margaret his wife, dau. and h. of William Peverel, Lord of Nottingham. The Arms of Peverel, assumed by the Ferrers's Earls of Derby, Vaire or and gu.

xxii. FERRERS's, Earls of Derby, (*original*) Sa. six horse shoes ar. three, two, and one.

xxiii. HUGH CYFEILIOC, Earl-Palatine of Chester, Az. six garbs or, three, two, and one.

xxiv. RANDLE GERNONS, Earl-Palatine of Chester, Gu. a lion ramp. ar.

xxv. RANDLE DE MESCHINES, Earl-Palatine of Chester, Or a lion ramp. gu.

xxvi. RICHARD, Earl-Palatine of Chester, Gu. semée of cross crosslets or, a wolf's head erased ar.

xxvii. HUGH LUPUS, Earl-Palatine of Chester, Az. a wolf's head erased ar.

xxviii. ROBERT FITZ-PARNELL, IV Earl of Leicester, Gu. a cinquefoil erm. pierced of the field.

xxix. WHITE OF DUFFIELD, co. Derby, Gu. a chev. betw. three goats' heads erased ar.

xxx. TALBOT DE BASHALL, of Bashall, co. York, senior line of the House of Shrewsbury, Ar. three lioncels saliant purpure.

xxxi. FERRERS OF EGGINTON, co. Derby, derived from William de Ferrers, III Earl of Derby, and Margaret his wife, dau. and heir of William Peverel, Lord of Nottingham.

xxxii. FERRERS, Earls of Derby, (*original*) Sa. six horse shoes ar. three, two, and one.

xxxiii. HALTON DE HALTON, Lord of Halton, co. York, Ar. two bars az.

xxxiv. DE KNOLL, Lords of Knollsmere, Wigglesworth, and Hellifield Peel, co. York, Ar. a bend cottised sa.

xxxv. DE ARCHES, of Wigglesworth, co. York, Gu. three arches ar.

Crest.—A dead Englishman's head in profile couped and bearded ppr.

Motto.—Heb Dduw, heb ddim Dduw a digon.

5th in descend,

GRIFFITH AP
RHYS.

From whom derived,
8th in descend,

ROBERT LLOYD,
Gent. of Ply-
mog, co. Den-
bigh, m. 25
May 1684,
bur. 4 Febru-
ary 1689.

de Halton
) and Anas-
and co-h. of
d of Knols-
Reginald de
ere, by Bea=
of Wiggles-

by Bashall
of John Ar-
Darwin, co.
qui ob. ante

James I. ob.

White, Esq.
, co. Derby,
the Long
t.

Earl-Palatine of Chester,
and Earl of Lincoln, (qui
ob. 1232,) she d. 1247.

William de Ferrers, VII=Margaret, 2nd wife, dau. and co-
Earl of Derby, had livery | h. (by Ellen, dau. and co-h. of
of Chartley Castle, co. Staf- | Alan, Lord of Galloway) of
ford, and the other lands of | **Roger de Quinci**, II Earl
his mother's inheritance | of Winchester, son and heir
upon doing homage 32 | of Saier, I Earl of Winches-
Hen. III. d. 12 March | ter, by Margaret, sister and
1254, 38 Henry III. | co-h. of **Robert Fitz=Par-
nell**, IV Earl of Leicester.

From whom derived

all, dau. and heir.=Edward Ferrers, Esq.

all, will dated 15=The sister and, in her issue, heiress of Rich.
ct. 1707. | Witton, Esq. of Wakefield.

ll, sister and co-=Richard Walmesley, Esq. of Coldcoates Hall,
rrers, Esq. of | and Eaves Hall, co. Lancaster, d. before
ch 1732) m. 22 | 1718.
Aug. 1737.

Esq. of Coldcoates and Bashall, d. 29 Aug. 1767, æt. 60.

EDWAR
Den
settl
May

HUGH- eir, bur. 26 May 1800.

RICHA q. d. 23 Nov. 1816.

I. RICHARD-WAL , of the Inner Temple, Esq. Barrister-=I. Dorothea, m.   II. Jane Lloyd,
LEY LLOYD, Esq. unger son of the late William Hughes, | 5 July 1832.   of Chester.
3 Aug. 1801, m. en-y-Clawdd, co. Denbigh, Representa-
Aug. 1828. male line of the **Hughes's of Gwerclas**,
f **Kymmer-yn-Edeirnion**, b. 6 Oct.

EDWARD-WALMES   Talbot de Bashall Hughes, b. 15 Dec. 1836.

Richard Walmesley Lloyd, Esq,

Representative of the Houses of

Plymog, Gwerclas, Coldcoates, & Bashall,

PLATE XLI.

Jackson, of Enniscoe and Carramore, co. Mayo.

GEORGE VAUGHAN JACKSON, of Carramore, Esq. M. A. a Magistrate and Deputy Lieutenant, and High Sheriff of Mayo in 1842, son of the late George Jackson, Esq. Colonel of the North Mayo Militia, by Sidney, his wife, only child and heir of Arthur Vaughan, of Carramore, Esq. a descendant of the Vaughans of Wales, descends from the ancient Devonshire family of Combhay, whose Arms he bears, quartered with those of CUFF, AUNGIER, RUTLEDGE, and VAUGHAN of Wales.

Arms.—Quarterly of six.—

I. Ar. on a chev. sa. betw. three hawks' heads erased az. as many cinquefoils of the field, for JACKSON.

II. Ar. on a bend indented sa. betw. two cottises az. bezantée three fleurs-de-lis of the field, for CUFF.

III. Erm. a griffin ramp. az. for AUNGIER.

IV. Ar. a stag pass. ppr. on a chief az. three estoiles or, for RUTLEDGE.

V. Or, a lion ramp. gu. for VAUGHAN.

VI. Sa. a goat ramp. feeding on an ivy tree ppr. for VAUGHAN of Wales.

Crest.—A horse pass. ar.

Motto.—Celer et audax.

George Jackson, of Enniscoe, co. Mayo, Esq.═Jane, dau. of the Right Hon. James Cuff, of Bal-
b. in 1717, great grandson of Francis Jackson, | linrobe, and, in her issue, heiress of James Cuff,
Esq. Captain of Dragoons in Cromwell's Army, | Lord Tyrawley. The Right Hon. James Cuff
a younger son of Joseph Jackson, of Sneyd Park, | was grandson of Sir James Cuff, Master of the
co. Kent, Esq. descended from Jackson of | Ordnance, and M. P. for co. Mayo in 1661, by
Combhay, co. Devon. | Alice, his wife, sister and co-h. of Ambrose
| Aungier, Earl of Longford.

George Jack-son, of Eniscoe, Esq. b. in 1761, m. in 1783, and d. in 1805. He was Col. of the North Mayo Militia, and member for the co. of Mayo in the Irish and Imperial Parliaments.	Maria, only dau. and h. of William Rutledge, of Foxford, co. Mayo, Esq.	James Jackson, a military officer, b. 1765, m. Mary, dau. of — Perry, of Cork, Esq. and d. in 1825, leaving two daus. Jane, wife of William de Mesurier, of Guernsey, and Mary-Pery.	Francis Jackson, b. in 1769, m. Eliza, dau. of John Martin, of Cleveland, co. Sligo, Esq. and d. in 1834, leaving George Francis, and other issue.	Oliver Jackson, m. in 1812, Sarah, dau. of Humphrey Jones, of Mullinabro', co. Kilkenny, Esq. and had George-Humphrey, and other issue.	Elizabeth Jackson, m. to John Ormsby, of Gortner Abbey, Esq. and d. in 1830.	Anne Jackson, m. to William Orme, of Abbeytown, co. Mayo, Esq.	Catherine Jackson, d. in childhood.

a   b   c   d   e   f   g

PLATE XLI.

a	b	c	d	e	f	g
William Jackson, of Enniscoe, Esq. Col. of the North Mayo Militia, *b.* in 1787, *d.* in 1822. = Jane Louisa, dau. of Colonel Blair, of Blair, co. Ayr, M.P. *d.* in 1827.	George Jackson, Esq. Col. of the North Mayo Militia, *m.* in 1804, and *d.* in 1836. = Sidney, only child and h. of Arthur Vaughan, of Carramore, co. Mayo, Esq.	James Jackson, Esq. Lt.-Col. 6th Dragoon Guards, has served in the Peninsula, at Waterloo, in India, &c.	Francis Jackson, Esq. Major 80th Regt. has served in Holland with distinction.	The Rev. Andrew Jackson, *m.* Mary Louisa, dau. of the Rev. Edwin Stock, son of Dr. Stock, Bishop of Waterford. — Issue.		Oliver Jackson, Esq.

1. Barbara Jackson, *m.* to Thomas Carey, of Rozel, Guernsey, Esq.
2. Jane Jackson, *m.* to Christ. Carleton, of Market Hill, Esq.

3. Mary Jackson.
4. Elizabeth Jackson, *m.* to Thomas Orme, of Abbeytown, Esq.

5. Anne Jackson, *m.* to Wm. Orme, of Glenmore, Esq.
6. Sarah Jackson, *d. unm.*
7. Belinda Cuffe Jackson.

Madeline Eglantine Jackson, only dau. and h. *m.* in 1834. = Mervyn Pratt, of Cabra Castle, co. Cavan, Esq.	1. George Vaughan Jackson, Esq. M.A. Camb. of Carramore, co. Mayo, *b.* 19 Sept. 1806, a Magistrate for the counties of Sligo and Mayo, and a Deputy Lieutenant of the latter.	2. The Rev. William Jackson. 3. Francis Jackson, in the Indian army.	4. Oliver Jackson, an officer in the 85th regiment.	5. James Sidney Jackson.	1. Maria Louisa Jackson.

Kelham, of Bleasby Hall, co. Nottingham.

ROBERT KELHAM KELHAM, of Bleasby Hall, co. Nottingham, Esq. son of the late Marmaduke Langdale, Esq. by Sarah Augusta, his wife, daughter of Robert Kelham, of Bush Hill, co. Middlesex, and of Great Gonerby, co. Lincoln, Esq. assumed, by Royal Licence in 1812, the Surname and Arms of KELHAM, in lieu of those of LANGDALE. His Paternal Ancestors, the Langdales of Longthorp, co. Northampton, descended traditionally from a younger branch of the Langdales of Houghton, co. York; his Maternal, the Kelhams, derive in a direct line from Richard Kelham, Esq. who resided at Allington, and possessed lands there in 1428.

Arms.—Quarterly, first, per pale gu. and az. three covered cups or, two and one, on a chief engr. as many estoiles sa. for KELHAM. Second, az. three covered cups or for KELHAM (ancient). Third, sa. a chev. betw. three estoiles ar. for LANGDALE. Fourth, az. a chev. betw. three falcons ar.

Crest.—A demi eagle displ. with two heads az. semée of erm. spots or, on each wing a covered cup of the last.

Motto.—Beneficiorum memor.

Phillipps, of Longworth, co. Hereford.

ROBERT BIDDULPH PHILLIPPS, of Longworth, Esq. High Sheriff in 1838, son and heir, by Mary-Anne, his wife, second daughter of Michael Biddulph, of Ledbury, Esq. of the late Robert Phillipps, of Longworth, Esq. M. P. for Hereford, who was third son of Thomas Phillipps, of Huntington and Lower

PLATE XLI.

Eaton, co. Hereford, Esq. by Sarah, his wife, daughter and heir of Robert Ravenhill, of Eaton Bishop, Esq. bears the quartered Coat of PHILLIPPS and RAVENHILL, and impales, in right of his wife, ELIZABETH, only daughter of the late JOHN BARNEBY, of Brockhampton, Esq. the quartered Arms of BARNEBY, LUTLEY, and BULKELEY. The Phillipps' of Eaton Bishop are traditionally derived from the junior branch of the Picton Castle family.

Arms.—Quarterly, first and fourth, or, a lion ramp. sa. collared and chained of the field, within a bordure of the second, charged with eight cross crosslets gold, for PHILLIPPS. Second and third, erm. three mounts vert, on each a raven sa. for RAVENHILL.

Impaling, Quarterly, I. quarterly, first and fourth, sa. a lion pass. guard. betw. three escallops ar. for BARNEBY. Second and third, quarterly, or and az. four lions ramp. counterchanged, for LUTLEY. II. Sa. a chev. betw. three bulls' heads caboshed ar. for BULKELEY.

Crest.—A demi lion sa. collared and chained, and holding betw. the paws a leopard's face jessant-de-lis or.

Motto.—Flecti sed non frangi.

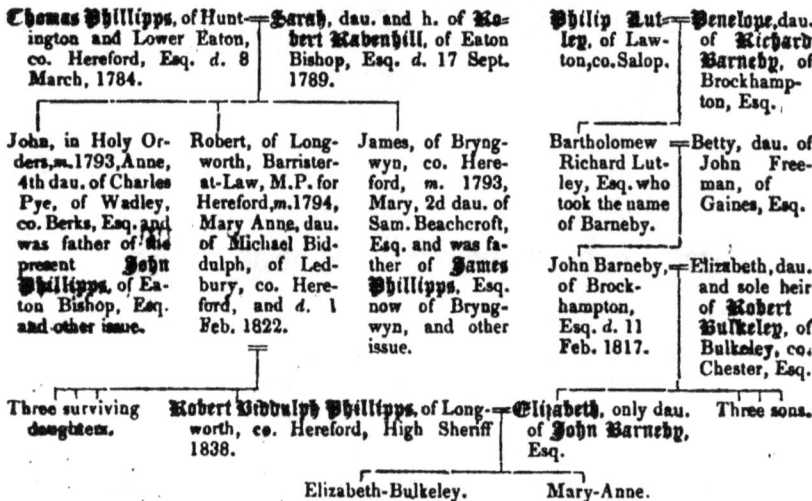

Thomas Phillipps, of Huntington and Lower Eaton, co. Hereford, Esq. d. 8 March, 1784. = Sarah, dau. and h. of Robert Ravenhill, of Eaton Bishop, Esq. d. 17 Sept. 1789.

Philip Lutley, of Lawton, co. Salop. = Penelope, dau. of Richard Barneby, of Brockhampton, Esq.

John, in Holy Orders, m. 1793, Anne, 4th dau. of Charles Pye, of Wadley, co. Berks, Esq. and was father of the present John Phillipps, of Eaton Bishop, Esq. and other issue.

Robert, of Longworth, Barrister-at-Law, M.P. for Hereford, m. 1794, Mary Anne, dau. of Michael Biddulph, of Ledbury, co. Hereford, and d. 1 Feb. 1822.

James, of Bryngwyn, co. Hereford, m. 1793, Mary, 2d dau. of Sam. Beachcroft, Esq. and was father of James Phillipps, Esq. now of Bryngwyn, and other issue.

Bartholomew = Richard Lutley, Esq. who took the name of Barneby.

Betty, dau. of John Freeman, of Gaines, Esq.

John Barneby, of Brockhampton, Esq. d. 11 Feb. 1817. = Elizabeth, dau. and sole heir of Robert Bulkeley, of Bulkeley, co. Chester, Esq.

Three surviving daughters.

Robert Biddulph Phillipps, of Longworth, co. Hereford, High Sheriff 1838. = Elizabeth, only dau. of John Barneby, Esq.

Three sons.

Elizabeth-Bulkeley.

Mary-Anne.

Hawley, of West Green House, co. Hants.

WILLIAM HENRY TOOVEY HAWLEY, of West Green House, Esq. eldest son and heir of the late Henry William Toovey Hawley, Esq. Lieutenant Colonel of the 1st or King's Dragoon Guards, by Catherine, his wife, daughter of George Jepson, of Lincoln, Esq. descends from the ancient Barons Hawley (see BURKE's *Landed Gentry*) of the Kingdom of Ireland, and bears their Arms.

Arms.—Vert, a saltire engr. ar.

Crest.—A winged thunder-bolt ppr.

Motto.—Et suivez moy.

PLATE LXI.

Norbury, of Sherridge, co. Worcester.

THOMAS NORBURY, of Sherridge, Esq. Justice of the Peace for the counties of Worcester and Hereford, and a Deputy Lieutenant of the former, son of Thomas Jones, Esq. by Ursula, his wife, third daughter of Benjamin Johnson, Esq. Alderman of the city of Worcester, assumed, by Royal Licence, his present Surname and Arms in lieu of those of JONES, in consequence of his marriage with Mary Anne, only child of Coningsby Norbury, of Droitwich, Esq.

Arms.—Sa. a chev. indented erm. betw. three bulls' heads cabossed ar. armed or.

Crest.—Out of a crown vallery or, a bull's head sa. armed or, in the mouth a trefoil vert.

GEORGE VAUGHAN JACKSON, ESQ.
CARRAMORE, CO. MAYO.

ROBERT KELHAM KELHAM, ESQ.
BLEASBY HALL, NOTTS.

ROBERT BIDDULPH PHILLIPPS, ESQ.
LONGWORTH CO. HEREFORD.

W. HENRY TOOVEY HAWLEY, ESQ.
WEST GREEN HOUSE, HANTS.

THOMAS NORBURY, ESQ.
SHELBRIDGE CO. WORCESTER.

PLATE LXII.

Craufuird, of Baidland,
and subsequently of Ardmillan, co. Ayr.

THOMAS CRAUFUIRD, of Grange, co. Ayr, Esq. Male Representative of the Craufuirds of Braidland, and the Kennedys of Ardmillan, bears the Quartered Coat of CRAUFUIRD and KENNEDY.

Arms.—Quarterly, first and fourth, Gu. on a fesse erm. betw. three mullets ar. two crescents interlaced of the field, for CRAUFUIRD, of Baidland. Second and third, Ar. a chev. gu. betw. three cross crosslets fitchée sa. for KENNEDY, of Ardmillan.

Crest.—A game hawk hooded and belled.

Motto.—Durum patientiâ frango.

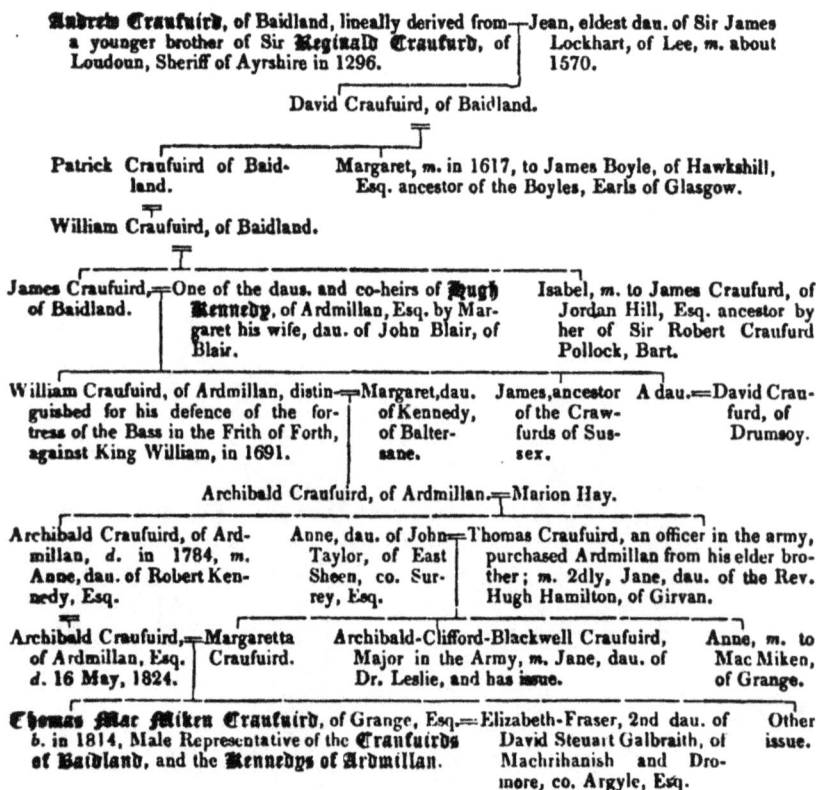

Andrew Craufuird, of Baidland, lineally derived from a younger brother of Sir Reginald Craufurd, of Loudoun, Sheriff of Ayrshire in 1296.═Jean, eldest dau. of Sir James Lockhart, of Lee, m. about 1570.

David Craufuird, of Baidland.

Patrick Craufuird of Baidland.

Margaret, m. in 1617, to James Boyle, of Hawkshill, Esq. ancestor of the Boyles, Earls of Glasgow.

William Craufuird, of Baidland.

James Craufuird,═One of the daus. and co-heirs of Hugh Kennedy, of Ardmillan, Esq. by Margaret his wife, dau. of John Blair, of Baidland. Blair.

Isabel, m. to James Craufurd, of Jordan Hill, Esq. ancestor by her of Sir Robert Craufurd Pollock, Bart.

William Craufuird, of Ardmillan, distinguished for his defence of the fortress of the Bass in the Frith of Forth, against King William, in 1691.═Margaret,dau. of Kennedy, of Baltersane.

James,ancestor of the Crawfurds of Sussex.

A dau.═David Craufurd, of Drumsoy.

Archibald Craufuird, of Ardmillan.═Marion Hay.

Archibald Craufuird, of Ardmillan, d. in 1784, m. Anne, dau. of Robert Kennedy, Esq.

Anne, dau. of John Taylor, of East Sheen, co. Surrey, Esq.═Thomas Craufuird, an officer in the army, purchased Ardmillan from his elder brother; m. 2dly, Jane, dau. of the Rev. Hugh Hamilton, of Girvan.

Archibald Craufuird,═Margaretta of Ardmillan, Esq. Craufuird. d. 16 May, 1824.

Archibald-Clifford-Blackwell Craufuird, Major in the Army, m. Jane, dau. of Dr. Leslie, and has issue.

Anne, m. to Mac Miken, of Grange.

Thomas Mac Miken Craufuird, of Grange, Esq.═Elizabeth-Fraser, 2nd dau. of b. in 1814, Male Representative of the Craufuirds of Baidland, and the Kennedys of Ardmillan. David Steuart Galbraith, of Machrihanish and Dromore, co. Argyle, Esq.

Other issue.

PLATE XLII.

Kelly, of Newtown House, co. Galway.

JAMES KELLY, of Newtown House, Esq. son of the late JAMES KELLY, of co. Cork, Esq. by Mary, his wife, daughter of Robert French, of French Grove, co. Mayo, Esq. and a descendant of the ancient Family of Kelly of Aughrim Castle, co. Galway, bears the Ensigns of the ancient Irish Sept of O'Kelly. (See BURKE's *Landed Gentry*.)

Arms.—Gu. on a mount vert, two lions ramp. supporting a tower ar.

Crest.—An Enfield passant ppr.

Motto.—Turris fortis mihi Deus.

Maude, of Moor House, co. York.

JOHN MAUDE, of Moor House, Esq. a Magistrate and Deputy Lieutenant for the West Riding of Yorkshire, Author of a "Visit to the Falls of Niagara in 1800," is the chief landed Representative in Yorkshire of the old and distinguished Baronial Family of MAUDE, and bears the ancient Arms which were proved and recorded in Glover's Visitation, A.D. 1585, by Arthur Mawhaut or Maude, of West Riddlesden. The Patriarch of the Family in England was EUSTACE DE MONTE ALTO, surnamed the "Norman Hunter," one of the soldiers of the Conquest in the immediate train of Hugh Lupus (see BURKE's *Landed Gentry*). The present head of the senior line is Cornwallis Maude, VISCOUNT HAWARDEN.

Arms.—Ar. three bars gemelles sa. over all a lion ramp. gu. charged on the shoulder with a cross crosslet fitchée or.

Crest.—A lion's head couped gu. charged with a cross crosslet fitchée or.

Motto.—De Monte Alto.

Welch, of Arle House co. Gloucester.

GEORGE ASSER WHITE WELCH, of Arle House, Esq. a Magistrate for the counties of Gloucester and Essex, and also a Deputy Lieutenant of the latter, son of John Gregory Welch, Esq. Justice of the Peace of Gloucestershire, by Frances-Asser, his wife, only surviving child and heir of the late Thomas White, Esq. and grandson of the late Walter Welch, of Arle, Esq. by Mary Gregory, his wife, bears a Coat quarterly of four, and the Arms of MANNOCK, on an Escutcheon of Pretence, in right of his wife Anne-Catherine-Gardiner, only child of the late Lieutenant Mannooch, of the 68th Regt. and niece of Vice-Admiral Sir Edward Brace, K. C. B.

PLATE XLII.

Arms.—Quarterly, first and fourth, az. on a fesse engr. betw. six mullets, a lion pass. Second, Per pale ar. and or, a chev. engr. chequy gu. and of the second betw. three roses of the third on a canton az. a fleur-de-lis. Third, Gu. a pale surmounted of two lions passant.

Crest.—An antelope's head arm[..] billettée, holding in the mouth a cross crosslet fitchée.

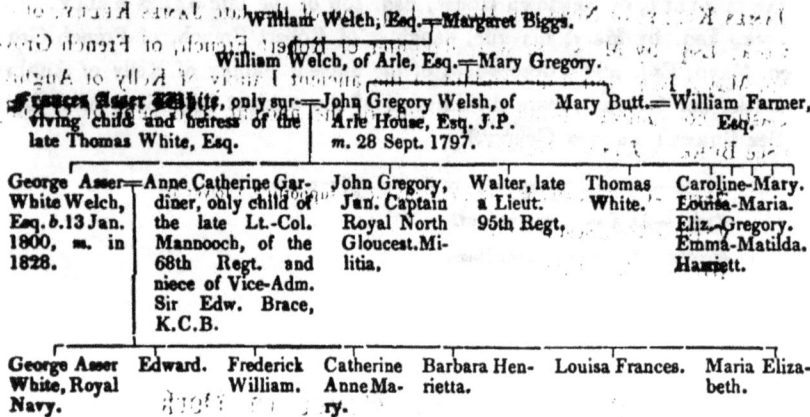

William Welch, Esq.═Margaret Biggs.				

William Welch, of Arle, Esq.═Mary Gregory.

| Frances Asser White, only surviving child and heiress of the late Thomas White, Esq. ═ | John Gregory Welsh, of Arle House, Esq. J.P. m. 28 Sept. 1797. | Mary Butt.═William Farmer, Esq. | | |

| George Asser White Welch, Esq. b. 13 Jan. 1800, m. in 1828. ═ | Anne Catherine Gardiner, only child of the late Lt.-Col. Mannooch, of the 68th Regt. and niece of Vice-Adm. Sir Edw. Brace, K.C.B. | John Gregory, Jan. Captain Royal North Gloucest. Militia, | Walter, late a Lieut. 95th Regt, | Thomas White. | Caroline-Mary. Louisa-Maria. Eliz.-Gregory. Emma-Matilda. Harriett. |

| George Asser White, Royal Navy. | Edward. | Frederick William. | Catherine Anne Mary. | Barbara Henrietta. | Louisa Frances. | Maria Elizabeth. |

Leche, of Carden, co. Chester.

JOHN HURLESTON LECHE, of Carden Park, Esq. High Sheriff of Cheshire in 1832, Representative of the very ancient Family of LECHE, bears a Shield of Six Quarterings.

Arms.—Quarterly, I. Erm. on a chief indented gu. three crowns or, for LECHE. Second, sa. a sling betw. two pheons ar. for CAWARDEN. Third, ar. two bars gu. a crescent for difference, for MAINWARING of Ightfield. Fourth, ar. four ermine spots in cross sa. for HURLESTON. Fifth, quarterly, gu. and or, in the first and fourth quarters, three fleurs-de-lis of the last, for MASSEY. Sixth as first.

Crest.—Out of a ducal coronet or, an arm erect ppr. grasping a snake, environed round the arm, vert.

John Leche, of Carden, Esq. great grand═Margaret, dau. and sole heir of George son of John Leche, by Lucy, his wife, Mainwaring, of Ightfield, co. Salop, 2nd dau. and co-h. of William de Esq. Cawarden.

From which marriage derived

John Leche, of Carden, Esq. High Sheriff═Mary, 2nd dau. and co-heir of John of Cheshire in 1753. Hurleston, of Newton, Esq.

William Leche, of Carden, Esq. High═Miss Hannah Newell, m. in 1805. Sheriff in 1774.

John Hurleston Leche, now of Carden, Esq.

THOMAS M. MIKEN CRAUFUIRD, ESQ.
GRANGE, CO. AYR.

JAMES KELLY, ESQ.
NEWTOWN HOUSE, CO. GALWAY.

JOHN MAUDE, ESQ
MOOR HOUSE, CO. YORK

GEORGE ASSER WHITE WELCH, ESQ.
ARLE HOUSE, CO. GLOUCESTER.

JOHN HURLESTON LECHE, ESQ
CARDEN PARK, CO. CHESTER.

PLATE XLIII.

Alston, of Neyland, co. Suffolk.

THE REV. GEORGE ALSTON, of Neyland, a descendant of the ancient Baronetical Family of Alston, whose Pedigree is traceable to the time of EDWARD I. bears the Arms of Alston impaled with the Coat of OXENDEN of Brome, in right of his wife, Anne Charlotte, third daughter of the late Sir Henry Oxenden, Bart. Sarah Alston, wife of John, fourth Duke of Somerset, was daughter and co-heir of Sir Edward Alston, of London, President of the College of Physicians.

> **Arms.**—Az. ten estoiles or, four, three, two, and one, for ALSTON; impaling, ar. a chev. gu. betw. three oxen sa. for OXENDEN.
>
> **Crest.**—A crescent ar. charged with an estoile or.
>
> **Motto.**—Immotus.

Rattray, of Barford House, co. Warwick.

JAMES RATTRAY, of Barford House, Esq. Captain R. N. a Magistrate for Warwickshire, son of David Rattray, M. D. by Dora, his wife, daughter of Richard Arnold, Esq. and great grandson of Sir Rullion Rattray, of Runy-gullion, co. Perth, Kt. descends from the very ancient Scottish Family of Rattray, and bears their Shield, impaled with that of VIVIAN, in right of his wife, EMILY, daughter of JOHN VIVIAN, of Claverton, co. Somerset, Esq.

> **Arms.**—Az. a fesse betw. six cross crosslets fitchée ar. impaling for VIVIAN, or on a chev. az. betw. three lions' heads erased ppr. as many annulets of the field, on a chief gu. three martlets ar.
>
> **Crest.**—A star ensigned by a flaming heart ppr.
>
> **Motto.**—Super sidera votum.

D'Arcy, of Hyde Park, co. Westmeath.

JOHN D'ARCY, of Hyde Park, Esq. Representative of the great Norman House of D'ARCY, bears the ancient Shield of the D'Arcys of Nocton, and Quarters BERTRAM, TUITE, NUGENT, JUDGE, and GRIERSON.

> **Arms.**—Quarterly :—
>
> I. Az. semée of cross-crosslets and three cinquefoils ar. for D'ARCY.
>
> II. Gu. an orle and eleven cross-crosslets or, for BERTRAM.

PLATE XLIII.

III. Quarterly, gu. and ar. for TUITE.

IV. Erm. two bars gu. for NUGENT.

V. Or a chev. vert for JUDGE.

VI. Ar. a fir tree growing out of the middle base vert, surmounted of a sword in bend az. hilt or, in the dexter and sinister chief an antique crown of the last, for GRIERSON.

Crest.—On a chapeau gu. turned up erm. a bull sa. armed or.

Supporters.—*Dexter*, a tiger ppr.; *Sinister*, a bull sa. armed or.

Motto.—Un Dieu, un Roy.

Norman D'Arcy, Lord of Nocton, co. Lincoln, *temp.* Conquestoris, living 1092.

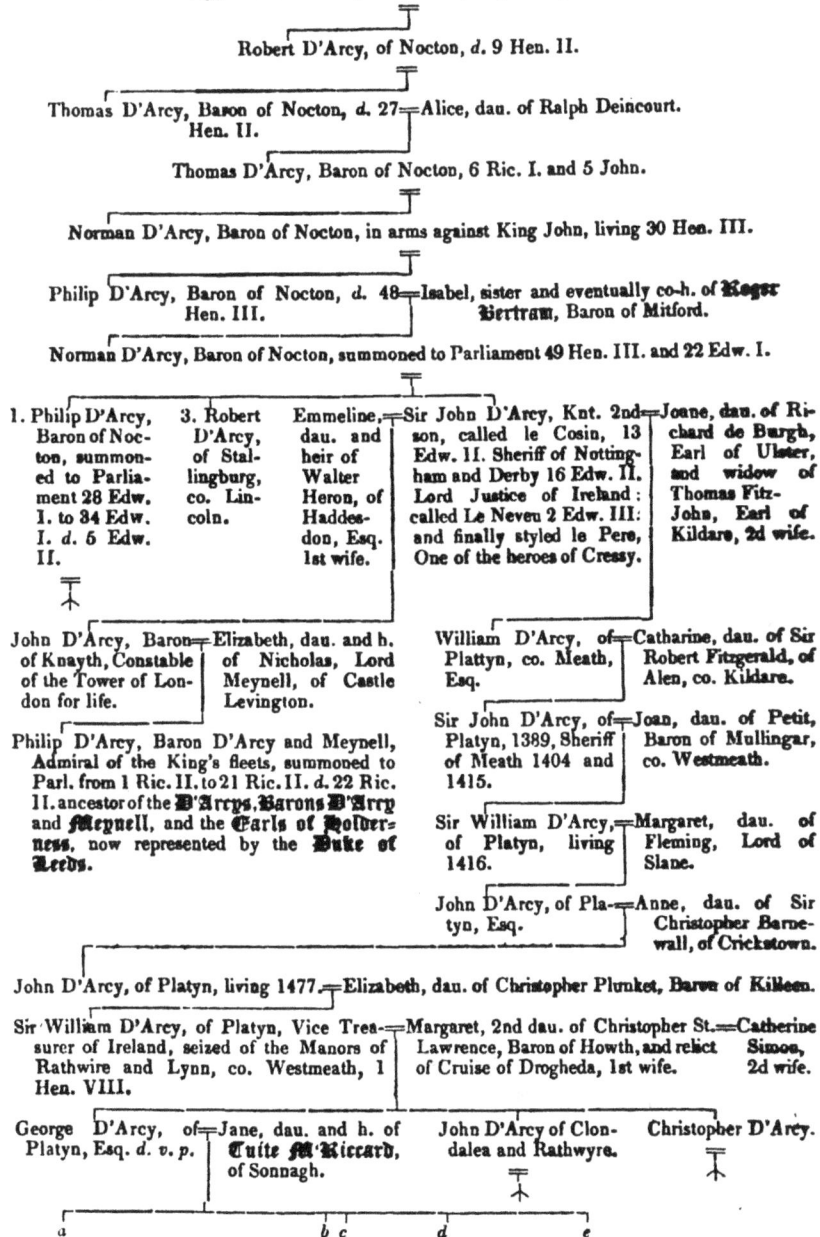

Robert D'Arcy, of Nocton, *d.* 9 Hen. II.

Thomas D'Arcy, Baron of Nocton, *d.* 27=Alice, dau. of Ralph Deincourt. Hen. II.

Thomas D'Arcy, Baron of Nocton, 6 Ric. I. and 5 John.

Norman D'Arcy, Baron of Nocton, in arms against King John, living 30 Hen. III.

Philip D'Arcy, Baron of Nocton, *d.* 48=Isabel, sister and eventually co-h. of Roger Hen. III. Bertram, Baron of Mitford.

Norman D'Arcy, Baron of Nocton, summoned to Parliament 49 Hen. III. and 22 Edw. I.

| 1. Philip D'Arcy, Baron of Nocton, summoned to Parliament 28 Edw. I. to 34 Edw. I. *d.* 6 Edw. II. | 3. Robert D'Arcy, of Stallingburg, co. Lincoln. | Emmeline, dau. and heir of Walter Heron, of Haddesdon, Esq. 1st wife. | Sir John D'Arcy, Knt. 2nd son, called le Cosin, 13 Edw. II. Sheriff of Nottingham and Derby 16 Edw. II. Lord Justice of Ireland: called Le Neveu 2 Edw. III: and finally styled le Pere, One of the heroes of Cressy. | Joane, dau. of Richard de Burgh, Earl of Ulster, and widow of Thomas Fitz-John, Earl of Kildare, 2d wife. |

John D'Arcy, Baron=Elizabeth, dau. and h. of Knayth, Constable of Nicholas, Lord of the Tower of London for life. Meynell, of Castle Levington.

Philip D'Arcy, Baron D'Arcy and Meynell, Admiral of the King's fleets, summoned to Parl. from 1 Ric. II. to 21 Ric. II. *d.* 22 Ric. II. ancestor of the D'Arcys, Barons D'Arcy and Meynell, and the Earls of Holderness, now represented by the Duke of Leeds.

William D'Arcy, of=Catharine, dau. of Sir Plattyn, co. Meath, Robert Fitzgerald, of Esq. Alen, co. Kildare.

Sir John D'Arcy, of=Joan, dau. of Petit, Plattyn, 1389, Sheriff Baron of Mullingar, of Meath 1404 and co. Westmeath. 1415.

Sir William D'Arcy,=Margaret, dau. of of Plattyn, living Fleming, Lord of 1416. Slane.

John D'Arcy, of Pla-=Anne, dau. of Sir tyn, Esq. Christopher Barnewall, of Crickstown.

John D'Arcy, of Platyn, living 1477.=Elizabeth, dau. of Christopher Plunket, Baron of Killeen.

Sir William D'Arcy, of Platyn, Vice Trea-=Margaret, 2nd dau. of Christopher St.=Catherine surer of Ireland, seized of the Manors of Lawrence, Baron of Howth, and relict Simon, Rathwire and Lynn, co. Westmeath, 1 of Cruise of Drogheda, 1st wife. 2d wife. Hen. VIII.

| George D'Arcy, of=Jane, dau. and h. of Platyn, Esq. *d. v. p.* Tuite M'Riccard, of Sonnagh. | John D'Arcy of Clondalea and Rathwyre. | Christopher D'Arcy. |

a   b   c   d   e

PLATE XLIII.

a   *b*   *c*   *d*   *e*

Sir William D'Arcy, of Platyn, Knt. will dated 18 Jan. 1545, ancestor of the **D'Arcys** of Platyn, co. Meath, now extinct. | Robert. Walter. | Edmund, of Martry, Balrish, Halton, and Stidalt. | Thomas D'Arcy, of = Margaret, Dunmow, Esq. next brother of Sir William D'Arcy, of Platyn, Knt. | dau. of Richard Kiltole, of Trim.

John D'Arcy, of Dunmow, Esq. *d.* 20 = Elizabeth, dau. of . . . . .
Sept. 1639.

William D'Arcy, of Dunmow, Esq. *d. v. p.* = Margaret, dau. of Brandon, and niece of Thomas Brandon, of Dundalk, *d.* 14 Car. II.

Thomas D'Arcy, of Dunmow, Esq. heir to = **Alicia**, dau. and heir of **Nugent** of New his grandfather. Haggard, co. Meath.

George D'Arcy, Esq. declared an innocent = Alicia, dau. of Thomas Nugent, of Clonpapist 20 Aug. 1663, *d.* 1718. lost, co. Westmeath.

Thomas D'Arcy, of Dunmow, Esq. only = Jane, dau. of Bellew of Bellewstown. son and heir.

John D'Arcy, Esq. *d.* at Dunmow, March = Elizabeth, dau. and co-h. of **Thomas** 1758. **Judge**, of Grangebegg, co. Westmeath, Esq.: will proved 1773.

Judge D'Arcy, of Dunmow and Grangebegg, Esq. = Eliza, dau. of Richard Nugent of Robinstown. | Francis, of Bath, *d. s. p.* in 1813. Arthur, *d. unm.* Thomas, *d. s. p.* Lavallen, *d. unm.* | James D'Arcy, of = Martha, dau. Hyde Park, co. Westmeath, Esq. *d.* about 1803. | and h. of **William Grierson**, of Deanstown, co. Dublin, Esq.

Eliza-Judge, only dau. and h. *m.* Gorges Marcus Irvine, of Castle Irvine, co. Fermanagh, Esq.

Emily, dau. = **John D'Arcy**, = Mary of Thomas of Hyde Park, Anne, Purdon, of co. West- dau. of Hunting- meath, Esq. Thomas don, co. Cary, West- Esq. meath, Esq. | Rev. Joshua D'Arcy, Rector of Killalon, co. Westmeath, *m.* 28 Aug. 1811, Sarah, dau. of Capt. Fleming, of Hermitage, co. Kildare, and sister of Robert Crowe Fleming, of Nutfield, co. Clare, Esq. | Thomas = Eliza, dau. Seve- D'Arcy, of Wm. ral Major in Buchan- daus. the Army, an, Esq. Inspector Gen. of Police Province of Ulster, *d.* 1836.

George-James Norman, eldest son and heir, *b.* in 1820. | John Samuel, of Bagatelle, co. Westmeath, eldest son, *m.* in 1834, Louisa, only dau. of William Handcock, of Carrintrilly, Esq. and has issue. | William-James, Barrister-at-law, eldest son.

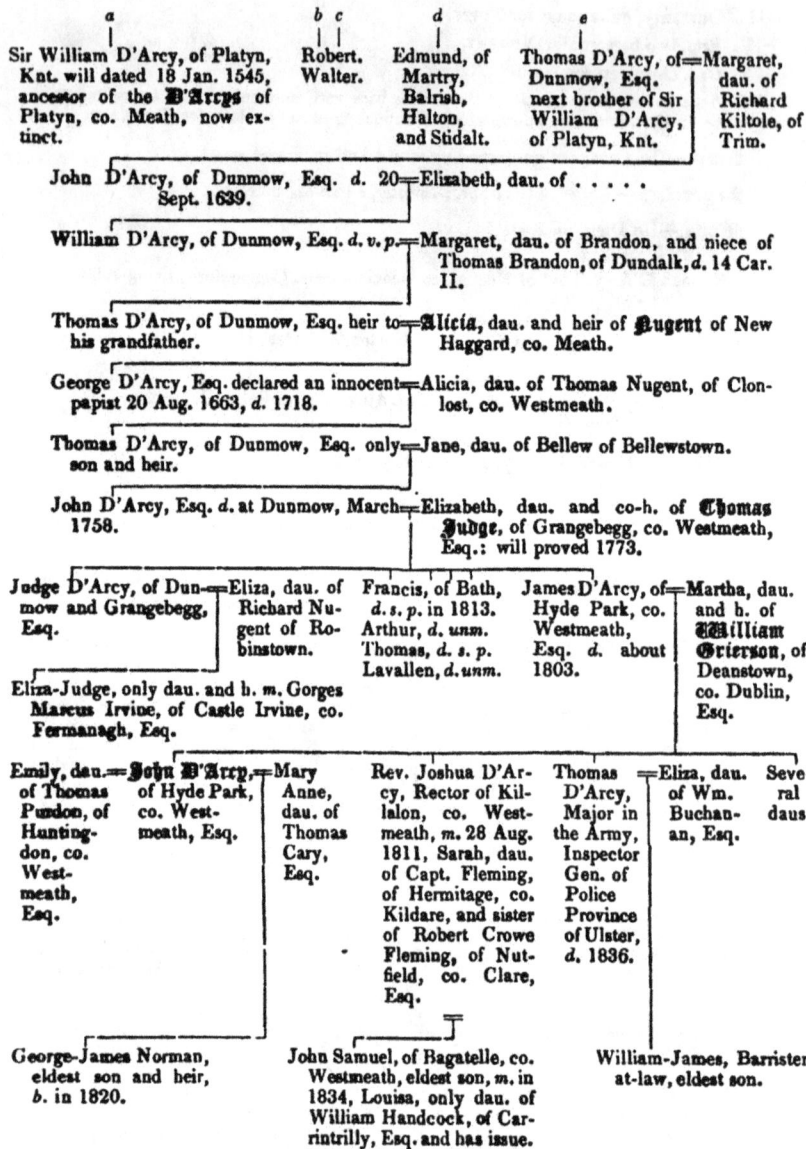

Galbraith, of Machrihanish and Drumore, co. Argyll.

David Steuart Galbraith, of Machrihanish and Drumore House, Esq. a Magistrate and Deputy Lieutenant for Argyllshire, descends from the Galbraiths of Grigha, derived, themselves, from a scion of Galbraith of Baldernock, one of the oldest Families in Scotland. (See Burke's *Dictionary of the Landed Gentry.*)

Arms.—Gu. a fesse chequy ar. and az. betw. three bears' heads erased of the second, muzzled of the third.

Crest.—A lion's head erased.

Motto.—Vigilo et spero.

PLATE XLIII.

Hayman, of Youghal.

THE Haymans of Youghal descend from a younger son of the Somersetshire branch of the ancient Baronetical family of Heyman, of Somerfield, co. Kent. The present Representative of the Irish branch is MATTHEW HAYMAN, of South Abbey, co. Cork, Esq. son and heir of the late Samuel Hayman, Esq. M.D. by Melian, his wife, second daughter and co-heiress of Matthew Jones, Esq. Collector of Youghal, and grandson of the Rev. Atkin Hayman, by his first wife, Elizabeth, daughter of Thomas Atkin, of Leadington, Esq. (See BURKE's *Landed Gentry.*) Mr. Hayman *married*, 1816, Helen, daughter of Arundel Hill, of Doneraile, Esq. and has issue surviving, viz. I. Samuel, in Holy Orders. II. Matthew Jones, an Ensign in the 18th Royal Irish. I. Melian. II. Helen. III. Elizabeth. IV. Maria Lucy Anne. V. Susan.

> **Arms.**—Ar. on a chev. engr. az. betw. three martlets sa. as many cinquefoils pierced or.
>
> **Crest.**—A demi Moor, full faced, wreathed about the temples, holding in the dexter hand, a rose slipped and leaved, all ppr.
>
> **Motto.**—Cœlum, non solum.

PLATE XLIII.

THE REV. GEORGE ALSTON,
NEYLAND, CO. SUFFOLK.

JAMES RATTRAY, ESQ. CAPT. R.N.
BARFORD HOUSE, CO. WARWICK.

JOHN D'ARCY, ESQ.
HYDE PARK CO. WESTMEATH.

DAVID STEUART GALBRAITH, ESQ.
MACHRIHANISH & DRUMORE HOUSE CO. ARGYLL.

MATTHEW HAYMAN, ESQ.
SOUTH ABBEY, YOUGHAL.

PLATE XLIV.

Giffard, of Chillington, co. Stafford.

THOMAS WILLIAM GIFFARD, of Chillington, Esq. Representative of the great House of Giffard, derived from WALTER GIFFARD, Count of Longueville, living in 1025, (see BURKE's *Landed Gentry*,) bears a Quartered Coat, first and fourth, CHILLINGTON; second and third, BUCKINGHAM.

Arms.—Quarterly, first and fourth, az. three stirrups with leathers or, two and one; second and third, gu. three lions pass. ar.

Crest.—A tiger's head couped, full faced, spotted, flames issuing from his mouth ppr. and a demi archer bearded and couped at the knees in armour ppr. from his middle a short coat paly ar. and gu. at his middle a quiver of arrows or, in his hands a bow and arrow drawn to the head or.

Motto.—Prenez halcine tirez fort.

Francklin, of Gonalston, co. Notts.

JOHN FRANCKLIN, of Gonalston, Esq. son and heir of the late Richard Francklin, of Great Barford, co. Bedford, Esq. by Judith Reddall, his wife, third daughter and co-heir of Sir Philip Monoux, of Sandy Place, Bart. and representative of the ancient Family of FRANCKLIN, (see BURKE's *Landed Gentry*), bears a Quartered Coat, first, FRANCKLIN; second, FOSTER; third, MONOUX; and fourth, WALSH.

Arms.—Quarterly, first, ar. on a bend engr. betw. two lions' heads erased gu. a dolphin embowed of the field betw. two birds close or, for FRANCKLIN; second, sa. on a chev. betw. three bugle horns or, as many pheons az. for FORSTER; third, ar. on a chev. sa. betw. three oak leaves vert as many bezants, for MONOUX; fourth, sa. a bend ar. betw. three columbines of the second, for WALSHE.

Crest.—A dolphin's head in pale or, erased gu. betw. two sprigs vert.

Motto.—Sinceritate.

Dickinson, of Farley Hill, co. Berks.

CATHERINE, widow of the late CHARLES DICKINSON, of Farley Hill, Esq. and daughter of the late THOMAS ALLINGHAM, of the city of London, Esq. by Mary, his wife, second daughter and co-heir of JOHN TAYLOR, of Furzeyhurst, in the Isle of Wight, Esq. which John Taylor was son of Richard Taylor, of Newport, M. D. by Grace, daughter and co-heir of JOHN CHEKE, of Newport, Esq. son of Edward Cheke, of Merston, Esq. bears the Arms of DICKINSON impaled with the quartered Coat of ALLINGHAM, TAYLOR, and CHEKE. The family of Cheke

PLATE XLIV.

descended from Richard Cheke, by the daughter of Lord Montacute, and about the time of Edward VI. and Queen Elizabeth was of great distinction. Sir John Cheke, Knt. was Tutor to the former Monarch, and his sister, Mary Cheke, was married to Lord Burleigh, the celebrated Lord Treasurer. The Chekes of Moston, from whom Mrs. Dickinson derives, were the senior line, and sprang from an uncle of Sir John Cheke.

Arms.—Or, a bend engr. betw. two lions ramp. gu. for Dickinson.

Impaling—Quarterly, first and fourth, bendy of eight or and ar. in base a lion ramp. az. in chief two chaplets vert. roses gu. for Allingham; second, per pale sa. and ar. in base a lion pass. and in chief three annulets, all counterchanged, for Taylor; third, ar. three crescents gu. for Cheke.

Gregory.

A. E. Gregory, Esq. formerly High Sheriff of Bedfordshire, descended from a younger son of the ancient Family of Gregory, of Ashfordsby, co. Leicester, now represented in the senior line by Arthur Francis Gregory, of Stivic Hall, co. Warwick. Esq. bears a Shield of Six Quarterings.

Arms.—Quarterly:—
I. Or two bars az. in chief a lion pass. of the last, for Gregory.
II. Sa. a lion ramp. ar. ducally crowned or, debruised by a bend gu. for Seagrave.
III. Erm. a fess paly of six or and gu. for Malyn.
IV. Sa. two lions pass. ar. crowned or, for Dymoke (Champion of England).
V. Az. three lions pass. guard. in pale ar. for Ludlow.
VI. Vairy az. and ar. a fess gu. fretty or, for Marmion.

Crest.—A demi bear ramp. sa. collared or.

Motto.—Vigilamur.

Jones, of Hartsheath, co. Flint.

William Jones, of Hartsheath, co. Flint, and Cefn Coch, co. Denbigh, Esq. High Sheriff of the latter shire in 1831, thrice M.P. for Denbigh, son of the late John Jones, of Cefn Coch, Esq. by Elizabeth, his wife, daughter and heir of Edward Wilson, of Liverpool. Esq. grandson of Maurice Jones, of Cefn Coch. Esq. by Catherine, his wife, daughter and heir of Peter Williams, of Ruin. Esq. and great grandson of Hugh Jones, of Dole, co. Merioneth, Esq. by his wife, the daughter and heir of Maurice Lewis, of Pant Glas, co. Denbigh, Esq. bears a Shield of Six Quarterings, and an Escutcheon of Pretence in right of his wife, Cecil. daughter of the late John Carstairs, of Warboys, co. Huntingdon, Esq. F.R.S.

Arms.—Quarterly, first and sixth, ar. three boars' heads erased sa.; second, vert a chev. betw. three wolves' heads ar.; third, per pale fesse sa. and ar. a lion ramp. counterchanged; fourth, gu. a fess betw. three boars' heads couped or; fifth, sa. a wolf salient ar. in chief three escutcheons of the last.

An Escutcheon of Pretence for Carstairs—Az. on a chev. ar. betw. three green covers slipped ppr. three roundels of the field.

Crest.—A wolf's head erased sa. langued gu. transfixed by an arrow.

Motto.—Heb nefol nerth nid rhyl saeth. In English, Without help from above, the arrow flies in vain.

PLATE XLVII.

THOMAS WILLIAM GIFFARD, ESQ.
CHILLINGTON, CO. STAFFORD.

JOHN FRANCKLIN ESQ
GONALSTON, CO NOTTS.

MRS DICKINSON
FARLEY HILL, BERKS.

A. E. GREGORY, ESQ.
FORMERLY HIGH SHERIFF OF BEDFORDSHIRE.

WILSON JONES, ESQ.
HARTSHEATH, CO. FLINT.

PLATE XLIV.

descended from Richard Cheke, by the daughter of Lord Montacute, and about the time of EDWARD VI. and QUEEN ELIZABETH was of great distinction. Sir JOHN CHEKE, Knt. was Tutor to the former Monarch, and his sister, MARY CHEKE, was married to LORD BURLEIGH, the celebrated Lord Treasurer. The Chekes of Moston, from whom Mrs. Dickinson derives, were the senior line, and sprang from an uncle of Sir JOHN CHEKE.

> **Arms.**—Or, a bend engr. betw. two lions ramp. gu. for DICKINSON.
> **Impaling**—Quarterly, first and fourth, bendy of eight or and ar. in base a lion ramp. az. in chief two chaplets vert, roses gu. for ALLINGHAM ; second, per pale sa. and ar. in base a lion pass. and in chief three annulets, all counterchanged, for TAYLOR ; third, ar. three crescents gu. for CHEKE.

Gregory.

A. E. GREGORY, Esq. formerly High Sheriff of Bedfordshire, descended from a younger son of the ancient Family of GREGORY, of Ashfordsby, co. Leicester, now represented in the senior line by ARTHUR FRANCIS GREGORY, of Stivic Hall, co. Warwick, Esq. bears a Shield of Six Quarterings.

> **Arms.**—Quarterly :—
> I. Or two bars az. in chief a lion pass. of the last, for GREGORY.
> II. Sa. a lion ramp. ar. ducally crowned or, debruised by a bend gu. for SEAGRAVE.
> III. Erm. a fess paly of six or and gu. for MALYN.
> IV. Sa. two lions pass. ar. crowned or, for DYMOKE (CHAMPION OF ENGLAND).
> V. Az. three lions pass. guard. in pale ar. for LUDLOW.
> VI. Vairy ar. and az. a fess gu. fretty or, for MARMION.
>
> **Crest.**—A demi boar ramp. sa. collared or.
> **Motto.**—Vigilanter.

Jones, of Hartsheath, co. Flint.

WILSON JONES, of Hartsheath, co. Flint, and Cefn Coch, co. Denbigh, Esq. High Sheriff of the latter shire in 1831, thrice M.P. for Denbigh, son of the late John Jones, of Cefn Coch, Esq. by Elizabeth, his wife, daughter and heir of EDWARD WILSON, of Liverpool, Esq. grandson of Maurice Jones, of Cefn Coch, Esq. by Catherine, his wife, daughter and heir of PETER WILLIAMS, of Bala, Esq. and great grandson of Hugh Jones, of Dole, co. Merioneth, Esq. by his wife, the daughter and heir of Maurice Lewis, of Pant Glas, co. Denbigh, Esq. bears a Shield of Six Quarterings, and an Escutcheon of Pretence in right of his wife, CECIL, daughter of the late JOHN CARSTAIRS, of Warboys, co. Huntingdon, Esq. F.R.S.

> **Arms.**—Quarterly, first and sixth, ar. three boars' heads erased sa.; second, vert a chev. betw. three wolves' heads ar.; third, per pale fesse sa. and ar. a lion ramp. counterchanged; fourth, gu. a fess betw. three boars' heads couped or; fifth, sa. a wolf saliant ar. in chief three estoiles of the last.
> An Escutcheon of Pretence for CARSTAIRS.—Az. on a chev. ar. betw. three green roses slipped ppr. three buckles of the field.
> **Crest.**—A boar's head erased sa. langued gu. transfixed by an arrow.
> **Motto.**—Heb nevol nerth nid sier saeth. *In English*, Without help from above, the arrow flies in vain.

THOMAS WILLIAM GIFFARD, ESQ.
CHILLINGTON, CO. STAFFORD.

JOHN FRANCKLIN, ESQ.
GONALSTON, CO. NOTTS.

MRS. DICKINSON.
FARLEY HILL, BERKS.

A. E. GREGORY, ESQ.
FORMERLY HIGH SHERIFF OF BEDFORDSHIRE.

WILSON JONES, ESQ.
HARTSHEATH, CO. FLINT.

PLATE XLV.

Corbet, of Moreton Corbet, and Acton Reynald,
co. Salop, Bart.

Sir Andrew Vincent Corbet, of Moreton Corbet and Acton Reynald, Bart. Representative of that most ancient and distinguished family, bears a Shield of twenty-five Quarterings.

Arms :—

    I. Or, a raven sa. for Corbet.

    II. Or, an escarbuncle sa. for Turett.

    III. Az. two lions pass. or, for Erdington.

    IV. Gu. a lion ramp. or, within an orle of cross crosslets of the second, for Hopton.

    V. Gu. a mermaid ppr. for Guros.

    VI. Vairè ar. and sa. a canton gu. for Erdington.

    VII. Az. six lions ramp. ar. three, two, and one, within a bordure engr. or, for Leybourne.

    VIII. Gu. two lions pass. ar. within a bordure engr. or, for Strange.

    IX. Per bend az. and gu. a bend betw. two crescents or, for Langbergh.

    X. Paly of six sa. and or: on a chief of the second two palets of the first: an inescutcheon barry of six erm. and gu. for Burley.

    XI. Barry of six or and az. a bend gu. for Penbruge.

    XII. Or, three roses gu. for Younge.

    XIII. Or, an eagle displ. vert, oppressed with a bend gobonated ar. and gu. for Sibton.

    XIV. Barry nebulée of six or and vert, for Hawburk.

    XV. Gu. semée of cross crosslets, three lucies haurient ar. for Lucy.

    XVI. Ar. three chev. sa. for Archdeacon.

    XVII. Gu. three roches naiant ar. for Roche.

    XVIII. Ar. three bends sa. for Haccombe.

    XIX. Gu. a lion ramp. or, oppressed by a bend az. all within a bordure engr. of the second, for Talbot.

    XX. Barry of six ar. and vert, eighteen fleurs-de-lis, three, three, three, three, three, and three, counterchanged, for Mortimer.

    XXI. Gu. two bars vair, for Say.

    XXII. Gu. ten bezants, four, three, two, and one, a label az. for Zouch.

    XXIII. Gu. a saltire or, surmounted of a cross engr. erm. for Prince.

    XXIV. Ar. on a bend az. betw. two cornish choughs sa. three garbs or, for Wickstead.

    XXV. Or, a raven sa. for Corbet.

Crests.—First, an elephant ar. armed or, on his back a castle triple-towered of the last, trappings or and sa. Second, a squirrel sejant or.

Mottoes.—Under the Arms, Deus pascit corvos. Above the first Crest, Virtutis laus actio. Above the second, Dum spiro spero.

PLATE XLV.

Sir Richard Corbet, Knt. son of Roger=Joan, dau. and heir of Bartholomew
Corbet of Wattlesborough, co. Salop.   Curett, of Moreton, co. Salop.
From whom derived

Sir Roger Corbet, of Moreton Corbet, co.=Margaret de Erdington, beiress of Shaw-
Salop, Knt. living *temp.* Edward III.   bury, co. Salop.

Robert Corbet, of Moreton Corbet, Esq.=Margaret, dau. of Sir William Mallory,
High Sheriff of Shropshire in 1419.   Knt.

Sir Roger Corbet, of Moreton Corbet, Knt.=Elizabeth, dau. and sole heir of Thomas
son and heir.   Hopton, of Hopton Castle, co. Salop, Esq.
  [which marriage brought into the Corbet
From whom derived   family nineteen quarterings.]

Andrew Corbet, of Moreton Corbet, Esq.=Frances, dau. and heir of William
d. in 1757.   Prince, of Shawbury, Esq.

Richard Prince Corbet, Esq. *d.* 30 Jan.=Mary, dau. and heir of John Birk-
1779.   stead, of Wem, co. Salop, Esq.

Sir Andrew Corbet, of Moreton Corbet,=Mary, eldest dau. of Thomas Taylor, of
created a BARONET in 1808: *d.* 5 June   Lymme Hall, co. Chester, Esq.
1835.

Sir Andrew Vincent Corbet, of Moreton Corbet and Acton Reynald, Bart.: *b.* in 1800, *m.* 19 Sept. 1820.	=Rachel-Stephens, sister of Rowland Viscount Hill.	Richard Corbet, of Adderley Hall, co. Salop, Esq. *b.* in 1804: *m.* in 1830, Eleanor, youngest dau. of the Rev. C. Johnson.	Robert Corbet, *d. unm.* in 1829. Judith, *d. unm.* in 1829.	Vincent Roger Corbet, *m.* 1 May 1838, Maria, dau. of — Humberston, of Chester, Esq.

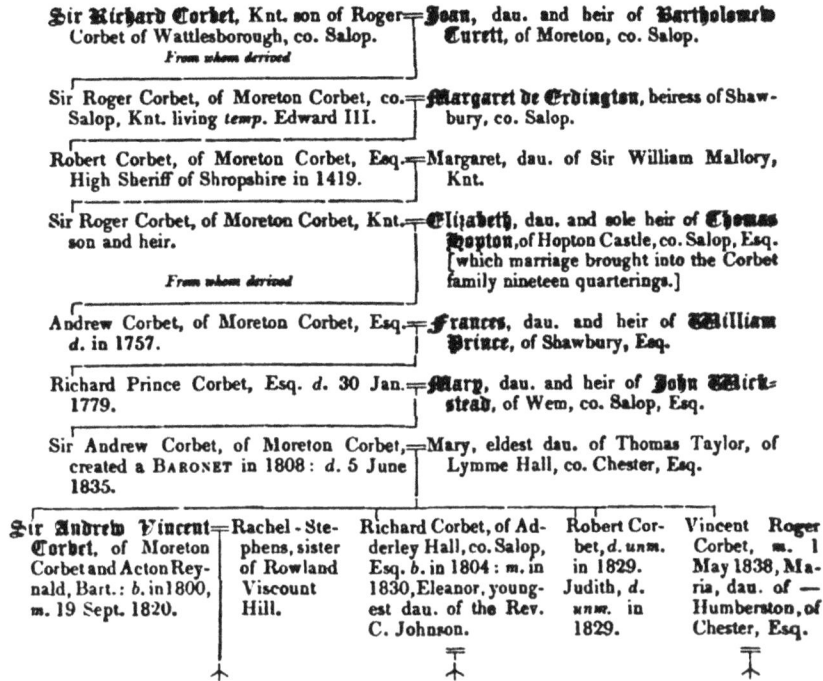

Colston, of Roundway Park, co. Wilts.

EDWARD FRANCIS COLSTON, of Roundway Park, Esq. son and heir of the late Edward Francis Colston, of Filkins Hall, co. Oxford, Esq. by Arabella, his wife, daughter of Michael Clayfield, of Bristol, Esq. and grandson of the Rev. Alexander Colston, Vicar of Broadwell and Henbury, who was great-grandnephew of the ever memorable philanthropist, EDWARD COLSTON, of Bristol, bears a Shield of four Quarterings: first and fourth, COLSTON; second, EDWARDS; and third, HAYMAN.

   Arms.—Quarterly, first and fourth, ar. betw. two dolphins haurient respecting each other an anchor, all ppr. for COLSTON. Second, per bend sinister erm. and ermines, over all a lion ramp. or, for EDWARDS. Third, ar. on a chev. engr. az. betw. three martlets sa. as many cinquefoils or, for HAYMAN. On an Escutcheon of Pretence or, a lion ramp. reguard. sa. for JENKINS.

   Crest.—A dolphin embowed ppr.

   Motto.—Go and do thou likewise.

Mary Colston, dau. of William Colston,=Sir William Hayman, Knt. Mayor of
Sheriff of Bristol, and sister of Edward   Bristol.
Colston the philanthropist.

   Mary Hayman.=Thomas Edwards, of Filkins Hall, co. Oxford, Esq.

Sophia Edwards.=Alexander Ready, of the Inner Temple, Esq. who assumed the surname of Colston.

The Rev. Alexander Colston, Vicar of=Louisa Minshull, dau. of Paul George Elers,
Broadwell and Henbury, 1744.   of Black Bourton, co. Wilts, Esq.

Edward Francis Colston, of Filkins Hall,=Arabella, dau. of Michael Clayfield, of
co. Oxford, Esq. Lieut.-Col. in the army.   Bristol, Esq.: she *d.* 24 Feb. 1812.

Edward Francis Colston, of Roundway=Marianne, only child of William Jenkins,
Park, co. Wilts, Esq.   Esq.

PLATE XLV.

Rodick, of Gateacre.

THOMAS RODICK, of Gateacre, co. Lancaster, and Woodclose, co. Westmoreland, Esq. one of her Majesty's Justices of the Peace for the former county, bears for

Arms.—Gu. a chev. party per pale wavy ar. and or, betw. two roses in chief and one in base of the second, all barbed and seeded vert, a crescent for difference.

Crest.—In her nest ar. a pelican and young sa. winged or, vulning herself gu. charged on the breast with a crescent as in the arms.

Motto.—Omnia vincit amor.

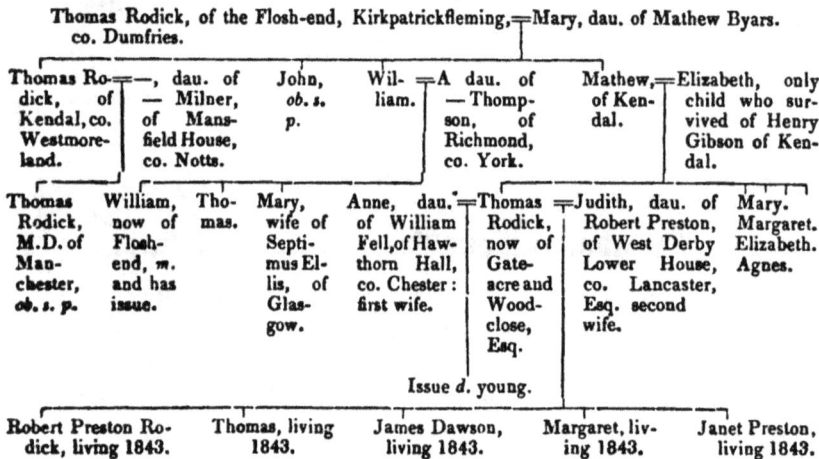

Thomas Rodick, of the Flosh-end, Kirkpatrickfleming, co. Dumfries. = Mary, dau. of Mathew Byars.

Thomas Rodick, of Kendal, co. Westmoreland. = —, dau. of — Milner, of Mansfield House, co. Notts.	John, ob. s. p.	William. = A dau. of — Thompson, of Richmond, co. York.	Mathew, of Kendal. = Elizabeth, only child who survived of Henry Gibson of Kendal.

Thomas Rodick, M.D. of Manchester, ob. s. p.	William, now of Flosh-end, m. and has issue.	Thomas.	Mary, wife of Septimus Ellis, of Glasgow.	Anne, dau. of William Fell, of Hawthorn Hall, co. Chester: first wife. = Thomas Rodick, now of Gateacre and Woodclose, Esq. = Judith, dau. of Robert Preston, of West Derby Lower House, co. Lancaster, Esq. second wife.	Mary. Margaret. Elizabeth. Agnes.

Issue d. young.

Robert Preston Rodick, living 1843.	Thomas, living 1843.	James Dawson, living 1843.	Margaret, living 1843.	Janet Preston, living 1843.

SIR ANDREW VINCENT CORBET, BART.

MORETON CORBET AND ACTON REYNALD, CO SALOP

EDWARD FRANCIS COLSTON, ESQ.

ROUNDWAY PARK, CO WILTS

THOMAS RODICK, ESQ

GATEACRE, CO. LANCASTER

PLATE XLVI.

Parbury, of London.

GEORGE PARBURY, of Mansfield House, Russell Square, Esq. M.R.A.S. (eldest son of the late Charles Parbury, of London, Esq. and grandson of George Parbury, Esq. by Mary, his wife, daughter of Edward Pollen, of New Inn, Esq. son of Edward Pollen, elder brother of John Pollen, Esq. M.P. the father of the 1st Sir John Pollen, Bart.) bears the paternal Arms of Parbury, with the Ensigns of the family of ELLIS, on an Escutcheon of Pretence, in right of his wife, Mary-Anne-Joanna, only child of Edward Ellis, of the Priory, Hertford, Esq. several times Mayor of that town.

Arms.—Or, on a bend engr. cotised, also engr. az. betw. six torteaux, five escallops ar. on an Escutcheon of Pretence for ELLIS, or, on a cross sa. five crescents ar.

Crest.—Two branches of laurel in saltire ppr. surmounted by a pelican or, semée of torteaux, in her nest ppr. feeding her young gold.

Motto.—Cras mihi.

Gay, of Thurning Hall, co. Norfolk.

JAMES GAY, of Thurning Hall, Esq. who formerly filled the appointments of Under Secretary to the Government of Ceylon, and Second Commissioner for the Affairs of the Kandyan Provinces, is younger son of the late John Gay, of Alborough, Esq. by Frances, his wife, daughter of Richard Johnson, of Clay-next-the-sea, Merchant, and bears the Ensigns which his ancestors, settled at Thurgarton and Alborough since the time of ELIZABETH, have used for a long series of generations. (See BURKE's *Dictionary of the Landed Gentry*.)

Arms.—Ar. on a fess, per pale or and gu. betw. three mullets of the third, a demi lion ramp. betw. two fleurs-de-lis counterchanged.

Crest.—A fleur-de-lis or.

Motto.—Toujours gai.

PLATE XLVI.

O'Kelly.

EDMUND DE PENTHENY O'KELLY, Esq. *b.* 5 Feb. 1800, *m.* 16 July 1822, Blanche Arundell, a Countess of the German empire, second daughter of the Hon. Raymond Arundell, brother of James-Everard, 9th Lord Arundel of Wardour, and has issue, I. Augustus, *b.* 3 March 1825. II. Arundell Clan-Eugene, *b.* 27 Jan. 1828. III. Pentheny, *b.* 25 Dec. 1831. IV. Raymond, *b.* 13 Jan. 1834. I. Blanche. II. Emily. For a history of the O'KELLY Family, *see* BURKE's *Landed Gentry.*

Arms.—Quarterly, first and fourth, for O'KELLY. Second and third, for DE PENTHENY, sa. a chev. erm. betw. three pheons, ar. on a bordure of the last, engr. thirteen roundlets az.

Crests.—First, for O'KELLY. Second, for DE PENTHENY, on a wreath of the colours sa. and ar. an oak tree ppr. fructed or.

Mottoes.—First, for O'KELLY. Second, for DE PENTHENY, Malo mori quam fœdari.

Peter de Repentenye, A.D. 1252, was the first of the family that appears to have settled in Ireland. The name is from Pentney, near Lynne in Norfolk, and was introduced into England by Robert de Repentheny, styled "de vallibus," founder of the Priory of Pentney, *temp.* William the Conqueror, A.D. 1066, et seq. (See DUGDALE's *Monasticon.*)

Raymond le Repenthenye, A.D. 1266, Kinsman of Peter.

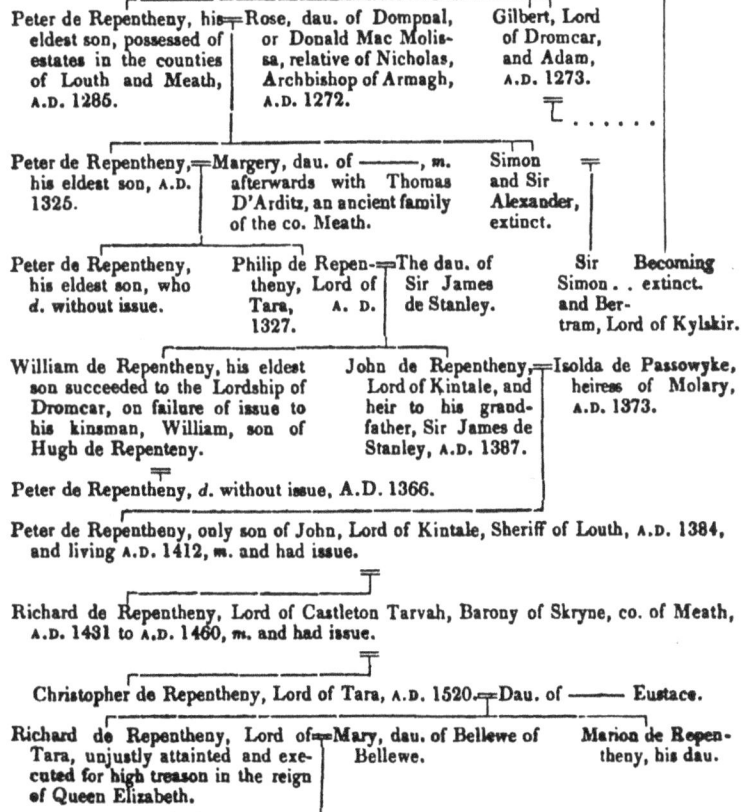

Peter de Repentheny, his eldest son, possessed of estates in the counties of Louth and Meath, A.D. 1285.==Rose, dau. of Dompnal, or Donald Mac Molissa, relative of Nicholas, Archbishop of Armagh, A.D. 1272.

Gilbert, Lord of Dromcar, and Adam, A.D. 1273.

Peter de Repentheny, his eldest son, A.D. 1325.==Margery, dau. of ———, *m.* afterwards with Thomas D'Arditz, an ancient family of the co. Meath.

Simon and Sir Alexander, extinct.

Peter de Repentheny, his eldest son, who d. without issue.

Philip de Repentheny, Lord of Tara, A.D. 1327.==The dau. of Sir James de Stanley.

Sir Simon . . and Bertram, Lord of Kylskir.

Becoming . . extinct.

William de Repentheny, his eldest son succeeded to the Lordship of Dromcar, on failure of issue to his kinsman, William, son of Hugh de Repenteny.

John de Repentheny, Lord of Kintale, and heir to his grandfather, Sir James de Stanley, A.D. 1387.==Isolda de Passowyke, heiress of Molary, A.D. 1373.

Peter de Repentheny, d. without issue, A.D. 1366.

Peter de Repentheny, only son of John, Lord of Kintale, Sheriff of Louth, A.D. 1384, and living A.D. 1412, *m.* and had issue.

Richard de Repentheny, Lord of Castleton Tarvah, Barony of Skryne, co. of Meath, A.D. 1431 to A.D. 1460, *m.* and had issue.

Christopher de Repentheny, Lord of Tara, A.D. 1520.==Dau. of ——— Eustace.

Richard de Repentheny, Lord of Tara, unjustly attainted and executed for high treason in the reign of Queen Elizabeth.==Mary, dau. of Bellewe of Bellewe.

Marion de Repentheny, his dau.

a

PLATE XLVI.

a

Edward de Repentheny, restored by King James I. to his = Catherine, dau. of Michael Barnwall, Esq. of Athronan, co. Meath.
father's estates, who was declared to have been wrongfully attainted.

| Mathew, forfeited his estates in the Great Rebellion of 1641, which were granted to James, Duke of York. | = Elinor, dau. of Christopher Cruise, Esq. of the Naul. | 2. Gilbert, who *d.* young, *s. p.* | 3. Francis de Pentheny, chief of his name, A. D. 1641. | = Elizabeth, dau. of Luke de Bathe, of Waterside, co. Meath. Esq. | James, 4th son, and five daughters. Mary. Elinor. Elizabeth. Margaretta. Margery. |

Issue extinct.

Luke de Pentheny, = Margaretta, dau. his only son. of Ashe of Ashfield, co. Meath.

Catherine, *m.* to Plunkett, of Tullo, co. Kildare.

Luke, who *d.* young, *s. p.*

II. Christopher de Pentheny, who = Elizabeth, dau. of James Gaynor, *d.* A.D. 1768, great-grandfather of Black-Castell, co. Meath, of the present representative. Esq.

| John, *d.* at his residence at Kill, co. Meath. | = Mary, dau. of Michael Dease, of Tourbotstown, Esq. | II. Peter de Pentheny, chief of his name, grandfather of the present representative. | = Mary, relict of Charles O'Mally, of Castle-Mally, Esq. | III. James. IV. Augustine. V. Mary. VI. Elinor. |

| Peter. Michael. James. Elizabeth. Catherine. extinct. | Elizabeth, *d.* young. | II. Maria de Pentheny, heiress of the above, *m.* to George - Bourke - Kelly O'Kelly. (See BURKE's *Landed Gentry.*) | III. Elinor, co-heiress with her sister Maria, relict of William Bourke, of Springfield St. Croix, Esq. *s. p. v.* |

Edmund de Pentheny, their eldest son, is the present representative of this family, A.D. 1843.

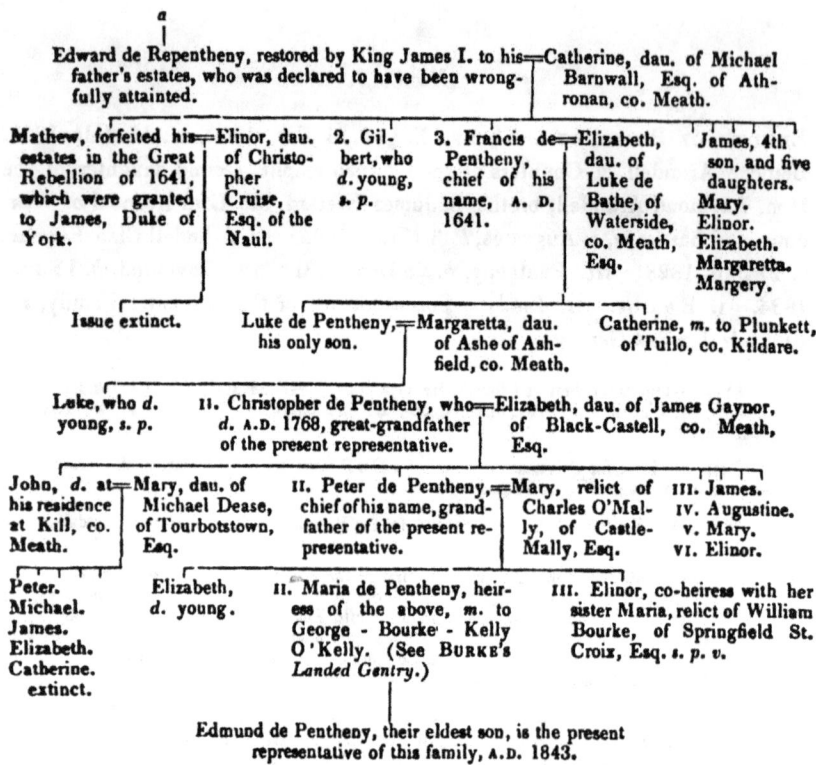

Johnson, of Runcorn, co. Chester.

JOHN JOHNSON, of Runcorn, co. Chester, Esq. (See BURKE's *General Armory*) bears for

Arms.—Or, a saltire vair betw. two cocks' heads erased in pale sa. combed and wattled gu. and two pheons in fesse of the third.

Crest.—On a wreath of the colours a crescent or, issuant therefrom a pheon, the whole betw. two wings sa.

Motto.—Servabo fidem.

Wilder, of Purley Hall, and Sulham, co. Berks.

THE Wilders has been seated in Berkshire since the time of HENRY VII. (See BURKE's *Landed Gentry*) and have intermarried with heiresses of the families of SAUNDERS and BOYLE, through which they Quarter the Ensigns of SAUNDERS, BOYLE, GARTH, BEAUFOY, and HUGFORD.

PLATE XLVI.

Arms.—Quarterly, first, gu. from a fesse or, charged with two barrulets az. a demi lion ramp. issuant of the second for WILDER. Second, per. chev. sa. and ar. three elephants' head erased, counterchanged for SAUNDERS. Third, per bend crenellée ar. and gu. for BOYLE. Fourth, or, two lions pass. betw. three cross crosslets fitchée sa. for GARTH. Fifth, erm. on a bend az. three cinquefoils ar. for BEAUFOY. Sixth, vert on a chev. betw. three stags' heads caboshed or, three mullets gu. for HUGFORD.

Crest.—A savage's head affrontée, couped at the shoulders, the temples entwined with woodbines, all ppr.

Motto.—Virtuti mœnia cedunt.

Henry Wilder, Esq. of Nunhide, co. Berks ; buried at Sulham, 10 June, 1755.	Elizabeth, younger dau. and co-heir of Thomas Saunders, Esq. of Purley, co. Berks ; she d. in 1741.

John Wilder, of Nunhide, Esq. Magistrate and Deputy Lieutenant of Berkshire ; buried at Sulham, 13 July, 1772.	Beaufoy, eldest dau. and co-heir of Colonel William Boyle, (brother of Henry, Earl of Shannon), by Martha Beaufoy, his wife, dau. and heir of Sir Samuel Garth, Knt. by Martha, his wife, dau. and heir of Beaufoy of Edmundscote.

The Rev. Henry Wilder, LL.D. of Parley Hall, Berks, Rector of Sulham, b. in Sept. 1744, d. 22 Jan. 1814.	Joan, dau. of William Thoyts, of Sulhamstead, Esq. ; she d. aged 89, in 1837.

John Wilder, of Purley Hall, Esq. eldest son and heir, bapt. at Sulham in 1769, d. 22 Feb. 1834.	Harriet, dau. of the Rev. Edwards Beadon, Rector of North Stoneham, co. Hants ; she d. 4 Oct. 1825, aged 52.

The Rev. Henry Watson Wilder, of Parley Hall, Rector of Sulham, b. 3 Nov. 1798 : m. in 1829, Augusta, sister of Sir Charles-Joshua Smith, of Suttons, Bart. and was drowned together with his wife, 2 July, 1836.	II. John, late Fellow of Eton College, and now Rector of Sulham, b. 9 July, 1801.	Mary, dau. of the Ven. Gilbert Heathcote, Archdeacon of Winchester, m. 26 July, 1831.	III. Charles, Fellow of King's College, Cambridge, d. in 1838, aged 30.	IV. Frederick, d. in infancy.	I. Jane. II. Harriet, d. young in 1823.

Frederick, of Purley Hall, b. 2 July, 1832.   Henry Beaufoy, b. 25 Oct. 1834.

PLATE LVI.

GEORGE PARBURY, ESQ.

MANSFIELD HOUSE, RUSSELL SQUARE.

JAMES GAY, ESQ.

THURNING HALL, CO. NORFOLK.

DE PENTHENY O'KELLY.   O'KELLY.   ARUNDELL DE WARDOUR.

JOHN JOHNSON, ESQ.

RUNCORN, CO. CHESTER.

WILDER OF PURLEY HALL AND SULHAM,

CO. BERKS.

PLATE XLVII.

___

Lecky, of Castle Lecky, co. Londonderry, and Ballyholland House, co. Down.

THE family of Lecky came originally from Stirlingshire in Scotland, and settled in the counties of Derry and Carlow: the former branch is now represented by HOLLAND LECKY, of Castle Lecky, and Ballyholland House, Esq. only son of the late Averell Lecky, Esq. Capt. 14th Light Dragoons, by Jane, his wife, daughter of the late Hyacinth Daly, of Killimur Castle, co. Galway, Esq. and the latter by John James Lecky, of Ballykealy, co. Carlow, Esq. (See BURKE's *Dictionary of the Landed Gentry.*)

Arms.—Az. a chev. betw. three mullets or.
Crest.—A wild boar's head erased ppr.
Motto.—Semper paratus.

Tatton, of Withenshaw, co. Chester.

THOMAS WILLIAM TATTON, of Withenshaw, Esq. son of the late Thomas William Egerton, Esq. who assumed the surname and arms of TATTON, on inheriting the Withenshaw Estate, bears the Tatton Arms impaled with the quartered Coat of PARKER and TOWNLEY, in right of his wife, a daughter of Robert Townley Parker, of Cuerden, Esq. The family of Tatton is of great antiquity, and was in early times of Tatton, in Cheshire.

Arms.—Quarterly, ar. and gu. four crescents counterchanged, impaling, first and fourth, gu. a chev. betw. three leopards' heads or, in the mouth of each an arrow fesse-ways, ar. Second and third, ar. a fesse sa. charged with a mullet of the first, in chief three mullets of the second, for TOWNLEY.
Crest.—A greyhound sejant ar. collared and tied to a tree ppr.
Motto.—Crescent.

Robertson, of Inshes, co. Inverness.

ARTHUR JOHN ROBERTSON, of Inshes, Esq. Representative of the second branch of the great house of STROWAN, unquestionably one of the oldest and most distinguished in Scotland, descends from and is connected with many of the first Scottish Nobles, the SINCLAIRS of Rattar, Earls of Caithness, the MACKENZIES, Lords Kintail, the BALFOURS, Lords Burleigh, the MURRAYS of Philiphaugh, the DOUGLAS's of Cavers, the PATTERSONS of Inshes, the ELPHINSTONES, Lords Balmerino, &c. &c.

Inshes quarters PATTERSON, SINCLAIR, and MACKENZIE.

PLATE XLVII.

Arms.—Gu. three wolves' heads erased ar. armed and langued az. within a bordure of the last.

Crest.—A swan ppr. This was the original Crest of the descendants of DUNCAN I. King of Scotland, and is still borne by the present ROBERTSON of Inshes, who sprang from the Strowan family previous to the acquisition, by that house, of the Crest of " the imperial crown held up by a dexter hand," which was awarded for the services rendered after the King's murder, by Robert, the 4th Baron of Strowan.

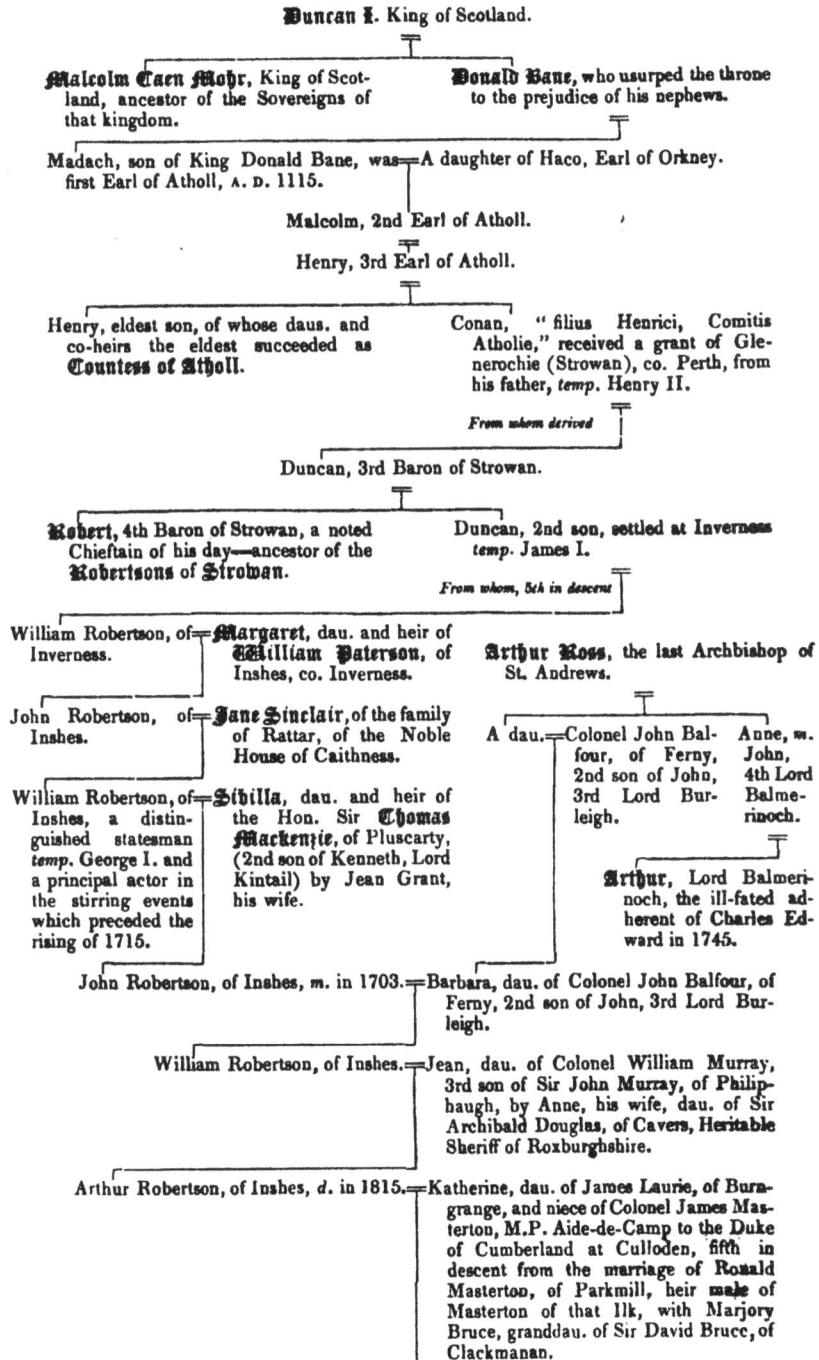

Duncan I. King of Scotland.

Malcolm Caen Mohr, King of Scotland, ancestor of the Sovereigns of that kingdom.

Donald Bane, who usurped the throne to the prejudice of his nephews.

Madach, son of King Donald Bane, was first Earl of Atholl, A. D. 1115. ═ A daughter of Haco, Earl of Orkney.

Malcolm, 2nd Earl of Atholl.

Henry, 3rd Earl of Atholl.

Henry, eldest son, of whose daus. and co-heirs the eldest succeeded as **Countess of Atholl**.

Conan, " filius Henrici, Comitis Atholie," received a grant of Glenerochie (Strowan), co. Perth, from his father, *temp.* Henry II.

From whom derived

Duncan, 3rd Baron of Strowan.

Robert, 4th Baron of Strowan, a noted Chieftain of his day—ancestor of the **Robertsons of Strowan**.

Duncan, 2nd son, settled at Inverness *temp.* James I.

From whom, 5th in descent

William Robertson, of Inverness. ═ **Margaret**, dau. and heir of **William Paterson**, of Inshes, co. Inverness.

Arthur Ross, the last Archbishop of St. Andrews.

John Robertson, of Inshes. ═ **Jane Sinclair**, of the family of Rattar, of the Noble House of Caithness.

A dau. ═ Colonel John Balfour, of Ferny, 2nd son of John, 3rd Lord Burleigh.

Anne, m. John, 4th Lord Balmerinoch.

William Robertson, of Inshes, a distinguished statesman *temp.* George I. and a principal actor in the stirring events which preceded the rising of 1715. ═ **Sibilla**, dau. and heir of the Hon. Sir **Thomas Mackenzie**, of Pluscarty, (2nd son of Kenneth, Lord Kintail) by Jean Grant, his wife.

Arthur, Lord Balmerinoch, the ill-fated adherent of Charles Edward in 1745.

John Robertson, of Inshes, m. in 1703. ═ Barbara, dau. of Colonel John Balfour, of Ferny, 2nd son of John, 3rd Lord Burleigh.

William Robertson, of Inshes. ═ Jean, dau. of Colonel William Murray, 3rd son of Sir John Murray, of Philiphaugh, by Anne, his wife, dau. of Sir Archibald Douglas, of Cavers, Heritable Sheriff of Roxburghshire.

Arthur Robertson, of Inshes, *d.* in 1815. ═ Katherine, dau. of James Laurie, of Burngrange, and niece of Colonel James Masterton, M.P. Aide-de-Camp to the Duke of Cumberland at Culloden, fifth in descent from the marriage of Ronald Masterton, of Parkmill, heir male of Masterton of that Ilk, with Marjory Bruce, granddau. of Sir David Bruce, of Clackmanan.

PLATE XLVII.

a

| Masterton Robertson, of Inshes, *d.* in 1822. | = | Mary Sherer, of an ancient Stirlingshire family. |

| Arthur John Robertson, now of Inshes, Esq. *m.* 1st in 1824, and 2ndly in 1840. | = 1st wife, Marianne, only child of Richard Patison, of Petite Cote, Canada, Esq. by Julia Shobert, his wife, only child of Deputy Governor Shobert, Upper Canada, *d.* 16 Sept. 1836. | = 2nd wife, Charlotte-Maria-Bearda, dau. of T. B. Batard, of Sydenham, co. Kent, Esq. *m.* 18 Sept. 1840, *d.* 10 February 1842. |

| Arthur-Masterton, younger, of Inshes, *b.* 9 Jan. 1826. | Thomas Gilzean. *b.* in 1827. | Julia Isabella. Ellen Rose. | Charlotte-Caroline-Bearda. |

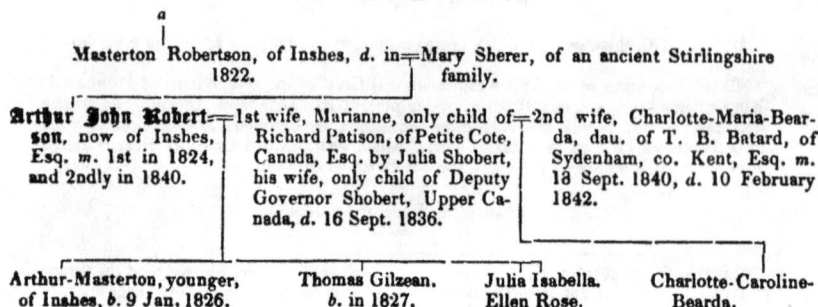

Power, of Edermine, co. Wexford.

JAMES POWER, of Edermine, M.P. for the County of Wexford, Esq. son and heir of Sir JOHN POWER, of Roebuck House, co. Dublin, Bart. bears, in addition to his paternal Arms, the Ensigns of TALBOT, on an Escutcheon of Pretence, in right of his wife, Jane, daughter and coheir of JOHN HYACINTH TALBOT, of Talbot Hall, Esq.

Arms.—Per saltire or and ar. three lions ramp. az. armed and langued gu. in the centre chief section an open helmet affronté, unbarred ppr. on a chev. gu. three escallops ar. on an Escutcheon of Pretence : gu. a lion ramp. within a bordure engr. or.

Crest.—A buck's head cabossed quarterly gu. and or, betw. the horns counterchanged a cross Calvary-erect gu.

Motto.—Per crucem ad Coronam.

Reay, of Gill, co. Cumberland.

JOHN REAY, of Gill House, parish of Bromfield, co. Cumberland, Esq. is representative of the very ancient family of REAY, which is stated by tradition to have had a grant of the lands of Gill, then very extensive, from WILLIAM the Lion, King of Scotland, in the 12th Century. The tradition records that the Chief of the house received this favour in recompense for his fidelity to the Monarch, and his extraordinary swiftness of foot in pursuing the buck, and that the conditions of the grant were, that he and his descendants should pay a peppercorn annually, and that the name of William, after their Royal Patron, should, if possible, be preserved in the family, which, with the exception of the existing representative, and his immediate predecessor, has ever been the case. The present JOHN REAY, Esq. inherited Gill House, at the decease of his grandfather, the late JOHN REAY, of Gill, Esq. (See BURKE's *Landed Gentry*.)

Arms.—Ar. three bucks courant gu.

Crest.—A buck, statant, guard. gu.

Motto.—In omnia promptus.

PLATE LXXV.

HOLLAND LECKY, ESQ

BALLY HOLLAND, HOUSE, CO. DOWN.

AND CASTLE LECKY, CO. LONDONDERRY.

THOMAS WILLIAM TATTON, ESQ

WITHENSHAW, CO. CHESTER.

Robertson.

Paterson.

Sinclair.

Mackenzie.

ARTHUR JOHN ROBERTSON, ESQ.

INSHES, CO. INVERNESS.

JAMES POWER, ESQ. M.P.

EDERMINE, CO. WEXFORD

JOHN REAY, ESQ

GILL HOUSE, CO. CUMBERLAND.

PLATE XLVIII.

Welles, of the Grange, West Moulsey, co. Surrey.

EDWARD LIONEL WELLES, of the Grange, Esq. youngest son of the late
Dymoke Welles, of Grebby Hall, co. Lincoln, Esq. by Anne, his wife, daughter
and coheir (with her sister Elizabeth, wife of Thomas Massingberd, of Candlesby
House, Esq.) of Thomas Waterhouse, of Beckingham Hall, Esq. High Sheriff of
Nottinghamshire in 1787, and great-grandson of the Rev. Thomas Welles,
Rector of Willingham, by Elizabeth, his wife, only daughter and eventual heir of
ROBERT DYMOKE, of Grebby Hall, Esq. grandson of Sir Edward Dymoke, of
Scrivelsby, Knt. Champion at the Coronation of CHARLES II., bears a Shield of
Sixteen Quarterings, and Impales, in right of his wife Mary-Ann, daughter of
John Galliers, of Stapleton Castle, co. Hereford, Esq. the Quartered Coat of
GALLIERS and VAUGHAN.

Arms—Quarterly—I. Or, a lion ramp. sa. for WELLES. II. Sa. two lions pass. ar.
crowned or, for DYMOKE. III. Az. three lions pass. reguard. ar. for LUDLOW. IV. Vairé
az. and ar. a fesse fretty gu. for MARMYON. V. Sa. a sword erect in pale ar. hilted or,
for KILPEC. VI. Erm. five fusils in fesse gu. for HEBDEN. VII. Gu. on a bend ar. three
rye stalks and ears sa. for RYE. VIII. Or, a lion ramp. double queued sa. for WELLES.
IX. Barry of six erm. and gu.; over all, three crescents sa. for WATERTON. X. Gu. a
fesse dancettée or, betw. six cross crosslets of the last, for ENGAYNE. XI. Ar. six sparrows
sa. three two, and one, on a chief indented gu. two swords in saltire betw. as many wolves'
heads erased or, for SPARROW. XII. Ar. a saltire gu. on a chief of the second three
escallops of the first, for TALBOYS. XIII. Gu. two bends or, for FITZWITH. XIV. Gu.
a cinquefoil ar. within an orle of eight cross crosslets or, for UMFREVILLE. XV. Gu. a
chev. or, betw. nine cross crosslets ar. for KYME. XVI. Or, a pale engr. sa. in base two
fountains ppr. for WATERHOUSE. Impaling, quarterly, first and fourth, paly of six or
and sa. on a chief of the first three cocks gu. for GALLIERS. Second and third, az. three
boys' heads, couped at the shoulders, the necks entwined with snakes ppr. for VAUGHAN.

Crests.—First, a demi lion ramp. sa. Second, A sword erect ar. pomel and hilt or.

Motto—Semper paratus.

Sir John Dymoke, Knt. M.P. for Lincolnshire, 46 and 47 Edw. III. Champion at the Coronation of Rich. II.	Margaret de Ludlow, heiress of Scrivelsby, co. Lincoln, dau. and heir of Sir Thomas de Ludlow, Knt. by Joan, his wife, dau. and co-heir of Philip de Marmion; she d. 2 Henry V.
Sir Thomas Dymoke, K.B. of Scrivelsby, Champion to Henry V. d. last year of that reign.	Elizabeth, dau. and heir of Sir Richard Hebden, Knt. by his wife, the dau. and heir of Rye.
Sir Philip Dymoke, Knt. Champion of Henry VI.	Joan, dau. of Sir Christopher Conyers, of Sokeburn.
Sir Thomas Dymoke, of Scrivelsby, Knt. beheaded temp. Henry VI.	Margaret, 2nd dau. and co-heir of Lionel, Lord Welles, by Joane, his wife, dau. and heir of Sir Robert Waterton, of Waterton.
Sir Robert Dymoke, Knight Banneret, of Scrivelsby, Champion at the Coronations of Richard III. Henry VII. and Henry VIII.	Jane, dau. and co-heir of John Sparrow, of London, 2nd wife.
Sir Edward Dymoke, of Scrivelsby, Knt. Champion at the Coronations of Edward VI. Mary, and Elizabeth, d. in 1506.	Anne, dau. of Sir George Talboys, and sister and co-heir of Gilbert, Lord Talboys, of Kyme.
Robert Dymoke, of Scrivelsby, Esq. d. in 1580.	Bridget, eldest dau. and co-heir of Edward, Lord Clinton.

PLATE XLVIII.

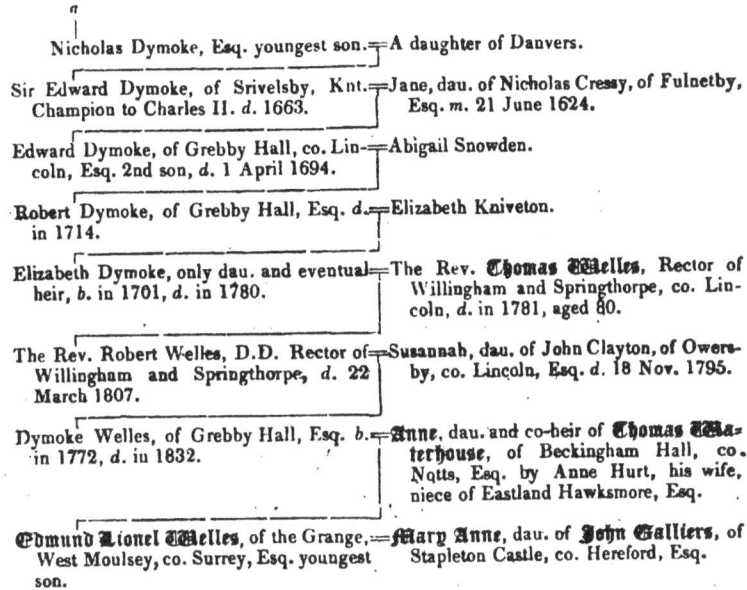

Nicholas Dymoke, Esq. youngest son.╤A daughter of Danvers.

Sir Edward Dymoke, of Srivelsby, Knt.╤Jane, dau. of Nicholas Cressy, of Fulnetby,
Champion to Charles II. *d.* 1663. | Esq. *m.* 21 June 1624.

Edward Dymoke, of Grebby Hall, co. Lin-╤Abigail Snowden.
coln, Esq. 2nd son, *d.* 1 April 1694.

Robert Dymoke, of Grebby Hall, Esq. *d.*╤Elizabeth Kniveton.
in 1714.

Elizabeth Dymoke, only dau. and eventual╤The Rev. **Thomas Welles**, Rector of
heir, *b.* in 1701, *d.* in 1780. | Willingham and Springthorpe, co. Lin-
coln, *d.* in 1781, aged 80.

The Rev. Robert Welles, D.D. Rector of╤Susannah, dau. of John Clayton, of Owers-
Willingham and Springthorpe, *d.* 22 | by, co. Lincoln, Esq. *d.* 18 Nov. 1795.
March 1807.

Dymoke Welles, of Grebby Hall, Esq. *b.*╤**Anne**, dau. and co-heir of **Thomas Wa-**
in 1772, *d.* in 1832. | **terhouse**, of Beckingham Hall, co.
Notts, Esq. by Anne Hurt, his wife,
niece of Eastland Hawksmore, Esq.

Edmund Lionel Welles, of the Grange,╤**Mary Anne**, dau. of **John Galliers**, of
West Moulsey, co. Surrey, Esq. youngest | Stapleton Castle, co. Hereford, Esq.
son.

Russell.

THOMAS JOHN RUSSELL, Esq. Representative of a distinguished branch of the noble Family of Russell, which held for many centuries the dignity of BARON of KILLOUGH, in Ulster, (*see* BURKE'S *Landed Gentry*), bears for

Arms.—Ar. a lion ramp. gu. on a chief sa. three escallops of the first.

Crest.—A goat passant ar. armed.

Motto.—Che sara sara.

Rolls, of the Hendre, co. Monmouth.

JOHN ETHERINGTON WELCH ROLLS, of the Hendre, Esq. High Sheriff of Monmouthshire in 1842, eldest son of the late JOHN ROLLS, of Bryanston Square, London, Esq. by Martha, his wife, only daughter and heir of Jacob Barnett, Esq. and grandson of JOHN ROLLS, of the Grange, co. Surrey, Esq. High Sheriff of Monmouthshire in 1794, by Sarah, his wife, daughter of Thomas Coÿsh, of Camberwell, Esq. bears a Shield, quarterly of four, and impales, in right of his wife, Elizabeth-Mary, third daughter of Walter Long, of Preshaw, co. Hants, Esq. the Quartered Coat of LONG.

Arms.—Quarterly, first and fourth, or, on a fesse dancettée with plain cottises betw. three billets sa. each charged with a lion ramp. of the field, as many bezants, for ROLLS. Second, Gu. an eagle displ. barry of six erminois and az. for COYSHE. Third, Or a saltire sa. in chief a leopard's face of the second, for BARNETT.
Impaling LONG, quartering TRENCHARD, ASHFORDBY, HIPPISLEY, &c.

Crest.—Out of a wreath of oak a dexter cubit arm, vested or, cuff sa. the arm charged with a fesse dancettée, double cottised of the second, charged with three bezants, in the hand ppr. a roll of parchment ar.

Motto.—Celeritas et veritas.

PLATE XVII.

EDMUND LIONEL WELLES. ESQ

THE GRANGE. WEST MOULSEY. CO SURREY

THOMAS JOHN RUSSELL. ESQ.

REPRESENTATIVE OF THE BARONS OF KILLOUGH

JOHN ETHERINGTON WELCH ROLLS. ESQ

THE HENDRE. CO MONMOUTH

PLATE XLIX.

Porcher, of Clyffe, co. Dorset.

CHARLES PORCHER, of Clyffe, co. Dorset, Snare Hill, co. Norfolk, and Borough Green, co. Cambridge, Esq. third son of the late Josias Du Pré Porcher, of Winslade House, co. Devon, Esq. M. P. for Old Sarum, by Charlotte, his wife, second daughter of Admiral Sir William Burnaby, Bart. and the descendant of an ancient and noble Family of the kingdom of France, where, on the banks of the Loire, the Counts Porcher of Richebourg still exist (*see* BURKE's *Dictionary of the Landed Gentry*), bears his Paternal Coat, impaled with that of REDHEAD, in right of his wife Ellinor, only daughter of the late Thomas Redhead, of Snare Hill, Esq.

> **Arms.**—Per pale ar. and gu. barry of eight counterchanged, a cinquefoil erm. for PORCHER; impaling, sa. a bend engr. or betw. two cottises ar. on a canton of the last a saltire gu. for REDHEAD.
>
> **Crest.**—A lion ramp. or, charged with three bars gu. holding betw. the paws a cinquefoil, as in the arms.
>
> **Motto.**—Pro Rege.

Garnett, of Quernmore Park and Bleasdale,
co. Lancaster.

WILLIAM GARNETT, of Quernmore Park and Bleasdale, Master Forester of Her Majesty's Forest of Bleasdale, and High Sheriff of Lancashire in 1843, bears for

> **Arms.**—Gu. a lion ramp. ar. ducally crowned or, within a bordure nebulée, also or, a canton of the last, thereon an eagle displayed with two heads sa.
>
> **Crest.**—A demi lion ar. gorged with a wreath of oak ppr. holding betw. the paws an escutcheon gu. charged with a buglehorn or.
>
> **Motto**—Diligentiâ et honore.

Rose, of Kilravock.

THE Family of Roos, or ROSE, was settled in Nairnshire in the reign of King Alexander III. Hugh Rose of Geddes, by marriage with Elizabeth Byset, acquired the lands of Kilravock, and had a Crown Charter of the Barony from King John (Balliol). From that period the estate has descended lineally to the present proprietor, HUGH ROSE, of Kilravock, Esq.; and what is uncommon, every link of the pedigree is proved by documents in public records or in the family charter chest. In 1640 Hugh Rose, then of Kilravock, by a license from the Lord of the Isles, built the present Castle, which stands on the bank of the river Nairn.

The Baron of Kilravock in 1560 used a Seal of the Family Arms, with the inscription " *S. hugonis ros baronis*," a style very unusual in Scotland, but which seems to have been adopted by many of the Lairds of Kilravock.

> **Arms.**—Or, three water bougets, az.
>
> **Crest.**—A hawk's head couped ppr.
>
> **Supporters.**—Two hawks ppr.
>
> **Mottoes.**—*Under the Arms*, Audeo. *Above the Crest*, Constant and true.

PLATE XLIX.

Norton, of Kings Norton, co. Worcester.

ROBERT NORTON, of the city of Dublin, Esq. Barrister-at-law, eldest son of the late Brett Norton, Esq. one of the Commissioners of Bankrupts, and great-grandson of Colonel Robert Norton, of Sherington, co. Bucks, Major of Duke Schomberg's Regiment of Horse at the Boyne, represents the ancient Family of Norton, of King's Norton, co. Worcester, derived from Theobald de Ryngville, the Norman, and bears a Shield of Eleven Quarterings.

Arms.—Ar. on a bend betw. two lions ramp. sa. three escallops of the first, quartering ST. LOE, RUSSELL, DE LA RIVIERE, &c. &c.

Crest.—A greyhound's head or, gorged with a fesse engr. betw. two bars gu. the fesse ringed behind of the first.

Thomas Norton, of Hingston, co. Cambridge, and of Hundon, co. Suffolk, Esq. grandson of Richard Norton, of King's Norton, Esq. and representative of Theobald de Ryngville, the Norman, d. 41 Eliz. == Margaret, only dau. and heir of Sir William St. Loe, Capt. of Queen Elizabeth's Guard, grandson of Sir John St. Loe, Knt. and Isabel de la Riviere, his wife, heiress of Tormaton.

William Norton, of Sherrington, co. Bucks, and of Hundon, co. Suffolk, Esq. d. in 1642. == Ann, dau. of Sir John Brett, Knt. of Edmonton, co. Middlesex.

Brett Norton, of Sherrington, Esq. b. 1626. == Sarah Lamby, m. 1647.

Col. Robert Norton, of Sherrington, Major of Schomberg's Regt. of Horse at the Boyne, and a distinguished officer of Marlborough's campaigns, d. in Ireland in 1730. == Anne Smithwick, m. 26 Aug. 1716, d. in Dublin in 1756.

Robert Norton, b. 1719, d. 1778. == Sidney, dau. of Patrick Sandys, of Dublin, Esq.

Brett Norton, Esq. barrister-at-law, and one of the Commissioners of Bankrupts, b. 1747, d. 1791. == Bridget, only dau. of Luke Eife, of Donnymore, co. Meath, Esq. == Francis Talbot, Esq. 2nd husband.

| Robert Norton, of Dublin, Esq. Barrister-at-law. | Other issue deceased. | John Norton, Esq. late Captain 34th Regt. served in six campaigns under the Duke of Wellington, and is distinguished by his valuable inventions. | Mary Anne, m. Rev. H. R. Robinson, M.A. of Granard. = | Bridget-Sidney, m. William Clarke, of Dublin, Esq. | Grace. | Other issue deceased. | Letitia Talbot, wife of the Rev. James George Purcell. |

George-Augustus-Frederick Robinson, b. in 1821.   Bridget-Elizabeth.

Hall, of Grappenhall Hall, co. Chester.

WILLIAM HALL, of Grappenhall, Esq. an acting Magistrate for the counties of Lancaster and Chester, descends from the Family of Hall, which has been settled at Warrington for nearly a century, and which derived from the Halls of Beverley, co. York. (*See* BURKE's *Dictionary of the Landed Gentry.*)

Arms.—Sa. three poleaxes ar.

Crest.—An embowed arm holding a poleaxe.

Motto.—Finem respice.

PLATE III.

CHARLES PORCHER, ESQ.

CLYFFE, CO. DORSET.

WILLIAM GARNETT, ESQ.

BLEASDALE AND QUERNMORE PARK, CO. LANCASTER.

HUGH ROSE, ESQ.

KILRAVOCK CASTLE, CO. NAIRN.

ROBERT NORTON, ESQ.

OF THE CITY OF DUBLIN.

WILLIAM HALL, OF GRAPPENHALL,

CO. CHESTER.

PLATE L.

Harvey, of Castle Semple, co. Renfrew.

Lieutenant Colonel James Harvey of Castle Semple, K.H. (whose patronymic was Lee) assumed his present surname and arms agreeably to the provisions of the Settlements by which he and his wife (Margaret, daughter and heiress of the Honourable John Harvey, of the Island of Grenada) succeeded to the extensive estates of Mr. Harvey. (See Burke's *Landed Gentry*.)

Arms.—Gu. on a bend erminois, three trefoils slipped vert, on a chief ar. a buck's head cabossed az. betw. two mullets of the first, and for distinction, in the sinister chief point of the field, a cross pattée of the fourth :—Impaling, gu. on a bend erminois, three trefoils slipped vert, on a chief ar. a buck's head cabossed az. betw. two mullets of the first, all within a bordure wavy of the second.

Crest.—Issuant out of a crescent or, charged with a buck's head as in the arms, a cubit arm ppr. the hand grasping a trefoil slipped, erect, vert; and for distinction, the arm charged with an ermine spot gold.

Motto.—Omnia Bene.

Dolling, of Magheralin.

Robert Holbeach Dolling, Esq. Barrister-at-Law, and Justice of the Peace, son and heir of the Rev. Boughey William Dolling, of Magheralin, co. Down, Rector of Magheralin, &c. and great-grandson of James Dolling, of London, Esq. by Mary his wife, only child and heiress of the Honourable J. Ratcliffe, of Stockport, co. Chester, and Hatton Garden, London, cousin german of the ill-fated Earl of Derwentwater, bears the quartered Coat of Dolling and Ratcliffe.

Arms.—Quarterly, first and fourth. Per fesse ar. and az. a fesse dancettée, per fesse dancettée sa. and of the first, for Dolling. Second and third ar. a bend engr. sa. for Ratcliffe.

Crests.—First, a buck's head ppr. attired or, gorged with two bars dancettée ar. for Dolling. Second, a bull's head erased gu. ducally gorged or, for Ratcliffe.

Motto.—Spero.

PLATE L.

Fitzgerald, Knight of Glin.

JOHN FRAUNCEIS FITZGERALD, Knight of Glin, of Glin Castle, co. Limerick, High Sheriff thereof in 1830, is Representative of Sir JOHN FITZ-JOHN Knt. second son of JOHN FITZ-THOMAS FITZGERALD, Lord of Decies and Desmond. This Lord of Decies, by Virtue of his Royal Seigniory, as a Count Palatine, created three of his sons, by his second marriage, KNIGHTS, and their descendants have been so styled in Acts of Parliament, Patents under the Great Seal, and all Legal Proceedings up to the present time. From the eldest of these sons derived the WHITE KNIGHTS, from the second, the KNIGHTS OF GLIN, and from the third, the KNIGHTS OF KERRY.

> Arms.—Erm. a saltire gu.
> Crests.—First, a boar passant gu. bristled and armed or. Second, a castle with two towers, issuant from the sinister tower, a knight in armour, holding in his dexter hand a key, all ppr.
> Supporters.—Two griffins, collared and chained.
> Motto.—Shanit a Boo.

Greg, of Norcliffe Hall.

ROBERT HYDE GREG, of Norcliffe Hall, co. Chester, Esq. a Magistrate for that Shire, and formerly M.P. for Manchester, is son of the late Samuel Greg, Esq. and great-grandson of John Greig, Esq. who migrated from Scotland, and settled in the North of Ireland, at Belfast. (*See* BURKE's *Landed Gentry*.)

> Arms.—Ar. a fir tree growing out of a mount vert, in base, surmounted by a sword in bend ppr. on a dexter canton az. a royal crown ppr.
> Crest.—An arm embowed in armour, grasping a scimitar az. pommel and hilt or.
> Motto.—Ein doe and spair not.

Whitehurst, of the Mount, near Shrewsbury.

BRANCHES of the Family of WHITEHURST have been resident in the Counties of Denbigh, Salop, and Herts, for several generations; the direct Elder Line is represented by JOHN WHITEHURST, of the Mount, near Shrewsbury and of Wornerton Park, near Church Stretton, Esq. and a younger branch, by the Rev. EDWARD WHITEHURST.

> Arms.—Long borne by the family, and confirmed 8 GEO. III. Per chev. ar. and gu. a chev. counterchanged betw. two garbs in chief ppr. and a horse in base ar.
> Crest.—On a mural crown ar. a knight's helmet plumed, pierced with a javelin, the point dropping blood ppr.
> Motto.—Je crains Dieu.

LIEU. COL. JAMES HARVEY, K.H.
CASTLE SEMPLE. CO. RENFREW.

ROBERT HOLBEACH DOLLING. ESQ.
MAGHERALIN. CO. DOWN.

JOHN FRAUNCEIS FITZGERALD.
KNIGHT OF GLIN.

ROBERT HYDE GREG. ESQ.
NORCLIFFE HALL. CO. CHESTER.

JOHN WHITEHURST. ESQ.
THE MOUNT. SHREWSBURY.

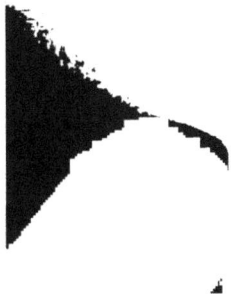

PLATE LI.

Evans, of The Hill Court.

KINGSMILL EVANS, of The Hill Court, co. Hereford, Esq. Justice of the Peace and Deputy Lieutenant, formerly an Officer in the First Foot Guards, and High Sheriff of the County of Hereford in 1816, bears the quartered Coat of EVANS, CLARKE, and KYRLE.

Arms.—Quarterly, First and fourth, per pale, az. and gu. three lions ramp. ar. armed and langued or, for EVANS; second, or, a fesse erm. betw. three trefoils slipped vert, for CLARKE; third, vert, a chev. betw. three fleurs-de-lis or, for KYRLE.

Crest.—Out of an earl's coronet a dexter arm embowed naked, brandishing a dagger, pommelled and hilted or, blade ar. guttée de sang.

Walter Kyrle, of The Hill, co. Hereford, Esq. eldest son and heir of Walter Kyrle, of "the Hulle," Esq. temp. Henry VII.

Alice Kyrle, dau. and sole heir, m. temp. = **Christopher Clarke**, Esq. Henry VII.
From whom derived fifth in descent,

Richard Clarke, of The Hill, Esq. living, = Alice, dau. of John Vele, of Longford, co. aged 46, in 1683. Gloucester, Esq.

Alice Clarke, in her = **Thomas Evans**, of Langattock, co. Monmouth, Esq. living in issue, heiress of Hill 1699; son and heir of Herbert Thomas Walter Evans, of the Court, m. Jan. 1, same place, Esq. by Frances, his wife, dau. of Giles Morgan, 1696. of Pencraig House, near Newport, Esq. and grandson of Thomas ap Ivon ap Jenkin Herbert, of Langattock, temp. Elizabeth.

Thomas Evans, = Sybil, dau. of	Mary, dau. of William Adams, of = Kingsmill Evans, of
of Langattock, Penry Wil-	the Anchor Hill, Esq. and sister Lydiert House, co. Mon-
eldest son and liams, of	of William Adams Williams, of mouth, Esq. Barrister-
heir, living in Penpont, co.	Langibby Castle, Esq. at-law, second son.
1729. Brecon, Esq.	

Thomas Evans,	Mary, m. to Her-	Kingsmill Evans, of Lydi- = Catherine, dau. of Wil-
of Langattock,	bert Phillipps,	ert House, Esq. colonel in liam Durham, of Mau-
d. unm. in 1808,	Esq. and had	the 1st foot guards, d. of gusbury, co. Gloucester,
aged 78.	one son, Thomas	wounds received at Lincelles Esq. by Catherine, his
	Phillipps, Esq.	in France in 1793. wife, dau. of John
		Blewitt, of Llantarnam
		Abbey, Esq.

Kingsmill Evans, Esq. = Anne-Rosalia-Eliza-	Joseph Blew-	Anne, m. in	Cathe-
justice of the peace and de- beth, eldest dau. of	ett, capt. 1st	1819 to lieut.-	rine.
puty lieutenant, b. 1 July, Thomas Thoroton, of	foot guards,	gen. Sir Man-	Mary.
1784; inherited in 1806, on Flintham House, co.	d. unm. in	ley Power,	
the death of his cousin Jane, Notts, Esq. M.P. m.	France in	K.C.B. lieut.	
last surviving child of the 19 Sept. 1810.	1815.	governor of	
late Joseph Clarke, Esq. the		Malta.	
estate of The Hill Court.			

PLATE LI.

Gilbert, of Devon and Cornwall.

WALTER RALEIGH GILBERT, Esq. Major-General in the Honourable East India Company's Service, second son of the late Rev. Edmund Gilbert, Descendant and Representative of the ancient and highly eminent Family of Gilbert of Compton Castle, co. Cornwall, (see BURKE's *Dictionary of the Landed Gentry*,) impales with his paternal Coat of GILBERT, the Arms of Ross, in right of his wife, Isabella, daughter of Major Ross, Royal Artillery, by Isabella, his wife, fifth daughter of John Macleod, tenth Baron of Rasay.

> **Arms.**—Ar. on a chev. sa. three roses of the first, leaved ppr. impaling, Ar. the sea, thereon a ship, sails furled and flags flying, all ppr. ; on a chief embattled gu. three lions ramp. of the first for Ross.
>
> **Crest.**—A squirrel sejant, feeding on a bunch of nuts, ppr.
>
> **Motto.**—Mallem mori quam mutare.

Cantillon of Ballyhigue, co. Kerry.

ANTOINE SYLVAIN DE CANTILLON, Chevalier Baron de Ballyhigue, Lieutenant-Colonel of Hussars in the French Service, Officer of the Legion of Honour, Knight of St. Louis, &c. is Representative of the ancient Irish Family of Cantillon, and as such bears their Armorial Ensigns.

> **Arms.**—Az. a lion ramp. or, armed and langued gu. betw. two arrows in pale of the second, the points in base ar. feathered ppr.
>
> **Crest.**—A naked dexter arm embowed, the hand grasping an arrow.
>
> **Supporters.**—Dexter, a wolf reguardant, sinister, a lion reguardant.
>
> **Motto.**—Fortis in bello.

SIR HENRY DE CANTILLON, Knight, Lord of Cantelon in Normandy, accompanied the Conqueror to England, and being wounded at the Battle of Hastings, received from that Monarch in return for his services, an Estate in Devonshire. This property Sir Henry Cantillon called Cantelon, subsequently corrupted into Cantelupe. One of his descendants became established in the County of Kerry in Ireland, towards the year 1169, from him derived

Roger de Cantillon, Lord of Ballyhigue, co. Kerry, *b.* in 1533, *m.* Elizabeth Stuart, niece of Alexander, Lord of Garlies, ancestor of the Earls of Galloway.

David de Cantillon, Lord of Ballyhigue, *b.* in 1579, *m.* Maria Fitz Gerald, of the family of the Earls of Kildare, ancestors of the Duke of Leinster.

Philip Cantillon, of Belview, *b.* in 1611, *m.* Barbara, dau. of Samuel Pigot, of Disart, Esq. and Margaret Perceval, his wife, of the noble family of Egmont.	Valentine Cantillon, Esq. an officer in the army of Charles I. was wounded at the Battle of Naseby in 1645. He *m.* in Flanders, Marie Messéan, and *d.* there in 1649.	Richard Cantillon, of Kerry, Esq. who received from Charles I. as reward for services, confirmation and grant of several lands situated in the Barony of Clanmaris ; the charter dated 7, Sept. 1636. He *m.* Mary ———, of the county of Kerry.
a		*b*

PLATE LI.

a   *b*

| James Cantillon, de Belview, *b.* in 1650, capt. in the guards of James II. whom he accompanied to France. He received eleven wounds at the Battle of Malplaquet in 1709, and was created a Knight of St. Louis by Louis XIV. = Jane, dau. of Sir Thomas Harold, Governor of Limerick and M.P. in 1689, grand-dau. through her father of Elizabeth Seymour, of the noble houses of Somerset and Hertford, and through her mother of Mary Mac Mahon. | 2. Richard Cantillon, Esq. banker at Paris in 1710, *m.* Maria-Anne Bulkeley, of Beaumaris, Isle of Anglesey, of the family of Lord Bulkeley. | 1. Philip Cantillon, Esq. banker in Paris in 1730. | 3. Robert Cantillon, of Limerick, Esq. *m.* Mary, dau. of John O'Bryen, of the co. of Kerry, Esq. |

| Thomas Cantillon, capt. in Bulkeley's regiment in 1754, was wounded at the Battle of Fontenoi, and made a Knight of St. Louis by Louis XV. = Elizabeth Seymour. | Philip Cantillon, Esq. Lord of Bishecourt in Surrey. = Rebecca, dau. of William Newland, of Sutton, co. Surrey, Esq. | Henrietta Cantillon, *m.* 1st, in 1743, to William Howard, 3rd Earl of Stafford, and 2ndly, in 1759, to Robert 1st Earl of Farnham, and by the latter had one dau. Henrietta, *m.* in 1780 to the Rt. Hon. Denis Daly, of Dunsandle, co. Galway, M.P. | Elizabeth Cantillon, *m.* to the Count de Bulkeley, Lieut.-gen. in the service of France, and brother-in-law of the Marshal Duke of Berwick. | Mary Cantillon, *m.* to Maurice O'Connell, of Derrynane, co. Kerry, Esq. uncle of Daniel O'Connell, Esq. M.P. |

| Antoine Joseph Cantillon, Chevalier, of Paris, *d.* in 1831, aged 96. = Marie Louise Brot. | Elizabeth Cantillon, of Bishecourt, *m.* to Chevalier Denis O'Sullivan, Advocate General to the Supreme Council of Brabant in 1767. The grandson of this marriage, Baron O'Sullivan, is Ambassador from Belgium in Austria. |

| Antoine Sylvain de Cantillon, Chevalier, Baron de Ballyhigue, (by letters patent from the King of the French, dated 18 Nov. 1839,) *b.* at Paris, lieut.-col. of Hussars, officer of the Legion of Honour, Chevalier of St. Louis, and of the second class of St. Ferdinand of Spain, present representative of the senior branch of this family. = Mademoiselle de Léval, *m.* in 1831. | Charles Cantillon, of Paris, Esq. *m.* to Mademoiselle Rose Cassart. | William |

| Alfred de Cantillon, *b.* at Amiens in 1832. | Francois Edward Eugene de Cantillon, *b.* at Niort in 1834. Bernard-Edward Howard Duke of Norfolk, and Frances Lady Stafford, stood sponsors in consideration of the ancient alliance of the family of Cantillon with the illustrious house of Howard. | Auguste de Cantillon, *b.* at Niort in 1836. | Louise. Laure. Théonie. Marie. Henriette. | Daughters. |

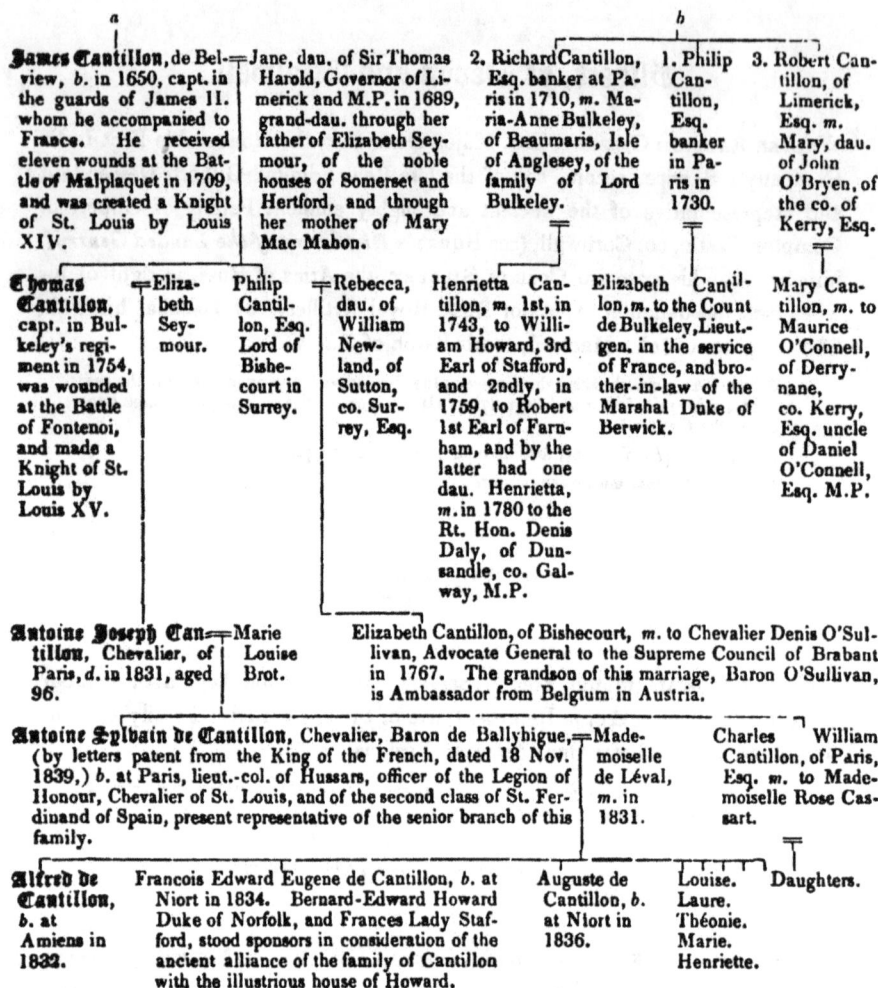

Selby, of Biddleston, co. Northumberland.

WALTER SELBY, of Biddleston, Esq. (son of the late Walter Selby, Esq. of the same place, by Alicia, his wife, daughter of Thomas Swarbreck, Esq., grandson of Thomas Selby, of Biddleston, Esq. by CATHERINE, his wife, daughter and heir of RALPH HODSHON, of Lintz, co. Durham, Esq. and great-grandson by ELEANOR. his wife, daughter and coheir of NICHOLAS TUITE, Esq. of Thomas Selby, of Biddleston, Esq. who was son of Thomas William Selby, of Biddleston, Esq. by BARBARA, his wife, daughter and heir of CHRISTOPHER PERCEHAY, of Ryton, Esq. and Representative of the very ancient Northumbrian family of Selby,) bears a Shield of ten Quarterings. His cousin, JOHN THOMAS SELBY, Esq. only surviving son, by Teresa, his wife, sister of Charles, late Earl of Shrewsbury, of Robert Selby, Esq. fifth son of Thomas Selby, of Biddleston, Esq. by

PLATE LI.

Eleanor Tuite, his wife, is entitled to the same Quarterings, with the exception of HODSON and STRICKLAND.

Arms.—Quarterly, first, barry of eight or and sa. for SELBY; second, ar. a cross flory gu. for PERCEHAY; third, az. fretty ar. for LOUNDE; fourth, ar. a lion ramp. az. depressed by a bend or, for FAUCONBERG; fifth, ar. an inescutcheon sa. within an orle of eight cinquefoils gu. for D'ARCY; sixth, quarterly ar. and gu. a crescent sa. for difference for TUITE; seventh, erm. two bars gu. for NUGENT; eighth, ar. a saltire within a bordure gu. for FITZGERALD; ninth, per chev. embattled or and az. three martlets counterchanged, for HODSON; tenth, sa. three escallops ar. for STRICKLAND.

Crest.—A Saracen's head ppr. wreathed about the temples or and sa.

Motto—Semper sapit suprema.

Poley, of Boxted Hall, co. Suffolk.

GEORGE WELLER POLEY, of Boxted Hall, Esq. Representative of the ancient Knightly family of POLEY, which removed from Poley, Herts, to Boxted and Bradley, co. Suffolk, *temp.* Edward III. (see BURKE's *Landed Gentry*,) is grandson of GEORGE WELLER, Esq. who, as heir to his maternal ancestors, assumed the Surname and Arms of POLEY.

Arms.—Quarterly.—

I. Or, a lion ramp. sa. for POLEY.

II. Sa. two chevronels betw. three roses ar. for POLEY,

III. Ar. on a bend sa. three crosses pattée of the first, ancient Arms borne by Sir HUMPHREY DE POLEY *temp.* Henry I.

IV. Sa. a chev. engr. or, betw. three mullets ar. for BADWELL.

V. Az. a saltire or, betw. four billets ar. for LEYES.

VI. Barry of six sa. and or, for KNIGHTON.

VII. Erm. on a cross gu. five escallops ar. for WEYLAND.

VIII. Gu. three fusils in fesse erm. betw. three martlets ar. for ROCKELL.

IX. Erm. on a bend gu. three pheons ar. for BLYANT.

X. Ar. a chev. betw. three lozenges ermines, for SHAA.

Crest.—A lion ramp. sa. collared and chain reflexed over the back or.

Motto.—Fortior qui se.

PLATE 21

KINGSMILL EVANS. ESQ.
THE HILL COURT. CO. HEREFORD.

MAJOR GEN. WALTER RALEIGH GILBERT
E. I. C. SERVICE.

THE CHEVALIER ANTOINE SYLVAIN DE CANTILLON
BARON DE BALLYHIGUE

WALTER SELBY. ESQ.
MIDDLESTON. CO. NORTHUMBERLAND

GEORGE WELLER POLEY. ESQ.
BOXTED HALL. CO. SUFFOLK

PLATE LII.

Wilson, of Stowlangtoft, co. Suffolk.

HENRY WILSON, of Stowlangtoft Hall, Esq. late M.P. for West Suffolk, only
son of Joseph Wilson, of Highbury Hill, co. Middlesex, and Stowlangtoft, co.
Suffolk, Esq. who was second son* of Thomas Wilson, of Highbury Place, Esq.
impales, with his own Arms, the Ensigns of FITZROY, in right of his wife,
Caroline, only daughter of the late Lord Henry Fitzroy, and niece of the Duke
of Grafton.

> **Arms.**—Sa. a wolf salient or, on a chief of the last a pale of the first, charged with a
> fleur-de-lis ar. betw. two pellets : **Impaling,** for FITZROY, quarterly, first and fourth,
> France and England, quarterly, second, Scotland ; third, Ireland : over all, a sinister
> baton compony, ar. and az.
>
> **Crest.**—A demi wolf or, the sinister paw resting on a pellet charged with a fleur-de-
> lis gold.
>
> **Motto.**—Wil sone wil.

Hippisley, of Lamborne Place, co. Berks.

HENRY HIPPISLEY, of Lamborne Place, Esq. High Sheriff of Berks in 1840,
second son of the late Rev. Henry Hippisley, M.A. of Lamborne Place, by
ANNE, his wife, daughter and coheir of LOCK ROLLINSON, of Chadlington, co.
Oxford, Esq. and sixth in direct descent from the marriage of John Hippisley,
of Stone Easton, Esq. (son of John Hippisley, Esq. of the same place, by ELIZA,
his wife, daughter and heir of JOHN ORGAN, of Lamborne, Esq.) with MARGA-
RET, daughter and heiress of JOHN PRESTON, of Crickett, co. Somerset, Esq.
bears a Quartered Shield, HIPPISLEY, ORGAN, PRESTON, and ROLLINSON, and
an Escutcheon of Pretence, quarterly NELSON and HEYDON, in right of his wife,
Elizabeth Agnes, daughter and heir of the Rev. John Nelson, Prebendary of
Heytesbury, by Catherine his wife, daughter and coheir of Richard Heydon, of
Bodicote Grange, co. Oxford, Esq.

> **Arms.**—Quarterly, first, sa. three mullets, pierced in bend, betw. two bendlets or, for
> HIPPISLEY. Second, per saltire or and erm. over all a cross couped gu. for ORGAN.
> Third, az. ten bezants, four, three, two, and one, on a chief ar. two lions passant counter-
> passant sa. for PRESTON. Fourth, ar. a cinquefoil az. on a chief gu, a lion passant guard.
> or for ROLLINSON.
>
> **An Escutcheon of Pretence.**—Quarterly, first and fourth, per pale ar. and sa. a chev.
> betw. three fleurs-de-lis counterchanged, for NELSON. Second and third, quarterly, ar.
> and az, a cross engr. counterchanged, for HEYDON.
>
> **Crest.**—A hind's head erased or, gorged with a collar sa. charged with three mullets
> of the first.

---

* The eldest son is THOMAS WILSON, of Highbury Place, Esq. and the only daughter, Mary,
wife of Samuel Mills, of Russell Square, Esq.

PLATE LII.

Kennedy, of Bennane and Finnarts, co. Ayr.

HEW FERGUSSONE KENNEDY, of Bennane, Esq. Representative in the male line of the Chiefs of the name, derives in direct descent from Roland de Carrick, A. D. 1250.

Arms.—Quarterly, first and fourth, ar. a chev. gu. betw. three crosses crosslet fitchée sa. for KENNEDY. Second and third, az. three fleurs-de-lis or (*the Royal Arms of France*).

Crest.—A fleur-de-lis or, issuing out of two oak leaves ppr.

Supporters.—Dexter, a female in the costume of the sixteenth century; sinister, a wyvern ppr.

Motto.—Fuimus.

Soltau, of Little Efford, co. Devon.

GEORGE WILLIAM SOLTAU, of Little Efford, Esq. son and heir of the late George Soltau, of Little Efford, Esq. by Elizabeth-Maria, his wife, daughter of William Symons, of Chaddlewood, Esq. (see BURKE's *Landed Gentry*) bears, on his Paternal Shield, an Escutcheon of Pretence, quarterly, first and fourth, CULME; second and third, GODDARD, in right of his wife, Frances Goddard, daughter and coheir of the Rev. Thomas Culme, of Tothill, son of John Culme, of Tothill, Esq. by his wife, the daughter and heir of the Rev. William Goddard, of Berkshire.

Arms.—Per bend sinister az. and ar. on the dexter side three ears of wheat on one stalk or; on the sinister side, three fleurs-de-lis of the first.

An Escutcheon of Pretence.—Quarterly, first and fourth, az. a chev. betw. three pelicans vulning themselves or, for CULME. Second and third, gu. a chev. vairé betw. three crescents ar. for GODDARD.

Crest.—A demi lion arg. within two branches of roses ppr.

Motto.—Miseris succurrere disco.

Hodges, of Hemsted, co. Kent.

THOMAS LAW HODGES, of Hemsted, Esq. late M. P. for Kent, eldest son of the late Thomas Hallett Hodges, Esq. High Sheriff of that county in 1786, by Dorothy, his wife, youngest daughter of John Cartwright, of Marnham, co. Notts, Esq. and grandson of Thomas Hodges, Esq. Governor of Bombay, (*see* BURKE's *Dictionary of the Landed Gentry*,) bears, on his hereditary Coat, an Escutcheon of Pretence, in right of his wife, Rebecca, only child of Sir Roger Twisden, of Bradbourn Park, Bart.

Arms.—Or, three crescents sa. on a canton of the second a ducal crown of the first.

An Escutcheon of Pretence.—Gyronny of four ar. and gu. a saltire betw. four cross crosslets all counterchaiged, a crescent for difference, for TWISDEN.

Crest.—Out of a ducal coronet or, an heraldic antelope's head ar. horned and tufted gold.

Motto.—Mala prævisa pereunt.

HENRY WILSON. ESQ.
STOWLANGTOFT. CO SUFFOLK

HENRY HIPPISLEY. ESQ.
LAMBORNE PLACE. CO. BERKS.

CAPT HEW FERGUSSONE KENNEDY.
BENNANE AND FINNARTS CO. AYR

GEORGE WILLIAM SOLTAU. ESQ.
LITTLE EFFORD. CO. DEVON

THOMAS LAW HODGES. ESQ
HEMSTED CO. KENT

PLATE LIII.

Tucker, of Coryton Park, co. Devon.

WILLIAM TUCKER, of Coryton Park, Esq. a Magistrate for the Counties of Devon, Somerset, and Dorset, son of the late WILLIAM TUCKER, of Coryton Park, Esq. and great-grandson of William Tucker, of Coryton, Esq. by Mary, his wife, only dau. of Thomas Marwood, of Widworthy, Esq. bears a quartered coat and two crests.

> **Arms.**—Quarterly, first and fourth, barry wavy of six ar. and az. a chev. embattled or, gutteé sa. betw. three sea-horses of the third; second and third, az. on a chev. embattled betw. three sea-horses ar. as many hearts gu.
>
> **Crests.**—A lion's gamb, erased and erect gu. charged with three billets in pale or, holding in the foot a battle-axe ar. handle of the second. A demi sea-horse reguard. ar. holding in his paws a heart gu.
>
> **Motto.**—Auspice Teucro.

Prodgers, of Bromfield.

THE REV. EDWIN PRODGERS, B.D. Rector of Ayot St. Peter, Welwyn, co. Herts, and a magistrate for Surrey, descends from the ancient family of Proger, or Progers, of Gwarindee, co. Monmouth, which derived from Jenkin ap Guillim, eldest son of William ap Jenkin, *alias* Herbert, Lord of Gwarindee, *temp.* Edward III. and brother of Howell ap Guillam, ancestor of the Herberts. (See BURKE's *Landed Gentry*.) The Rev. Gentleman bears, on an Escutcheon of Pretence, the Arms of Blades, in right of his wife, Caroline, daughter and coheir of the late John Blades, of Brockwell Hall, co. Surrey, Esq.

> **Arms.**—Per pale gu. and ar. three lions ramp. two and one ar. betw. three crosses patteé fitcheé in the foot, one and two, erminois.
>
> **An Escutcheon of Pretence.**—Az. two swords in saltire ar. pomels and hilts or, surmounted of the Roman fasces, paleways of the last, axe-headed of the second, interlaced with a double chain collar gold, on a chief erm. a bee volant, betw. two star pagodas ppr.
>
> **Crest.**—In front of a cross Calvary, or, a wivern with wings endorsed vert, in the mouth a sinister hand couped at the wrist gu. gorged with a collar and reflexed over the back gold, the dexter claw resting on a cross patteé of the last.
>
> **Motto.**—Devouement sans bornes.

Strachan, of Thornton.

THIS family is of great antiquity, and we find Walterus de Strachane, or Srathethyne, "cum consensu Rudolphi de Strachane heredibus sui," conveying lands to the Canons of St. Andrews, *circ.* 1160, in the reign of King Malcolm the Fourth; and John, the son of Rudolphus "filius ejus" makes over to the Abbot and Convent of Dunfermline, the lands of Belheldies, "pro salute suâ," and the deed is confirmed by Alexander the Third in 1278.

The present Baronet, SIR JOHN STRACHAN, of Thornton, Cliffden, Teignmouth, co. Devon, succeeded to the title from the failure and extinction of the previous heirs male, and is the nearest and lawful heir male in general, and re-

PLATE LIII.

presentative of the family of Strachan of Monboddo, and is also the nearest and lawful heir male in general to Sir Alexander Strachan, of Thornton, Kincardine-shire, Baronet, who was created and raised to the dignity of a Baronet by King Charles I. May 26, 1625, by Royal patent of that date. Sir John Strachan, *m.* Elizabeth, dau. of David Hunter, of Blackness, co. Forfar, Esq. and has had issue; 1. JOHN, *m.* Mary Anne, daughter of Isaac Elton, of Whitestaunton House, co. Somerset, Esq.; 2. James Graham, of the Civil Service Bombay, deceased; 3. Amelia, *m.* to the Rev. William Page Richards, LL.D. Rector of Stoke Abbas, co. Dorset; 4. Catherine Margaret, *m.* to John Cave, of Brentry House, co. Gloucester, Esq.

Arms.—Quarterly, first and fourth, or, a stag trippant az.; second and third, ar. on the sea a galley, her oars in saltire sa. within a bordure wavy az. **Impaling.** Ar. on a chev. gu. betw. three hunting-horns vert, a crescent ar. betw. two cinquefoils or, for HUNTER.

Crests.—First, a naked arm embowed ppr. holding a scimitar also ppr. pomel and hilt or. Second, on a rudder a man's head sidefaced, all ppr.

Supporters.—Two forresters ppr.

Mottoes.—*Above the first Crest*, For. D. ward. *Above the second*, Steer steady.

Warde, of Barford, and Clopton.

CHARLES THOMAS WARDE, of Clopton House, and Welcombe House, both in the co. of Warwick, only son of the Rev. THOMAS WARDE, Vicar of Weston-under-Weatherley, by Charlotte, his wife, daughter of John Lloyd, of Snitterfield, Esq. F.R.S. lineally descends from SERJEANT ROWLEY WARDE, an eminent Lawyer in the time of James I. who was eldest son, by Martha, his wife, daughter and heiress of Thomas Rowley, of Idlicot, co. Warwick, Esq. of THOMAS WARDE, of Barford, co. Warwick, Esq. third son of HENRY WARDE, of Pillerton, Esq. (See *Visitation of Warwickshire of* 1619.) He bears the Ensigns of WARDE and ROWLEY Quarterly; and impales, in right of his wife, Marianne, eldest daughter of John Lawes, of Rochampstead House, co. Herts, Esq. the Arms of LAWES.

Arms.—Quarterly, first and fourth, az. a cross patonce or, a mullet for difference, for WARDE. Second and third, ar. a fesse betw. three mullets sa. for ROWLEY; **Impaling,** or, on a chief az. three estoiles of the field, for LAWES.

Crest.—A wolf's head erased or, charged with a mullet for difference.

Firth, of Hartford Lodge, co. Chester.

THOMAS FIRTH, of Hartford Lodge, Esq. son of the late Thomas Firth, Esq. by Elizabeth, his wife, daughter of John Hemmingway, of Halifax, Esq. and great-grandson of George Firth, of Northowran, co. York, impales, with his own Ensigns, the Arms of HAND, in right of his wife, Anne, daughter of THOMAS HAND, of Middlewich, co. Chester, Esq.

Arms.—Az. a chev. engr. erm. betw. two battle-axes in chief, and a garb in base or. **Impaling,** sa. two bars, and in chief three crosses pattée ar. for HAND.

Crest.—On a mount vert, a griffin pass. sa. in front of a hurst of six trees, ppr.

Motto.—Deus incrementum dedit.

THOMAS FIRTH ESQ.
HARTFORD LARGE, CO. CHESTER.

WILLIAM TUCKER ESQ.
CORYTON PARK CO. DEVON.

SIR JOHN STRACHAN BART.
CLIFTON WIDENMOUTH
CO. DEVON.

THE REVᴰ EDWIN PRODGERS.
AYOT Sᵀ PETERS WELWYN. HERTS.

CHARLES THOMAS WARDE. ESQ
CLOPTON HOUSE AND WELCOME CO. WARWICK

Mottoes

TRANSLATED, WITH EXPLANATORY ILLUSTRATIONS.

Æquam servare mentem. Horace, Od. b. ii. 3. (To preserve an equal mind.) Mathew.

> " In adverse hours an equal mind maintain,
> Nor let your spirit rise too high,
> Though fortune kindly change the scene."— FRANCIS.

Amour avec loyaulté. (Love with loyalty.) Parr, of Lythwood.

A rege et victoriâ. (From the king and victory.) Barry, of Rocklaveston.

Asgre làn diogel ei pherchen. (A pure conscience is a safeguard to its possessor.) Jones, of Llanarth.

Aspera ad virtutem est via. (The road to virtue is rough.) Edwardes, of Gileston Manor.

Aspire, persevere, and indulge not. Adams, of Middleton Hall.

Audaces juvo. (I assist the daring.) Campbell, of Jura.

Audeo. (I dare.) Rose, of Kilravock.

> " I dare do all that may become a man."
> SHAKESPEARE.

Auspice Teucro. (Under the auspice of Teucer.) Tucker, of Coryton Park.

Bear up. Fulford, of Great Fulford.

Be as God will. Bracebridge, of Morville House.

Be mindful to unite. Brodie, of Lethen.

Beneficiorum memor. (Mindful of benefits.) Kelham, of Bleasby.

Benigno numine. (Under an auspicious divinity.) Meigh, of Ash Hall.

Boutez en avant. (Push forward.) Fowle, of Wiltshire.

    This is the motto also of the Earls of Barrymore, whence is derived the name of Buttevant, in the county of Cork, the second noble title of the family, under which they were the premier viscounts of Ireland.

Calm. M'Adam, of Ballochmorrie.

Caritas fructum habet. (Charity has fruit.) Burnell, of Beauchief Abbey.

> " . . . . Lasting Charity's more ample sway,
> Nor bound by time, nor subject to decay,
> In happy triumph shall for ever live,
> And endless good diffuse, and endless praise receive."— PRIOR.

Cave lupum. (Beware of the wolf.) Huband, of Ipsley—who bears a wolf for crest.

Celeritas et veritas. (Promptitude and truth.) Rolls, of the Hendre.

Certamine summo. (In the greatest contest.) Brisbane, bart.

Che sara sara. (What will be will be.) Russell.

Clarior e flammis. (Brighter from the flames.) Gray—who bears for crest a phœnix.

Clarior e tenebris. (Brighter from darkness.) Delaval Gray—who also bears a phœnix for crest.

Claris dextera factis. Virgil, Æn. vii. v. 474. (A right hand employed in glorious deeds.) Burgh Byam, Rector of Kew and Petersham.

Cnock Elachan. Colquhoun of that Ilk and Luss, Bart. This motto is the war cry of the Clan Colquhoun.

Cœlum non solum. (Heaven, not earth.) Hayman, of South Abbey.

Cognoies toy même. (Know thyself.) The old exhortation of Thales. Braddyl, of Cornished Priory.

> " Know then thyself, presume not God to scan,
> The proper study of mankind is man."— POPE.

Confido. (I trust.) Boyd, of Middleton Park. Boyd, of Merton Hall.

Conjunctio firmat. (Union strengthens.) Middleton, of Leam.

Conservabo ad mortem. (I will preserve to the death.) Jennings, of the Shrubbery.

Constant and true. Rose, of Kilravock.

Cras mihi. (The morrow for me.) Parbury, of Mansfield House, Russell Square.

Crescent. (They increase.) Tatton, of Withenshaw.

Crescit sub pondere virtus. (Virtue increases under affliction.) Chapman, of Whitby.
Cresco per crucem. (I rise through the cross.) Rowan.
Cruce dum spiro fido. (Whilst I breathe, I confide in the cross.) Dyson, of Willow Hall.
Crux mihi grata quies. (The cross a grateful rest for me.) M'Adam, of Ballochmorrie.
Dei dono sum quod sum. (By the blessing of God I am what I am.) Lumsden, of Pitcaple.
De monte alto. (From a high mountain.) Maude, of Moor House. The ancient name of the
    Maudes was Montalt, derived from Monte alto.
Deum cole regem serva. (Worship God, preserve the king.) Cole, of Brandrum.
Deus incrementum dedit. (God has given increase.) Firth, of Hartford Lodge.
Deus pascit corvos. See Psalm cxlvi. 9. (God feeds the ravens.) Corbet, bart.

> "He that doth the ravens feed,
> Yea, providentially caters for the sparrow,
> Be comfort to my age."—SHAKESPEARE.

Devouement sans bornes. (Devotion without bounds.) Prodgers.

> "Yield to the Lord with simple heart,
> All that thou hast, and all thou art."—COWPER.

Diligentiâ et honore. (With diligence and honor.) Garnett, of Bleasdale.
Domine dirige nos. Ecclesiast. xxxvi. 19. (O Lord direct us.) Brome, of Malling House.
Donec rursus impleat orbem. (Until it again fill its orb.) Scott, bart.
Dum memor ipse mei. Virgil, Æn. b. iv. 336. (While I am mindful of myself.) Irvine,
    bart.
Dum spiro spero. (While I breathe, I hope.)
Durum patientiâ frango. (I break what is hard with the aid of patience.) Crawfuird, of Grange.
Duw a digon. (God and enough.) Prytherch, of Abergole.
En Dieu ma foy. (In God my faith.) Maunton, of Longbridge.
Erectus non elatus. (Exalted, not elated.) Clarke, of Welton Place.
Esse quam videri. (To be, rather than to appear.) Croft, bart. Words used by Sallust in
    praise of Cato, when comparing that patriot with Cæsar, after their respective speeches in
    the History of the Catalinarian Conspiracy, Chap. 54.
Est concordia fratrum. (It is a concord of brothers.) Brown, of Beilby Grange.
Est pii Deum et patriam diligere. (It is the part of a pious man to love God and his country.)
    Atkinson, of Rehins.
Et suivez moi. (And follow me.) Hawley, of West Green House.
Fato prudentia major. Virgil, Georg. i. 416. (Prudence greater than fate.) Lomax, of
    Clayton Hall.

> "with heavenly souls
> Inspired, as man, who destiny controls."—DRYDEN.

> "Wisdom and fortune combating together,
> If that the former dare but what it can,
> No chance may shake it."—SHAKESPEARE.

Fax mentis honestæ gloria. (Glory is the incitement of a noble mind.) Nova Scotia Baronets.
Fear God. Brisbane, bart.
Ferar unus et idem. (I will be esteemed one and the same.) Michell, of Forcet Hall.
Ferendo et feriendo. (By bearing and striking.) Harrison, of Copford Hall.

> "*King Richard.* Norfolk, we must have knocks; ha! must we not?
> *Norfolk.* We must both give and take, my loving lord."—SHAKESPEARE.

Feros ferio. (I strike the brutal.) The Chisholm.
Fide et fortitudine. (With faith and fortitude.) Farquharson, of Invercauld.
Fidelis usque ad mortem. (Faithful until death.) Sutton, of Elton.
Fidelitas vincit. (Fidelity conquers.) Dunscombe, of Mount Desart.
Fidelité est de Dieu. (Fidelity is from God.) Mellor.
Fidus ad extremum. (Faithful to the end.) Forbes-Leith, of Whitehaugh.

> "Master, go on, and I will follow thee
> To the last gasp with truth and loyalty."—SHAKESPEARE.

Fight. Ashe, of Ashfield.
Finem respice. (Regard the end.) Hall, of Grappenhall.
Fixus adversa sperno (Firm I despise adversity.) Hamerton, of Hellifield Peel.
Flecti non frangi. (To bend, not to be broken.) Phillipps, of Longworth.
Floreo in ungue leonis. (I flourish in the claw of the lion.) King, of Staunton Park, whose
    crest is a lion rampant, bearing in its fore paw a rose, thus forming together the emblem of
    strength and beauty—the loveliest of flowers under the protection of the king of the forest,
    the noblest of animals.
Flourish. Rose Cleland, of Rath Gael House.
Follow me. Gurwood.
For d ward. Strachan, bart.
Fortis in bello. (Brave in war.) Cantillon, de Ballyhigue.
Fortiter. (Boldly.) M'Alester, of Loup.

MOTTOES.

Fortiter et fideliter. (Boldly and faithfully.) Norton, of Dublin, representing Norton, of Kings Norton. Wilson, of Knowle Hall.

Fortiter gerit crucem. (He boldly sustains the cross.) Allan, of Blackwell Grange and Blackwell.

Fortitudine. (With fortitude.) Moubray, of Cockairny House.

Frangas non flectes. (Thou mayst break, but canst not bend.) Duke of Sutherland.

Fuimus. (We have been.) Kennedy, of Bennane and Finnarts.

Garde ta bien aimée. (Protect thy well-beloved.) Maze, a name which in the old patois of southern France meant *my beloved* (*mazaimée*, abridged). An *s* or *z* is thus often interposed between two vowels there, as in Somersetshire. At the present day, *mise* (pronounced *mize*) means *mistress* in the dialect of Provence.

> " One sacred right of woman is protection.
> The tender flower that lifts its head elate,
> Helpless must fall before the blasts of fate,
> Sunk on the earth, defaced its lovely form,
> Unless your shelter ward th' impending storm."—BURNS.

Gaudet luce. (It rejoices in the light.) Galton, of Duddeston, Warley Hall, and Hadzor House.

Go and do thou likewise. St. Luke, x. 37. Colston, of Roundway Park. This motto, borrowed from the parable of the good Samaritan, is borne by the Colston family in commemoration of the eminent philanthropist, Edward Colston, of Bristol.

God be my bede. Beedham.
> Bede-house, now antiquated, signified a house of refuge or alms-house, meaning, therefore, God be my refuge.

God shield the right. Crawfurd, of Newfield.

Hæc aspera terrent. (These asperities terrify.) Moubray, of Cockairny House.

Heb dduw heb ddim dduw a digon. (Without God there is nothing, with God, enough.) Davies, of Eton House. Lloyd, of Plymogg.

Heb nevol nerth nid sier saeth. (Without help from above the arrow flies in vain.) Jones, of Hartsheath.

Homo proponit Deus disponit. (Man proposes, God disposes.) Starkey, of Wakefield.

Honi soit qui mal y pense. (Evil be to him who evil thinks; literally, Unlucky be he who thinks evil thereof.) Order of the Garter.

Honore et amore. (With honour and love.) Grantham, of Ketton Lodge.

Honore et virtute. (With honour and virtue.) Gillbanks, of Whitefield House.

I bide my time. Crawfurd, of Newfield.

Ich dien. (I serve.) Prince of Wales.
> " The King of Bohemia, who fell at the battle of Crecy, had three ostrich feathers for crest. and this *Ich dien* for motto. The ensign and legend were adopted by the Black Prince of Wales, the words probably on account of their apt allusion to the good service he did the day of that victory to his royal father and his country; and they have been continued by his successors as a lasting memorial of his triumph."—BURKE's *Peerage.*

I grow and wither both together. Bigg-Wither, of Manydown.

Illumino. (I enlighten.) Farquharson, of Haughton.

Immotus. (Unmoved.) Alston, of Neyland.

In ardua virtus. (Virtue for difficulties.) Leathes, of Herringfleet.

In candore decus. (Beauty in candour.) Chadwick, of Swinton Hall.

In cruce spero. (I hope in the cross.) Allardice, of Ury.

In cruce triumphans. (Glorying in the cross.) Raffles.

In Domino confido. Psalm x. 2. (I put my trust in the Lord.) Walker, of Norton Villa.

> " Yet then from all my griefs, O Lord,
> Thy mercy set me free;
> Whilst in the confidence of prayer
> My soul took hold of thee."—ADDISON.

Industriâ et virtute. (With industry and virtue.) Beaver, of Glyngarth.

In omnia promptus. (Ready for all things.) Reay, of Gill House.

In sanguine vita. (Life in blood.) Alluding to the crest—the head and neck of a pelican—which is shedding its own blood to feed its young. Cobbe, of Newbridge.

J'ay bonne cause. (I have good cause.) Botfield, of Norton Hall.

Je crains Dieu. (I fear God.) Whitehurst, of the Mount.

Je dis la verité. (I tell the truth.) Pedder, of Ashton Lodge.

> " I am as true as truth's simplicity,
> And simpler than the infancy of truth."—SHAKESPEARE.

Je pense a qui pense plus. (I think of him who is the most thoughtful of me.) Rose-Cleland, of Rath Gael.

Justum perficito nihil timeto. (Do what is just, fear nothing.) Rogers, of Yarlington.

> " Be just, and fear not."—SHAKESPEARE.

Kymmer yn Edeirnion. Hughes, of Gwerclas, Barons of Kymmer-yn-Edeirnion.

Libertas. (Liberty.) Bailey, of Glanusk Park.
Let the deed show. Moubray, of Cockairny House.
Loyal as thou fynds. Tempest, of Tong Hall.
Lux mea Christus. (Christ my light.) Newman, of Thornbury Park.
Mala prævisa pereunt. (Evils foreseen cease to exist.) Hodges, of Hemsted.
Mallam mori quam fœdari. (I would rather die than be disgraced.) Gilbert, of Devon.
Malo mori quam fœdari. (I had rather die than be disgraced.) Prior, of Rathdowney.

> "Here, on my knee, I beg mortality,
> Rather than life preserved with infamy."—SHAKESPEARE.

Mane prædam vespere spolium. (The stag, hunted in the morning, becomes the spoil of the
    evening.) Hurt, of Alderwasley.
Manu forti. See Exodus, xiv. 14. (With the strong hand.) Boyd, of Middleton Park.
Manus hæc inimica tyrannis. (This hand hostile to tyrants.) Hemsworth, of Shropham Hall.
    The whole passage which refers to Brutus is thus,

> "Manus hæc inimica tyrannis
> Ense petit placidam sub libertate quietem."

> "This hand, to tyrants hostile ever,
>   Grasps the sword that makes it free,
> And seeks, intent their bonds to sever,
>   Gentle rest in liberty."

    The Latin lines are more generally known as having been written by Algernon Sydney in the
album of the Copenhagen University, where he was delegated in 1660, to negotiate a peace
between Denmark and Sweden. The French ambassador, Terlon, who was employed on
the same pacific mission, tore the leaf from the book.

Marte et mari faventibus. (The war and the sea permitting.) Morris, of York.
Mea dos virtus. (Virtue my dowry.) Meadows, of Great Bealings.
Mea fides in sapientia. (My faith in wisdom.) Fryer, of the Wergs.
Memor esto majorum. (Let him be mindful of his ancestors.) Farquharson, of Haughton.
Militia mea multiplex. (My warfare manifold,) words used by Caius Marius. Tooke.
Miseris succurrere disco. Virg. Æn. 1. (I learn to succour the unfortunate.) Soltau, of Little
    Efford.
Moderata durant. (Moderate acquisitions are lasting.) Staunton, of Longbridge.
Mone sale. (Advise with wit.) Monsell, of Tervoe.
Moriens cano. (Dying I sing.) Cobbe, of Newbridge. Allusive to the swan in the Arms.

> "He makes a swan-like end,
> Fading in music."—SHAKESPEARE.

Mort en droit. (Death in the right.) Drax, of Charborough Park.
Mutare vel timere sperno. (I disdain to change or to fear.) Bythesea, of the Hill.
Natale solum dulce. (My native land is dear.) Taylor, of Todmorden Hall.
Ne tentes aut perfice. (Attempt not or accomplish.) Faunce, of Sharsted.
Nil desperandum auspice Deo. (Nothing is to be despaired of under the auspice of God.)
    Anderson, of Jesmond House.
Niti facere experiri. (To endeavour, to do, to experience.) Caldwell, of Linley Wood.
Noli me tangere. (Touch me not.) Græme, of Garvock.
Non nobis. (Not to us.) Woodd, of Yorkshire.
Non nobis sed omnibus. (Not to us, but to all.) Ashe, of Ashfield.
Non sibi. (Not for oneself.) Cleland, of Rath Gael House.
Nubem eripiam. (I will remove the cloud.) Shipperdson, of Piddinghall.
Nullius in verba. (To the words of no man.) Gabb, of Monmouthshire.
Omnia bene. (All's well.) Harvey, of Castle Semple.
Omnia vincit amor. Virgil, Ec. x. 59. (Love subdues all things.) Rodick of Gateacre.

> "In hell, and earth, and seas, and heaven above,
> Love conquers all; and we must yield to love."—DRYDEN.

Patria cara carior fides. (My country dear, my faith dearer.) Sir N. H. Nicolas, G.C.M.G.
Patriam hinc sustinet. Virgil, Geor. ii. 514. (Hence he sustains his country.) In allusion
    to the crest—a garb, or wheatsheaf. Higgins, Rector of Eastnor.
Per ardua stabilis esto. (Be firm through difficulties.) Dendy of Dorking.
Per crucem ad coronam. (Through the cross to a crown.) Power, of Edermine.
Per mare per terras. (Through sea, through land.) M'Alester, of Loup.
Persevere. Burrard, bart.

> "Perseverance, dear my lord,
> Keeps honour bright."—SHAKESPEARE.

Pour jamais. (For ever.) Colonel Gurwood.
Prenes haleine tirez fort. (Take breath, pull strong.) Giffard, of Chillington.
Pieux quoique preux. (Pious though valiant.) Long, of Preshaw. See annotations to Plate
    XXVIII.
Pro patria. (For my country.) Higgins, of Trafalgar Park.

MOTTOES.

Pro rege. (For the king.) Porcher, of Clyffe.

Pro rege, lege, grege. (For the king, the law, the people.) Bigg-Wither, of Manydown. Ponsonby, of Hale Hall.

Quod facio valde facio. (What I do, I do with energy.) Sykes, of Highbury.

> "Cæsar, after the triumph of Pharsalia, and in the plenitude of his power, heard, says Plutarch, the defence of an African Prince, a follower of Pompey, by Brutus, when struck with the ardour of the advocate's feelings and language, the dictator remarked : " I know not always what this young man desires, but whatever he wishes he wishes intensely." Πᾶν δε ο βουλεται σφοδρα βουλεται. (Plutarch, Life of Brutus, cap. vii.)

Quod justum non quod utile. (What is just, not what is useful.) The maxim of the Stoics.

Recte faciendo neminem timeas. (In doing rightly thou needst fear no one.) Robertson, of Inches.

Reparabit cornua Phœbe. Ovid's Metamorphoses, lib. i. 11. (The moon will renew her horns.) Scott, bart.

Salus per Christum. (Salvation through Christ.) Forbes, of Culloden. Forbes-Leith, of Whitehaugh.

Sapere aude incipe. (Dare to be wise, begin.) Claxson, of Eastgate.

Semper paratus. (Always ready.) Leckey, of Bally Holland House. Welles, of the Grange.

Semper sapit suprema. (His knowledge is ever of heavenly things.) Selby, of Biddleston.

Semper sidera votum. (The heavens always my wish.) Rattray, of Barford House.

> "The pious man
> In this bad world, when mists and couchant storms
> Hide Heaven's fine circlet, springs aloft in faith,
> Above the clouds that threat him, to the fields
> Of ether, where the day is never veil'd
> With intervening vapour."—KIRKE WHITE.

Servabo fidem. (I will preserve my faith.) Johnson, of Runcorn.

Shanet a Boo. (Shanet to victory.) Fitzgerald, Knight of Glin.

Si je puis. (If I can.) Colquhoun, bart. For an account of this motto refer to the annotations of Plate X.

Sinceritate. (With sincerity.) Francklin, of Gonalston.

Soies content. (Be content.) Charnock, of Charnock.

Sola salus servire Deo. (To serve God is the only means of salvation.) Hibbert-Ware, of Edinburgh.

Sola virtus invicta. (Virtue alone invincible.) Harris.

Spare nought. Brisbane, bart.

Spectemur agendo. (Let us be examined by our actions.) Duckett, of Duckett's Grove.

Spe posteri temporis. (In hope of the time to come.) Atcherley, of Marton.

Sperabo. (I will hope.) Annand, of Lutton.

> "Cease every joy to glimmer on my mind,
> But leave, oh ! leave the light of HOPE behind."—CAMPBELL.

Spero. (I hope.) Dolling, of Magheralin.

Steer steady. Strachan, Bart.

Stellis aspirate gemellis. (Aspire to the twin stars.) Tynning, of Bryn.

Studendo et contemplando indefessus. (Unwearied in study and contemplation.) Cardale.

Subditus fidelis regis et salus regni. (A faithful subject of the king, and a preserver of the monarchy.) Hopper, of Belmont.

> This motto is borne by the Hoppers in commemoration of the services rendered to King Charles II. after the battle of Worcester by Colonel William Carlos, one of their ancestors.

Sub libertate quietem. (Repose under liberty.) Walsham, bart. See above at Manus hæc, &c.

Templa quam dilecta. (How beloved are the temples.) Temple, bart. See the translation of this motto in BURKE's Peerage.

Teneo tenuere majores. (I hold, my ancestors have held.) Twemlow, of Hatherton.

The cross our stay. Parkhouse, of Eastfield Lodge.

Touch not the cat but a glove. Macpherson, of Cluny. Mackintosh, of that Ilk.

Toujours fidele. (Ever faithful.) Gynne-Holford, of Buckland.

Toujours gai. (Ever gay.) Gay, of Thurning Hall.

Towton. Mathew.

Transfigam. (I will transfix.) Colt, of Gartsherrie.

Tria juncta in uno. (Three joined into one.) The motto of the Order of the Bath.

> On the accession of James I. to the English throne, and union, in his person, of the three kingdoms (regna) these expressive words implied the event ; they have also been used to represent the concentration of the cardinal virtues, faith, hope, and charity, all three in the one and last, according to Scripture, (St. Paul, Corinth. i. 13.)

Treu und fest. (True and faithful.) H. R. H. PRINCE ALBERT.

Turris fortis mihi Deus. (God is to me a tower of strength.) Kelly, of Newtown House.

MOTTOES.

Turris prudentia custos. (Prudence is the safeguard of the tower.) Dick Lauder, bart.

Turris tutissima virtus. (Valour the safest tower.) Carlyon, of Tregrehan.

Un Dieu, un roy. (One God, one king.) D'Arcy, of Hyde Park.

Utcunque placuerit Deo. (Whenever it shall have pleased God.) Darby, of Colebrooke Dale.

Utile dulci. (The useful with the agreeable.) Hor. Art of Poetry, 343. Spedding of Summergrove.

Ut migraturus habita. (Dwell here as one about to depart.) Dick Lauder, bart.

Valor e lealdad. (Valour and loyalty.) Croft, bart.

Verus amor patriæ. (The true love of country.) Hughes, of Ely House.

Vi aut virtute. (By force or virtue.) The Chisholm.

Vi et armis. (By force and arms.) Armstrong, of Ballycumber.

Vi victus non coactus. (Overcome by force, not compelled.) Warter, of Cruck Meole.

Vigilanter. (Watchfully.) Gregory.

Vigilo et spero. (I watch and hope.) Galbraith, of Machrihanish.

Vim vi repellere licet. (It is lawful to repel force by force.) Gynne Holford, of Buckland.

Viresco vulnere. (I gain strength with the wound.) Oldfield, of Oldfield.

Virtus omnia vincit. (Virtue conquers all things.) White, of Charlton Marshall.

Virtus probata florescit. (Tried virtue flourishes.) Cologan, of Teneriffe.

Virtus vulnere virescit. (Its virtue increases with the wound.) Leith, of Whitehaugh.

Virtute et honore. (With virtue and honor.) Wells, Rector of Portlemouth.

Virtute et valore. (With virtue and valour.) Stamer, of Bath.

Virtute et veritate. (With virtue and truth.) Blathwayt, of Dyrham Park.

Virtute non verbis. (With virtue not with words.) Coulthart, of Collyn.

Virtuti. (To virtue.) Lauder, bart.

Virtutibus præmium honor. (Honor the reward for virtues.) Ffeilden, of Witton.

Virtuti mœnia cedant. (Let walls yield to valour.) Wilder, of Purley Hall.

Virtutis gloria merces. (Glory the recompense of valour.) Gyll, of Widdial Hall and Wyrardisbury.

Virtutis laus actio. (Action the delight of virtue.) Corbet, bart.

Vixi liber et moriar. (I have lived a freeman, and I will die one.) Gray.

Watch weel. Scott, bart.

Wil sone wil. Wilson, of Stowlangtoft.

Y fegynno dwy y fydd. (What God willeth shall be.) Mathew.

INDEX.

The Capital Letters indicate the Respective Family Shields: those in Roman Letters, the Quarterings and Impalements: the Figures refer to the Number of the Plate.

H. R. H. PRINCE ALBERT, OF SAXE COBURG.

INDEX.

INDEX.

INDEX.